NEW Blueprint
INTERMEDIATE

Brian Abbs & Ingrid Freebairn

Teacher's Book

Pearson Education Limited
Edimburgh Gate, Harlow
Essex CM20 2JE England
and Associated Companies throughout the world.
www.longman-elt.com

© Brian Abbs and Ingrid Freebairn 1995
All rights reserved. No part of this publication may be reproduced, stored in a retrieval system, or transmitted in any form or by any means, electronic, mechanical, photocopying, recording, or otherwise without the prior written permission of the copyright owners.

First published 1995
Seventh impression 2000

Set in 10/10½ point Times

Printed in Spain by Mateu Cromo

ISBN 0 582 24887 6

Project management by Desmond O'Sullivan.
ELT Publishing Services

Acknowledgement
We are very grateful to Elaine Walker and Steve Elsworth for their work on the Workbook sections of this Teacher's Book.

Contents

Introduction

The course   4
1. Level and components
2. General principles

The needs of the intermediate student   4
1. Progression
2. Revision
3. Variety
4. Fluency practice
5. Learning independence

How New Blueprint Intermediate meets these needs   5
1. The Students' Book
2. The Class Cassettes
3. The Student Cassette
4. The Workbook
5. The Teacher's Book
6. The Video

Special features of New Blueprint Intermediate   6
1. Rapid review
2. Character units
3. Grammar units
4. Communication units
5. Reading units
6. Topic units
7. Check units
8. Use your English
9. Progress tests

Methodology of New Blueprint Intermediate   7
1. Grammar
2. Reading
3. Speaking
4. Listening
5. Writing
6. Dialogues
7. Vocabulary
8. Speechwork
9. Pair work
10. Group work
11. Questionnaires and surveys
12. Roleplay
13. Error correction
14. Use of dictionaries
15. Self-monitoring
16. Alternative routes through the material

The first lesson   11
1. Preparation
2. Breaking the ice
3. Developing learning awareness
4. Introducing the course book
5. Starting the first unit

Abbreviations used in the Teacher's Book   12

Detailed Lesson notes   13
(including all tapescripts)

Grammar index   133

Vocabulary and expressions   136

Workbook key   139

Introduction

The course

1 Level and components
New Blueprint Intermediate is for students aged fifteen and over who have completed an elementary course. New Blueprint Intermediate provides approximately 90 to 120 hours of work. The course consists of a Students' Book, a Workbook, this Teacher's Book, a set of Class Cassettes and a separate Student Cassette. There is also a two-part video: 'Face the Music', with an accompanying Students' Workbook and Teacher's Manual, which may be used as an integrated part of the New Blueprint Intermediate course or as a free-standing video course.

2 General principles
The methodological approach of New Blueprint Intermediate is based on three principles:

1 *The outcome of learning should be communicative.*
   Whether focusing on grammar, functions or skills, the outcome should require students to communicate and put the language to active use. The communicative emphasis means that students are always given the opportunity to exchange information, to express ideas and to relate what they are learning to the own lives.
2 *The students should be actively involved at all times.*
   The approach ensures that students participate actively in their own learning in a variety of ways. They are involved practically in the active use of the language through conversation, roleplay and communicative activities. They are involved intellectually in the analysis and study of grammar, and in the interpretation of reading and listening texts. Finally, the students are involved critically when monitoring and correcting their own work.
3 *The material and methodology should be flexible.*
   It is important that teachers should not feel tied to fixed patterns of work and types of activity. The course allows for the teachers to organise different routes through the material and to experiment with different methodological styles to suit their own classes.

The needs of the intermediate student

An intermediate level class is rarely homogeneous. It is usually made up of students with different learning abilities and backgrounds, who have followed different courses with different syllabuses before they come together as a group. Although they may have met the main functions and structures of English before, they cannot necessarily use them accurately and confidently. They often feel that their learning progress has reached a plateau and that they are getting nowhere. They suddenly realise what lies ahead and the enormous amount there is still to learn. This can lead to a sense of frustration and despair. Against this background, five common needs emerge.

1 Progression
When starting a new coursebook, students need to feel a sense of direction and that they are learning something new. The balance between 'old' and 'new' has to be carefully established. The course must be seen to offer a definite sense of progression, not only in terms of new structures and functions but also in the equally important areas of vocabulary and skills development. Students need to feel they are learning not just 'new language' but also how to cope with more challenging reading and listening texts.

2 Revision
Intermediate students often do not feel confident that they have fully mastered the grammar that they have covered. It is vital, therefore, to reassure them by including a strong revision element in a programme of work. A thorough review of basic structures, as well as important features of pronunciation and stress, needs to be combined with a more analytical approach to language. The systematic recycling and closer study of familiar language will help students perform with a higher degree of accuracy and give them the confidence to tackle more challenging work.

3 Variety
At this level, students often complain of boredom because they seem to be covering familiar ground in familiar ways. In order to maintain students' motivation, it is essential to keep up the learning momentum. This can be achieved by variety in the range of activities and tasks, in the sequence and

patterns of work, and, if appropriate, through a combination of class and video work.

4 Fluency practice

One of the difficulties which intermediate students experience is in reproducing familiar language in new contexts. Regular fluency activities such as communication tasks, games and discussions, where the emphasis is on successful communication, encourage students to feel more at ease with the language.

5 Learning independence

If the students are going to progress in the language, they need to develop good learning techniques so that they can learn on their own and at their own pace. They must learn to guess meaning from context, to use dictionaries, to understand the meaning of certain prefixes and suffixes and to sort words into categories for easy learning. They should be shown how to observe and analyse what is going on at the structural level so that they can develop an awareness of how the system works, and they should also be given the opportunity to practise at length, aspects of English pronunciation and intonation.

How New Blueprint Intermediate meets these needs

1 The Students' Book

The Students' Book consists of fifty teaching units preceded by a short Rapid review section of basic grammar. To give students the feeling of progress, each unit covers no more than a single or double page. A unit corresponds to one or two 45 to 50-minute teaching periods.

The fifty units are grouped as five sections of ten units each. Each of these sections is introduced by an English-speaking character whose life and background provide a context for language practice and skills development.

The characters, in order of their presentation, are:

1. Nick, a student in his final year at a private boarding school.
2. Angie, a motorcycle courier who lives and works in London.
3. Glenn, an American student visiting Britain.
4. Eve, a jewellery maker from Wiltshire in the West Country.
5. Errol, a police officer from Bristol.

To provide variety, each ten-unit section offers a continual change of focus, which is indicated in the unit titles, e.g. *Grammar*, *Communication*, *Reading* and *Topic*. The focusing element means that a particular aspect of language learning can be concentrated on at different times within an integrated programme of work. To ensure that students feel they are making progress, every ten units of the book ends with a revision section containing Check, Use your English and Progress test. The Check unit gives students and teachers an opportunity to monitor in detail progress in the formal aspects of grammar and communication; Use your English offers students a chance to experiment more freely with the language through a combination of information gap tasks, and creative speaking and writing exercises. The Progress test is diagnostic by nature and aims to help teachers measure students' overall progress and ability in the language.

2 The Class Cassettes

The Class Cassettes contain the listening material from the Students' Book, including the listening tasks, the word stress exercises from the Vocabulary sections, the dialogues, and a dramatic reading of the six literary texts. The cassettes are an essential accompaniment to the course in that they provide exposure to a wide range of native speakers through dialogue and authentic listening passages, and they offer consistent word stress practice, an area which needs constant attention at this level.

3 The Student Cassette

The Student Cassette contains simplified listening comprehension material, and Speechwork exercises to practise pronunciation and intonation. It is specifically designed to allow students to work on their own at their own pace. Classroom directed listening practice can often leave slower learners perplexed. Giving them more control can help to develop greater confidence in listening. Speechwork is often neglected in the classroom for more 'important' work and is in many ways better suited to individual practice. The Student Cassette gives students a much-needed opportunity to concentrate on their own specific oral/aural problems.

4 The Workbook

The Workbook acts as a support for the Students' Book and the Student Cassette. It provides extra practice of key grammar, functions and vocabulary from the Students' Book and exercises linked to the listening practice and Speechwork material recorded on the Student Cassette. Each Workbook unit is linked linguistically and thematically to its corresponding unit in the Students' Book. All exercises are clearly labelled to show students the purpose of what they are practising. One version of the Workbook has a pull-out Answer Key to enable students to work on their own and check their own progress (otherwise the Answer Key is printed at

INTRODUCTION

the back of the Teacher's Book.) Speechwork is given special attention with exercises on contracted forms, elision in verb tenses and intonation patterns, all linked to recorded material on the Student Cassette.

5 The Teacher's Book

The Teacher's Book contains an introduction to and description of the course, a guide to general teaching procedures and unit-by-unit Lesson notes. These include suggestions for follow-up activities, the Students' Book answer keys, including the keys to the Check units and tapescripts of the recorded material for both the Students' Book and the Workbook.

6 The Video

The characters from the Students' Book are brought to life in a video entitled 'Face the Music'. There are ten episodes, each lasting between three and five minutes. Each pair of episodes relates to ten units of the Students' Book in terms of character focus and structural content. For teachers using the video as an integrated part of their course, it is therefore recommended that two episodes can be watched after ten units of the Students' Book.

Special features of New Blueprint Intermediate

1 Rapid review

The purpose of this section is to provide teachers and students with an opportunity for fast and efficient revision of basic grammar. The whole section can be used as a mini diagnostic test at the beginning of the course. Alternatively, teachers may prefer to select individual areas of grammar depending on the specific problems of the class. New Blueprint Intermediate assumes as a starting point that students are already familiar with these selected areas of grammar. The emphasis of the course is consequently on refining and building on to these familiar areas while extending the students' communication skills and knowledge of other, more complex areas of grammar.

2 Character units

These units provide human interest by presenting five young people who live and work in contemporary Britain. The texts which introduce each character incorporate the grammatical structures which are developed and practised in the subsequent Grammar units.

3 Grammar units

In a cycle of ten units there are four Grammar units. The first and third introduce or revise major grammatical structures. The second and fourth introduce more minor points of grammar. The Workbook provides additional practice of the grammar while the Teacher's Book Lesson notes for the unit include suggested extra activities for freer practice of the language.

4 Communication units

The Communication units introduce and practise social and communicative functions. They are self-standing in that they do not form part of the grammatical syllabus. Practice is contextualised through dialogues, problem situations and interactive roleplay. Special attention is given to aspects of style and register.

5 Reading units

Although reading texts regularly appear in all units, the reading skill is specifically developed every fifth unit, through a range of non-fiction and literary texts and a variety of challenging tasks. The texts provide a base for vocabulary study, language awareness tasks and general conversation.

6 Topic units

These units introduce a topic to link the second half of the ten unit cycle. The topics and discussion activities have been specially chosen to arouse interest and provoke a difference of opinion. As well as giving plenty of opportunity for fluency practice, the topic also provides a valuable opportunity for building specific topic-related word fields.

7 Check units

These units provide the students with a simple set of exercises to revise and test the most important grammatical and functional items from the preceding ten units. The exercises consist mostly of gap-filling, completion, matching and multiple-choice exercises, although the section ends with a more open-ended exercise of the type: *What would you say in these situations?* Keys to the Check exercises are contained in the Teacher's Book, with suggestions for alternative answers where appropriate.

8 Use your English

The Use your English sections consist partly of pair work communication tasks involving an information gap and partly of individual activities and tasks to encourage the freer use of language. Student A's role is printed on the same page whereas Student B's role is to be found at the back of the Students' Book.

9 Progress tests

The Progress tests focus on selected items of grammar, vocabulary and usage relating to the previous ten units. They are designed to help teachers and students locate areas of work which need remedial attention. The keys to the Progress tests are contained in the Teacher's Book. Whereas the exercises in the Check section may be set for class or homework, the teacher may find the Progress test more useful as a formal diagnostic test.

Methodology of New Blueprint Intermediate

The detailed Lesson notes for each unit explain how to handle the material step by step. The following notes provide an outline of the overall methodological approach adopted in New Blueprint Intermediate.

1 Grammar

The learning and revising of grammar is central to the course. Most grammar cannot be learnt in passing but has to be studied and thoroughly practised before students can produce it confidently and accurately in new contexts.

In the New Blueprint Intermediate Grammar units, students are asked first to compare and contrast forms and uses of language structures in a section called *What's the difference in meaning?* For example, to highlight the contrast between two verb tenses, students are asked to think about the difference in meaning between two sentences which are identical apart from the tense of the verb. The names of the different tenses are consciously taught so that students can more easily refer to them when discussing their meaning and their uses.

The *Focus* section summarises the main rules of use in as simple language as possible. It is intended for reference and as an occasional 'aide-memoire' for teachers and students during the lesson. After the initial study of the structure, the students are given a range of controlled and freer contexts in which to practise the grammar.

2 Reading

The importance of reading for intermediate students cannot be overestimated. Reading texts not only consolidate language already learnt, they also provide a context for learning new language and offer useful models for writing. It should be remembered that for students learning abroad, reading texts are often the only readily available source of language input. Developing good reading skills is essential not only for making progress in the language but also for the students' own educational and personal development.

In New Blueprint Intermediate, there are several types of reading texts. There are:

- specially written language presentation texts for close language study.
- texts for presenting cultural information.
- authentic material to support topics.
- topic-based texts for stimulating discussion.
- extracts from contemporary literature for students to enjoy examples of good writing and style.

All major reading texts in New Blueprint Intermediate are preceded by a *Before you read* section which prepares students for important vocabulary or for the issues and ideas which occur in the text. The reading activities which follow the text guide the students towards appropriate strategies such as skimming, scanning, guessing and inferring meaning from context. The aim is to lead students away from the need to understand every new item of language.

Most reading activities include the following:

Guess the meaning: a list of words which occur in the text and which should be guessable from the context. It is important that students are given time to think about the words and try to guess their approximate meaning before resorting to a dictionary.

Read and answer or *Read and find out*: exercises to check the comprehension of the main facts or gist of a text.

Read and think: questions to encourage students to make inferences and guess meaning beyond word level. The questions often have more than one answer and students are expected to justify their answers.

About you and *Talking point*: questions to encourage the students to exploit the text in conversation and discussion (see below – *Speaking*).

Style: sometimes the literary texts exhibit a point of style and its effect at a very simple level, e.g. sentence length or use of simile and metaphor. Students are asked to think about how the same effects are achieved in their own languages.

The non-fiction and literary texts in the Reading units are designed to be read mainly for gist. General comprehension is tested. The focal point of the lesson is the students' personal reaction to the text and its contents.

3 Speaking

Learning to speak a language is the most important aim of most language learners. As student talking time in class can be short, every opportunity should be taken to provide speaking practice.

In New Blueprint Intermediate this is achieved in a variety of ways. Controlled practice occurs in repetition of the Dialogues, and in question and answer pair work. There are also specific sections aimed at speaking practice within the units.

INTRODUCTION

Roleplay plays an important part (see *12 Roleplay* below) under the heading *Act it out*.

After the reading texts, the *About you* questions provide an opportunity for teachers to move away from the text and relate the content to the students' own lives and experiences. The questions give students a springboard for talking about themselves and about features of life in their own country, by inviting them to make comparisons.

This provides a contrast to the section *Talking point*, where the questions are more general and have been specially chosen to provoke discussion and disagreement. At the beginning of the course, special guidance is given to the students on the language of discussion, e.g. giving opinions, agreeing, disagreeing and giving examples.

Apart from this, students get plenty of fluency practice in the regular Use your English units and in the range of games, tasks and problem-solving activities suggested in the Teacher's Book Lesson notes for each unit, under the heading *Extra activities*.

4 Listening

For many students, understanding spoken language is a major source of difficulty. Listening practice which provides exposure to native speaker language is an important component in any language course. Students should learn to cope with material which is beyond their productive level and not be discouraged if they do not understand the meaning of every word.

In New Blueprint Intermediate the listening passages are a mixture of scripted and authentic recordings. Students listen for a variety of purposes: for gist, for information, for pleasure and occasionally to recognise specific usage.

It is essential to prepare students for the listening tasks. Suggestions on how to do this are given in the *Before you listen* section of the Students' Book or in the Teacher's Book Lesson notes. This preparation might involve asking the students to predict the content of the passage or raising questions which might be answered when they listen. Sometimes it is sensible to isolate difficult words and expressions and to check that the students know what they mean before they listen. When the listening task is a conversation or discussion, the students can be asked to perform the same conversation or discussion so that they can compare their performance with native speakers.

5 Writing

Writing is not only an aid to consolidating new language but is a meaningful activity in itself. The process of writing, of organising one's thoughts and expressing one's feelings logically and coherently, is as important and valuable as the final piece of writing.

In New Blueprint Intermediate the writing skill is developed consistently and thoroughly. In the Grammar units the writing is specifically aimed at consolidating the structure(s) in focus. In the Communication, Topic and Reading units, writing tasks are linked to the communicative focus or topic of the unit, and students are encouraged to used their imagination and full range of available language.

All the writing tasks should first be prepared orally to help students with the organisation of their writing, and special guidance and practice is given in the use of linking devices.

Suggestions for writing preparation are included in the *Before you write* section in the Students' Book or in the detailed Lesson notes in this Teacher's Book. When planning lessons, it is vital to allow adequate class time for this stage. Time should also be allowed for students to check their own work and identify any problems with which they would like help (see *15 Self-monitoring* below).

6 Dialogues

Short dialogues are included regularly throughout the course, especially in the Communication units. The content of the dialogue is indicated in the unit title, e.g. *Apologies*. All dialogues are recorded with a paused version for students to repeat and are a useful way of synthesising listening, speaking and reading.

Most teachers will have their own ways of handling dialogues but there are two important points to remember. Firstly, the students should be actively involved in the processing of the dialogue: by predicting the content, by listening or reading with a purpose and by noting and analysing key words and phrases. Secondly, dialogue study and practice should always lead to some form of creative output – in other words a roleplay or dialogue of the students' own making. Specific suggestions for making effective use of dialogues can be found in the relevant parts of the detailed Teacher's Book Lesson notes.

7 Vocabulary

New Blueprint Intermediate helps students to build their vocabulary through the study of word fields, prefixes and suffixes, derivation, compounds and synonyms and antonyms. After most texts, there is also a selected list of *Words to learn*.

Dictionary use is encouraged and practised on specific occasions (see *14 Use of dictionaries* below) but special attention is also given to the comprehension of unknown words in texts through *Guess the meaning* exercises.

The words which teachers will want students to

learn by heart for active use will obviously vary from course to course. All the words from the *Words to learn*, *Guess the meaning* and the specific *Vocabulary* sections are listed alphabetically with phonetic transcriptions at the back of the Students' Book. It is worth remembering that the acquisition of vocabulary is a very personal matter. Students will acquire different words depending on what associations the words have for them, or whether they like the sound of the word or not.

To develop good study habits, students should always be encouraged to keep a notebook for new words. These can be listen alphabetically, or in word fields or grammatical categories, e.g. nouns, verbs, adjectives. Ideally, the students should also add a sentence containing the new word in an appropriate context.

It is essential that new vocabulary and expressions are continually recycled. One way of doing this is to use flashcards of individual words and expressions for quick checks at the beginning of lessons. These flashcards can also be used for games and for building dialogues.

8 Speechwork

WORD STRESS

The learning of word stress patterns in New Blueprint Intermediate is linked directly with the learning of new words. Many of the Vocabulary exercises in the Students' Book are recorded so that students can hear the correct pronunciation and identify the main word stress. Guidance can be given to stress by underlining or using capital letters, e.g. phoTOGrapher or phot<u>o</u>grapher.

PRONUNCIATION AND INTONATION

Special pronunciation exercises relating to the Grammar units are included in the Workbook and are recorded on the Student Cassette. As well as this, key phrases and sentences from the Communication dialogues are selected for intonation practice in the Workbook and on the Student Cassette. A 'bleep' on the Student Cassette indicates that the tape must be paused to allow students time to respond. In class, intonation can be shown in sentences by using arrows, e.g.

I'm sorry. I'm terribly sorry.

When practising the intonation pattern of longer sentences, 'back-chaining' – where the sentence is built up in parts, starting from the end – can be an effective technique. In the case of the sentence *I'm terribly sorry*, the back chaining would be:

sorry – terribly sorry – I'm terribly sorry.

A general summary of the pronunciation points in the Speechwork exercises is included at the back of the Workbook.

9 Pair work

Many of the exercises, activities and roleplays in New Blueprint Intermediate require students to work in pairs. Pair work has the great advantage that it increases the students' talking time dramatically and helps to release tension. It is neither possible nor necessary to correct each student. With plenty of practice, major mistakes tend to disappear. If there is an uneven number in the class, the teacher can either make up a pair or ask some students to work in threes.

10 Group work

Group work, if used selectively, has several advantages. It offers students of mixed abilities a natural context for working together; shy students get a chance to talk informally; confident students get a chance to shine and develop their skills by acting as reporters and group secretaries; it offers a change of pace to a lesson; and, initially, it helps the students to get to know each other. However, some students may show resistance to group work. They feel that they are not learning English if their classmates are talking imperfect English. For this reason, group work in New Blueprint Intermediate is suggested for specifically group-orientated activities: for discussion of provocative issues, for problem-solving and for certain types of games.

Groups can be formed either by the teachers or by the students themselves. Different ways of forming groups can be based on position in the classroom, alphabetical order of names, colour of clothes, etc.

When setting up group work, always give clear instructions and set a time limit for each task. The students should appoint a group reporter if the task requires it. When the group work is in progress, it is best to monitor unobtrusively and contribute only when asked. Errors can be pointed out when the activity is finished, or at a later date (see *13 Error correction* below).

Recording the discussions live can be a good way of providing feedback on the students' individual performances at a later stage.

11 Questionnaires and surveys

A good way of revising and practising language in a realistic but controlled way is through the use of questionnaires and surveys. These work on the simple 'information gap' principle, where the seeking and giving of information provides a realistic context for language work. For example, in the questionnaire *How assertive are you?* in Unit 32, the *would you?* questions are a natural way of revising the second conditional.

Questionnaires can be devised to practise almost any verb tense. For example, a questionnaire to revise the present simple might include questions about leisure activities such as: *Which of the following magazines do you read? How often do you buy it/them? (Every week, Once a month, Occasionally, etc.) How much TV do you watch a night?* etc.

Surveys also provide meaningful practice in a different way. To revise a range of structures, the technique of a *Find someone who ...* survey is useful, e.g.

Find someone who:
- likes cold tea.
- went swimming yesterday.
- has seen a ghost.
- used to live in ... (town).

(See Unit notes for Units 7 and 22 under Extra activities.)

12 Roleplay

Roleplay is an ideal way of providing useful fluency practice if the students are not confused by instructions which are too complicated, or frightened off by roles which are too unfamiliar. The *Act it out* roleplays in New Blueprint Intermediate are straightforward and do not demand special acting skills. Students are only asked to play roles with which they can readily identify.

Cues for the roleplay chains are expressed in simple language and should not need to be translated. Examples can be elicited from the students before starting.

For the freer roleplays, where rolecards are provided for Students A and B, the students should be given time to read through the situation and instructions carefully, and to prepare their roles. Students who finish quickly can write down their conversations.

13 Error correction

Making mistakes is an important and positive part of learning a language. Only by experimenting with the language and receiving feedback can students begin to sort out how the language works. In general students like to be corrected, but it can be off-putting and demotivating to be stopped in free conversation whenever a mistake is made.

In controlled practice, where emphasis should be on accurate production, correction can be immediate. In roleplays and discussions, where emphasis is on communication and conversational fluency, students should not be interrupted. However, it is important to note any recurring or important mistakes for later comment and correction.

14 Use of dictionaries

At the intermediate level, perhaps more than any other, students should each be advised to have a good personal dictionary, such as the *Longman Dictionary of Contemporary English*, for active classroom use. They can then confirm the meaning of new words and expressions after they have initially tried to work them out from their context. The students should also be shown how to use the dictionary to find out further information about a vocabulary item, such as its headword, pronunciation, grammatical category, definition, and an example of how to use it.

headword
pronunciation
grammatical information
definitions and examples

blueprint /ˈbluːˌprɪnt/ *n* **1** a photographic copy of a plan for making a machine or building a house or other structure: *the blueprints of a new engine* **2a** a detailed programme of action: *a blueprint for victory* **2b** a plan, prototype: *The report is a blueprint for the reform of the tax system.*

15 Self-monitoring

An important need for intermediate students is to take increased responsibility for their own learning. Their work can be corrected in a variety of ways – not always by the teacher. Answers to exercises can be checked orally in a chain round the class, or students can correct their own or their partners' answers by using a key. For correcting written paragraphs, it is sometimes helpful to select a student's work (or parts of different students' work) and write it on the board for the class to see and correct together.

Students need to be reminded to check their written work systematically, for meaning, grammar and spelling, before handing it in. One way of doing this is for students to read their work aloud, either to themselves or to their partners. Alternatively, students can be asked to underline or note in the margin any points or sentences they are unsure of, where they would like the teacher to comment. In this way, the correction of their homework becomes a more personal dialogue between the teacher and the student.

For longer compositions, it is best to collect in and mark or comment on students' work individually. You may sometimes wish to write in corrections but it is generally better to get students to discover their own mistakes by using symbols (e.g. *vt = verb tense*) which both you and the students understand.

16 Alternative routes through the material

It is important to experiment occasionally with the teaching sequence suggested in the Students' Book, not just for the sake of variety but also as a means of finding the best way of handling the material in your own situation. For example, within a ten unit cycle, there are several possible sequences.

Sometimes teachers may want to teach the Grammar unit before the Character unit, or even to start a cycle with a Communication unit. Some teachers may wish to teach two Grammar units in sequence. Others may not always want to cover both Reading units. Students may themselves wish to decide on the order.

There can also be considerable variation within a unit. Not all teachers will prefer to start a Grammar unit with analysis and then proceed to practice. Sometimes it can be interesting to start a Reading lesson with the Vocabulary study, lead on from there to *About you* and then tackle the reading text. Opening a lesson with a roleplay can sometimes highlight a need for students which can then be solved by referring to the printed dialogue.

NOTE ON UNIT 1
Teachers with new students who have not worked with each other before, may like to teach Unit 2 before Unit 1. This will give students an opportunity to get to know each other and to get used to certain routine activities, like pair and group work, which you will be using throughout the course. Unit 1 can then be used as a follow-up text.

The first lesson

1 Preparation

AIMS
1 to break the ice and get to know each other
2 to develop learning awareness and a positive attitude to English
3 to introduce the course book
4 to start the first unit and to establish a friendly working atmosphere

AIDS
1 a board and a cassette player
2 also useful – a good monolingual dictionary (e.g. *Longman Dictionary of Contemporary English* or *Longman Active Study Dictionary*) and an atlas
3 a pin board display area for notices, students' work, and pictures which relate to the course book topics and themes
4 maps of the world, British Isles, USA
5 furniture arranged to facilitate the 'ice-breaker' activity you choose

2 Breaking the ice

Many teachers will have their own favourite 'ice-breaking' techniques to get the first lesson off to a good start. The chosen activity should be brief and uncomplicated. If you are new to teaching or to this technique, you may like to try one of the following ideas:

1 THE NAME CHAIN
(For classes of 15 or under)

Students give their names in turn round the class, including all the names that have gone before, e.g.

S1 (MARIA):   Maria.
S2 (CARLOS):   Maria, Carlos.
S3 (STEFAN):   Maria, Carlos, Stefan.

This continues until the last person (the teacher) has to remember all the names of the students in sequence. In a large class do this in two groups – but you have to do them all!

2 INTERVIEWS
Write cue words on the board so that students can interview each other in pairs, e.g.

Name and nationality: (if studying in the UK or the USA)
Job:
Family:
Hobbies:
Number of years learning English:

After the interviews, each person tells the class briefly about their partner.

3 FIND SOMEONE WHO ...

> Find someone who:
> – has a birthday this month.
> – likes milk in their tea.
> – keeps tropical fish.
> – owns a moped.
> – is learning another language as well as English.
> – is wearing something which was made in England.
> – went to Britain last summer.
> – has been to the USA/Australia/Canada.
> – had honey for breakfast.
> – watched television last night.
> – bought a newspaper today.

Make a list similar to the one above and photocopy it so that each student has a copy. Students have five minutes to ask questions like *Have you got a birthday this month?*. The object is to collect as many names as possible.

3 Developing learning awareness

The following questionnaires are to encourage students to think about how they learn and to prepare them for some of the learning activities which they will experience throughout the course. The questionnaires can be photocopied and distributed to the students.

If teachers feel that the questionnaires will take up too much class time during the first lesson, they can be set for homework and the responses discussed at the start of the next class.

INTRODUCTION

Alternatively, the questionnaires can be saved until a few weeks into the course when the students are more familiar with the methodology of the course.

LEARNING A LANGUAGE
Do you agree or disagree with
these statements?   Yes   No

1 I prefer not to speak because I don't like making mistakes in front of everyone.
2 I like to be corrected whenever I make a mistake.
3 You'll never learn unless you practise.
4 You speak more English when you're in groups.
5 I speak more in group work because I don't feel so shy.
6 I don't like working in pairs or groups because I think I'll learn bad English.
7 If you talk a lot of English, you will learn the grammar as you go along.
8 You can learn to speak a language just by learning grammatical rules.
9 It is important to understand the meaning of every word when you read or listen to a text.
10 Every time you meet a new word, you should look up its meaning in a dictionary.

LEARNING NEW WORDS
Answer the questions.

1 How do you remember new words?

    ....

2 When you record new words, do you put them in groups, in alphabetical order or as they occur in the book?

    ....

   Do you write sentences with the new words in them?

    ....

3 Apart from the meaning of a word, what other information can a dictionary give you?

    ....

4 Introducing the course book

For students to get the most out of the English course, it is important to familiarise them with the shape and contents of the course book. Ask the students to look first at the Contents list on pages 2–5 at the beginning of the Students' Book. The following questions can be photocopied in advance and given to the students. Alternatively, ask each question in turn to the class, allowing time for all students to locate the relevant information each time.

1 Who will you read about in Unit 1?
2 How many of the first ten units focus on grammar?
3 What is the grammar point in Unit 6?
4 What topic will you discuss in Unit 17?
5 In which unit will you learn how to make polite requests for information?
6 What will you listen to in Unit 32?
7 What will you write in Unit 38?
8 How many Progress tests are there?
9 What reference material is there at the back of the book?
10 What is the name of the section which starts on page 6?

5 Starting the first unit

The previous section directs students to the beginning of the Rapid review section which opens the book. It is assumed that most teachers will find it useful to assess their students' strengths and weaknesses before starting the course. The exercises are simply designed so that the students can work swiftly through them with the minimum of assistance from the teacher. However, some teachers may wish to make a start with Unit 1 and set the Rapid review as a homework task. Whatever the decision, it is important that students feel that they have started the book and done some 'proper work' before the end of the first lesson.

Abbreviations used in the Teacher's Book

T	Teacher
S	Student
T–S	Teacher speaks to student
S–S	Student speaks to student
S1–S2	First student speaks to second student and so on
OHP	Overhead projector
e.g.	for example
etc.	etcetera
i.e.	that is

Lesson notes

RAPID REVIEW

For the rationale behind the Rapid review, see under 'Special features of New Blueprint Intermediate' in the Introduction.

You should decide if you wish to use this section as a pre-course test to assess how much the students already know and where their problems lie. If you are short of time, or feel you want to start Unit 1 as soon as possible, you may wish only to select the grammar points which you know your students find difficult.

The first exercise in every section is designed to make students reflect on how the language is used and to draw conclusions about grammar and usage. The exercises which follow move from more to less controlled. The majority are keyed (see below). In some of the contextualised exercises, you may need to give an example before asking the students to continue with the exercise.

As the students work through the section, make a note of any special problems which arise and give some extra practice and consolidation of these points before starting the course.

Key

PRESENT SIMPLE

Exercise 1

1a 2a

Exercise 2

1 'Does he like chips?' 'Yes, he does.'
2 'Does she like fish?' 'No, she doesn't.'
3 'Do they like opera?' 'No, they don't.'
4 'Does it like dogs?' 'No, it doesn't.'
5 'Does he like studying?' 'No, he doesn't.'
6 'Does she like Kevin Costner?' 'Yes, she does.'

Exercise 3

1 does, mean 2 means 3 do, spell 4 doesn't look
5 don't understand 6 Do, remember 7 phones
8 don't open

ADVERBS AND ADVERBIAL PHRASES OF FREQUENCY

Exercise 1

1a 2b 3b 4a

Exercise 2

always usually often sometimes never

Exercise 3

1 I never go to bed before midnight.
2 She's usually had lunch by this time.
3 Do you ever go to discos?
4 I go to the dentist once a year.
5 She sometimes sees her boyfriend six days a week.
6 He is often very rude to people.
7 I've always like him.
8 We go to the cinema about twice a month.

Exercise 4

(Open exercise.)

PRESENT CONTINUOUS

Exercise 1

1 b, c, f 2 b

Exercise 2

1 Mr Gibson isn't watching television. He's sleeping.
2 Mrs Gibson isn't knitting or sewing. She's reading a magazine.
3 Luke isn't doing his homework. He's listening to his walkman.
4 Suzy isn't reading a book. She's talking to her boyfriend on the telephone.
5 The dog isn't sleeping beside the sofa. It's sleeping in front of the fire.
6 The cat isn't sitting by the window. It's sitting on Suzy's lap.

Exercise 3

1 She's leaving for Prague on Wednesday April 15th at 16.30 and returning on Friday April 17th at 15.30.
2 She's arriving in Prague at 19.45.
3 On Thursday morning she's meeting a representative from Prague Travel (at 10 a.m.).
4 On Thursday she's having lunch with Mrs Hlavka.
5 On Thursday evening she's going to a concert at Smetana Hall.
6 On Friday morning she's attending a conference at the Exhibition Hall.

Exercise 4

1 are you staying 2 'm spending 3 do you prefer
4 'm not answering 5 like 6 are you giving
7 Are you making 8 usually try 9 is coming along
10 hope

RAPID REVIEW

GOING TO AND *WILL*

Exercise 1
1c 2d 3e 4b 5a

Exercise 2
1 'll 2 won't 3 will 4 'll 5 'll 6 won't 7 'll 8 will

Exercise 3
1 'm going to; 'll
2 Are you going to; 'll
3 'm going to; 'll
4 're going to; 'll

PAST SIMPLE

Exercise 1
1 a 2 five minutes ago, last week

Exercise 2
walked, opened, liked, closed, wanted, watched, hoped, played, enjoyed, asked, answered, tried, died, happened, waited

Exercise 3
went, did, took, gave, wrote, make, rang, knew, found, left, thought, heard, said, got, sat

Exercise 4
1 did you leave 2 took 3 Did you come 4 caught 5 brought 6 changed 7 left 8 didn't realise 9 did 10 went

PAST CONTINUOUS

Exercise 1
1 a 2 b, c

Exercise 2
1 the baby was crying.
2 the children were fighting
3 the teenage daughter was playing loud music.
4 the telephone was ringing.
5 the supper was boiling over.
6 the dog was barking.

Exercise 3
1 was crossing 2 woke up, was pouring
3 did you get up 4 were you talking to
5 was having, saw

PRESENT PERFECT SIMPLE

Exercise 1
1b 2c 3b

Exercise 2
done, gone, been, had, brought, taken, made, read, written, spoken, driven, found, broken, got, bought, lost

Exercise 3
Present perfect adverbials: yet, so far today, just, never, already, ever, since 1987

Past simple adverbials: yesterday, two minutes ago, in 1983, last week, on Tuesday

Exercise 4
1 'Have you ever broken your leg?' ('Yes, I have. No, I haven't'.)
2 'Have you ever written a poem?' ('Yes, I have. No, I haven't'.)
3 'Have you ever sung in public?' ('Yes, I have. No, I haven't'.)
4 'Have you ever drunk champagne?' ('Yes, I have. No, I haven't'.)
5 'Have you ever seen a ghost?' ('Yes, I have. No, I haven't'.)
6 'Have you ever been to Africa?' ('Yes, I have. No, I haven't'.)
7 'Have you ever driven a racing car?' ('Yes, I have. No, I haven't'.)
8 'Have you ever stayed up all night?' ('Yes, I have. No, I haven't'.)

Exercise 5
1 've already had 2 did you get 3 have you eaten
4 did he arrive 5 have you ever tasted
6 have you worked 7 went 8 've seen

MODALS: *MUST, MUSTN'T, NEEDN'T, HAVE TO*

Exercise 1
1d 2a 3e 4c 5b

Exercise 2
must; needn't; mustn't; must; needn't

Exercise 3
1 don't have to 2 have to 3 didn't have to 4 had to
5 will have to

Exercise 4
Suggested sentences:

You must/have to look both ways before crossing the road.
You must/have to drive carefully / You mustn't stop. / You must keep your distance.
You mustn't smoke. / You mustn't walk about in the aeroplane.
You mustn't try and feed them. / You mustn't get too close.
You have to walk and speak quietly. / You mustn't smoke.

14

You have to be quiet. / You have to stop talking.
You mustn't change places. / You mustn't make any sudden moves.

VERBS FOLLOWED BY *TO* ... OR ...*-ING*

Exercise 1
Verb + infinitive with *to*: want, need, try, decide (*like*, *prefer*, *love* and *hate* can also be followed by *to* with a similar meaning but this is not exemplified in the sentences)

Verb + *-ing* (gerund): enjoy, like, prefer, love, finish, don't mind, hate, avoid

Exercise 2
1g 2b 3e 4h 5a 6c 7d 8f

Exercise 3
Suggested endings:
1 lying in front of the fire with a good book.
2 travelling first class.
3 to rest.
4 arriving late.
5 to buy some flowers for my mother.

ARTICLES, COUNTABLE AND UNCOUNTABLE NOUNS

Exercise 1
1b, c 2f 3g 4h 5e 6a 7i 8d 9j 10h

Exercise 2
1 a 2 – 3 – 4 the 5 – 6 an 7 – 8 the 9 a 10 – 11 the 12 the

Exercise 3
dogs, roads, countries, men, women, children, houses, churches, people, chickens, fish

Exercise 4
a/an: table, apple, suitcase, bag, chair, moon, church, kitchen
some: furniture, potatoes, luggage, sugar, butter, people, water, news, information, advice
the: government, police, moon, Alps, Pope, weather

Exercise 5
1 a 2 some 3 any 4 some 5 the 6 The 7 a, the 8 any, a, a

Exercise 6
1 an architect. 2 have breakfast
3 After leaving school
4 Have you finished the book
5 the Rocky Mountains 6 The information

EXPRESSIONS OF QUANTITY

Exercise 1
1b, c 2a, b, c 3a 4b 5a

Exercise 2
1 A: How many tomatoes are there in the fridge?
  B: There are plenty of tomatoes.
2 A: How much milk is there in the jug?
  B: There's not much milk.
3 A: How many people are there in the room?
  B: There are a lot of people.
4 A: How much fruit is there in the bowl?
  B: There's not enough fruit.
5 A: How much sport is there on TV?
  B: There's too little sport.
6 A: How many videos are there on the shelf?
  B: There aren't many videos.
7 A: How much money is there in the wallet?
  B: There's a lot of money.
8 A: How many eggs are there in the box?
  B: There are a few eggs.

PREPOSITIONS OF TIME AND PLACE

Exercise 1
a) in b) on c) at d) in e) at f) to g) by

Exercise 2
1 in, in 2 on 3 by 4 on, at 5 at 6 to
7 from, in, to, in 8 at 9 in 10 in, at

Exercise 3
1 in 2 in 3 at 4 at 5 From 6 to 7 at 8 in

COMPARISON OF ADJECTIVES

Exercise 1
nicer nicest; biggest; dirtiest; fatter, fattest; happier, happiest; best; worst; most, more.

Exercise 2
1 The Amazon is longer than the Mississippi.
  The Mississippi is shorter than the Amazon.
2 Mont Blanc is higher than the Matterhorn.
  The Matterhorn is lower than Mont Blanc.
3 A Ferrari is faster than a Mercedes 380SL.
  A Mercedes 380SL is slower than a Ferrari.
4 Gerry is older than Sue.
  Sue is younger than Gerry.
5 London is colder today than Barcelona.
  Barcelona is warmer today than London.
6 Peter is taller than Tom.
  Tom is shorter than Peter.
7 The brown leather coat is cheaper than the black one.
  The black leather coat is more expensive than the brown one.
8 My bag is heavier than yours.
  Your bag is lighter than mine.

Exercise 3
1 Which is the largest ocean in the world?
2 Which is the tallest building in New York?
3 Which is the most expensive car in this showroom?
4 Which is the best restaurant in this town?
5 Which is the worst time of year to go to Britain?
6 Which is the most interesting book you have ever read?
7 Which is the quickest way to the station?
8 Which is the hardest question on the exam paper?

Exercise 4
1 Jan is not as old as Tanya.
2 Carl Lewis is not as fast as Leo Burrell.
3 George Harrison is as rich as Rod Stewart.
4 *Sister Act* is not as long as *The Fugitive*.
5 Paris is as hot as Lisbon.
6 Leonard is not as intelligent as Kevin.

Exercise 5
1 the most interesting to visit 2 the most expensive
3 the liveliest 4 the most dangerous
5 the most relaxed

Nick

UNIT 1 Nick, a student

> BACKGROUND NOTES
>
> *'A' levels*: These are 'Advanced' level exams which students usually take at the age of eighteen. Students who choose to stay on at school after the age of 16 usually take between two and four 'A' levels in their chosen specialist subjects.
>
> *Eton*: A famous and exclusive private boarding school for boys. The students live and study there for the duration of each of the three school terms. The college is situated in Eton, a town about twenty miles west of London, close to Windsor. Private boarding schools are frequently called 'public schools' but the word 'public' should not be confused with 'state' schools, which are non-fee-paying.

Text about Nick

Ask the students to look at the picture of Nick and guess what sort of student he is (serious, lazy?) and what his hobbies and interests might be.

Make a chart on the board for students to copy. Students read the text silently and complete the chart. Point out that the information does not always come in the same order as the headings in the chart.

```
Name:
Age:
School:
'A' level subjects:
Spare time interests and activities:
Ambition:
```

KEY
Name:	Nick Harrington
Age:	18
School:	Eton
'A' level subjects:	Maths, Physics, Computer Studies
Spare time interests and activities:	Plays the guitar and piano; reads music magazines; plays in a band three evenings a week
Ambition:	Wants someone important from the music business to discover him

Words to learn

Ask students to find other words in the text and try to express the sentence in another way to show their meaning.

Exercise 1

Students ask and answer the questions in pairs. Give an example using the first question. Check the answers with the whole class afterwards.

KEY
1 He's taking Maths, Physics and Computer Studies.
2 Because he hasn't worked very hard for his 'A' levels and is spending too much time playing his guitar and reading music magazines.
3 He's supposed to revise for his exams.
4 He can play the piano as well as play the guitar. He can listen to any piece of music and then play it easily.
5 Because he goes to a private school.

Exercise 2

SUGGESTED ANSWERS
1 They are probably angry that he hasn't done more work for his exams, especially as they are paying a lot of money to send him to a private school.
2 He probably plays his guitar, listens to music, goes to the cinema, reads magazines, plays some sport, chats to his friends, etc.
3 He's not allowed to give any public performance in the town, so no one sees him perform outside the school.
4 They probably don't wear uniform; they get more freedom, etc.

Exercise 3

Students ask and answer the questions in pairs.

VOCABULARY

Exercises 2 and 3 prepare students to write and talk about their own education later in the lesson.

Exercise 1

Refer students back to the text about Nick to remind them of each phrase in context. Ask them to paraphrase them in their own words.

KEY
can't be bothered: not to have enough energy or enthusiasm (to do something)
see the last of: literally, see for the last time
have a good ear: be able to listen to a tune and then play it on an instrument without any effort

17

UNIT 1

to 'discover': to find and make famous
easier said than done: it is easy to say the words but making them come true is harder

Exercise 2

Students think of equivalent terms and expressions in their own language. Allow them to use a bilingual dictionary. After five minutes, discuss the terms with the whole class.

KEY
Students pay to go to a *private school* but a *state school* is free. Children go from home to a *day school* every day but students live in (*board*) at a *boarding school*.

Primary school is for children between the ages of five and eleven whereas *secondary school* is for children aged eleven and over. *To go to college* means you are a student at a college, e.g. *She went to college to study engineering*, whereas *to get into college* means you have passed a selection procedure, either by exam or by interview. Everybody *takes an exam*. Some people *pass* and some *fail*. The outcome of the exam, i.e. pass or fail, is the *result*. These results can be classified into *grades*, e.g. Grade A, B, C, etc., or 1, 2, 3. A *degree* is normally only given by a university or a college of higher education.

 ## Exercise 3

Play the tape and get students to repeat the first group of words chorally. Refer them to the second group and ask them to say which is the stressed syllable in each word. Give an example of a stress by saying *NIGHT school* aloud. Write it with the stressed syllable in capital letters. Tell the students to copy the other words and mark the stressed syllables.

KEY
NIGHT school   PRIvate school   EVEning class
PUBlic school   ENGlish class

TAPESCRIPT
Listen to how the following are stressed.

day school, state school, public school, boarding school

Write these words with the correct stress in capital letters and then say them aloud.

night school, private school, public school, evening class, English class

 ## LISTENING

Before you listen

Explain *approve of/disapprove of* and point out that not everyone in Britain approves of private education.

KEY
1 Disapproves 2 Approves 3 Disapproves
4 Approves 5 Disapproves

Listen

Write on the board and explain: *relate with* (also give *relate to*), *selective*, *on principle*, *perpetuates the class system*, *obstacle* and *mix with*. Ask students to tell you which words of each speaker helped them to form their conclusions.

KEY
1 Disapproves 2 Approves 3 Disapproves
4 Disapproves 5 Approves

TAPESCRIPT
Listen to people giving their opinions of public schools like Eton. Note whether the speakers approve or disapprove of these schools.

1 I'm not in favour of public schools. I think every child should have the same opportunity of going to school. It seems like they are … it's more serious, they are … they're grown up too soon.
2 Yes, I think the public school system is a better system of education. It takes one outside the parental home, so for a single child it's particularly beneficial, and it teaches you to relate with other people.
3 I think it's not equal as it is a selective system, so, er, the, the students they just stay in their own level with their own people and don't get so much in touch with other people.
4 I disagree on principle with the idea of private education, er, because I think it perpetuates the British class system which is one of the major obstacles to any progress in this country.
5 I mean, if I had enough money I'd definitely send him 'cause, er, they're mixing with a better sort of person, aren't they? I mean, they talk better and everything when they go there.

EXTRA ACTIVITIES

1 School survey

Students interview each other about their schooldays using the chart below. They may then write a paragraph about their partner's school days.

Type of school:	…
School subjects:	Best …
	Worst …
Teachers:	Favourite …
	Least favourite …
Sport:	Favourite …
	Least favourite …
Most embarrassing moment: …	
What I like most/least about school: …	

2 Categories: a sorting activity

Write on the board a list of words commonly associated with the classroom and ask students to work in pairs to sort the words into groups. The list of words might include: *board, chalk, cassette-recorder, desk, textbook, calculator, pen, pencil, school bag, video, eraser* (*rubber*), *compass, ruler, computer, notepad, file, pencil case, pencil sharpener, atlas* and *dictionary*.

The students may use any criteria they like to categorise the words, e.g. *furniture/electrical equipment/things used by a teacher/things used by a student/things you can write with*, etc. When they have finished, they compare their categories with other pairs.

UNIT 2 Grammar
Present simple and continuous

What's the difference in meaning?

The first sentence, using the present simple tense, implies that Nick plays the guitar as a hobby, whereas the second sentence, using the present continuous, means that he is playing a guitar at the moment, i.e. now. Point out that *now* also include the current period of time, as do expressions such as: *nowadays, these days* and *at the moment*.

As students find examples of the present simple and the present continuous tenses in the Unit 1 text about Nick, write a selection on the board.

FOCUS

Point out the important note at the end of the section – that you cannot use the present continuous with verbs of thinking and verbs of emotion. At this stage of the lesson you may like to play the grammar game – Number 1 in 'Extra activities'.

PRACTICE

Revise question formation in the present simple by asking students to make questions from a substitution table:

Where	do	you they	live?
	does	he she Nick	

Exercise 1

Go through the example with the whole class before students complete the exercise in pairs. Insist that any variations in the questions are grammatically accurate.

KEY
1 How old is Nick?
2 What subjects is he taking for 'A' levels?
3 Why does he hate revising?
4 What musical instruments can/does he play?
5 What does he do in his spare time?
6 How often does he play?
7 What sort of school does he go to?
8 When is he leaving school?

Exercise 2

> BACKGROUND NOTES
> *New Musical Express*: A weekly magazine for pop music fans.
> *The Face*: A weekly magazine mostly devoted to nightclubs, lifestyles and fashion.
> *Bath and Reading*: These are both large towns in south England. Reading, pronounced /redɪŋ/, is about thirty-five miles west of London. Bath, which is further west, was an important city in the time of Roman Britain. It is famous for its architecture and its mineral baths.

Refer students to the information chart. Select different students to ask and answer each question about Nick. Make sure that the present continuous tense is used for the heading 'Current activity'.

SUGGESTED QUESTIONS
Where does he live?
What's his favourite magazine?
What's his favourite food?
What does he enjoy doing in his spare time?
What exams/'A' level subjects is he studying at the moment?
Apart from 'A' levels, what else is he doing at the moment?
What does he want to be or do in the future?
What's him ambition?

Refer to the information about the other two people. Practise the pronunciation of: *Economics, journalist, Portuguese, travel courier*. Students work through the charts in pairs.

Exercise 3

Students make similar charts and interview their partners. They should make notes sot that they can summarise and report the information from memory. For additional practice of the 3rd person singular -*s*, students can play the game *Who is it?* ('Extra activities' 2).

🔊 LISTENING

Write the list of names below on the board for students to copy.

Charles	*Martha*	*Wendy*	*Wynne*
Linda	*Martin*	*Edna*	*Thomas*
Lydia	*Bill*	*Edwin*	*Ned*
Colin		*Edward*	*Ellen*
			Nell

UNIT 2

Play the tape for the first time and tell students to tick the names which they hear. (There are six names mentioned.) Students then copy an outline of a family tree into their notebooks.

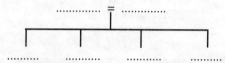

Play the tape for a second time. Students complete the family tree.

KEY

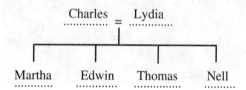

Play the tape for a third time to enable students to make notes about the characters. Encourage them to write more than one fact about each person.

TAPESCRIPT
Listen to an announcement for a new TV soap opera about a theatre family called 'The Hartleys'. Draw a family tree for the Hartley family and then write at least one fact about each person.

Come into the warm this winter and join the Hartley Family in ITV's new blockbuster series, 'The Hartleys'.

Enter the exciting world of London theatre life and meet the famous actor Charles Hartley – tall, grey-haired and handsome. Meet Lydia, his elegant actress wife. Together they are the most famous husband-and-wife team on the London stage.

Meet their children, the beautiful teenage twins Martha and Edwin, who are both hoping to become successful actors like their parents. The twins live at home. Their brother, Thomas, lives on his own and write plays. Their glamorous elder sister, Nell, is a dancer who is happily married to an architect.

However, things are not as happy as they seem. Charles is having money problems and is seeing another woman. Lydia wants a divorce. The magic world of the Hartleys is falling apart.

Be there when the drama begins next Thursday at 9 o'clock! Come into the warm world of 'The Hartleys'. Only on ITV!

WRITING

Exercise 1

Ask students what they already know about Nick's father before they read. They then read the text and tell you what else they have learned about him.

Draw attention to the linking devices: *and*, *but*, *so* and *because* and the time markers: *then*, *at the moment* and *next year*.

Exercise 2

Students plan their character sketch by making notes (five minutes). They can create an imaginary person if they wish.. Then students link the notes into connected paragraphs. This can be finished for homework.

EXTRA ACTIVITIES

1 Right or wrong?

For this grammar game, prepare ten sentences using the present simple and continuous tenses, half of which are grammatically wrong, e.g. *I am liking ice-cream*. Read each sentence aloud, being careful not to reveal which ones are wrong by your voice or expression. Students put a tick or cross against each number to indicate which are right and which are wrong.

2 Who is it?

This is a game to practice the 3rd person singular -s. Students work in pairs to choose a well-known TV character or personality, real or fictitious, and make notes about the character. Tell them to refer back to the paragraph about Nick's father. Each pair describes their character, taking turns to give a sentence. The rest of the class guesses who the person is.

3 True or false?

Each student thinks of three facts about themselves and their daily routine, one of which must be false. The aim is to try to disguise the false statement by choosing three unusual routines and activities, e.g.

I always drink a glass of hot water when I wake up in the morning.
I go back to bed after breakfast and read the paper.
I always brush my teeth before and after breakfast.

Divide the class into groups. In turn, each student reads out the three sentences and the others must confer before deciding which statement is false, e.g. *We think you are not telling the truth about brushing your teeth. We don't think you brush your teeth twice.*

Workbook tapescript

Unit 2

Exercise 3

Look at your book and listen. Label the photograph with the correct names.

FRIEND: So who's that one, Sarah? He's good-looking.

SARAH: Oh, the one drying himself? That's my cousin Jack. Yes, he's married now and he has a child.
FRIEND: Really? Is that his wife there, holding the ball?
SARAH: No, he wasn't married then. That's Helen. She was his girlfriend when this photo was taken. She's really nice. She lives in Brighton now and I sometimes go and visit her.
FRIEND: So who's the girl next to you? And why's she making that funny face?
SARAH: Oh, that's my friend Alice. I think she's just tried to eat a sandwich full of sand. Haven't you met Alice? She works in my office.
FRIEND: No, I don't think I have. And I suppose that's your brother Peter running out of the water?
SARAH: Yes, that's right.
FRIEND: Does he still play football?
SARAH: Oh yes, he plays for his local team now.
FRIEND: Do you ever go and watch him?
SARAH: No, now I have my own business. I don't really get the time.

Exercise 4
Listen again and write about the people.

Unit 2
Speechwork: Pronunciation
Present simple question forms

Exercise 5
A
Listen to this question.
Where do you work?
Now listen and repeat.
do you [bleep] do you [bleep]
Where do you work? [bleep]

Listen to this question.
Where do they live?
Now listen and repeat.
do [bleep] do they [bleep]
Where do they live? [bleep]

Listen to this question.
What does she do?
Now listen and repeat.
does [bleep] does she [bleep]
What does she do? [bleep]

Listen to these questions and repeat.
Where do you come from? [bleep]
What does she do?]bleep]
Where do they work? [bleep]
Do you like it? [bleep]

B
Now you make questions. Listen to the example.
Where does she live?
He
Where does he live?
Now you do it.
Where does she live?
He [bleep]
Where does he live?
They [bleep]
Where do they live?
You [bleep]
Where do you live?
She [bleep]
Where does she live?

Unit 2
Exercise 6
Look at your book and tick the sentences which you hear.

Example: They live here.

1 I know you.
2 Do you drive this car?
3 Do we have to stay here?
4 They all study English.
5 You work very hard.

UNIT 3 COMMUNICATION
Shopping

Photograph and questions

Ask the students to describe what is happening in the photograph. Ask the questions printed in the book and let the conversation develop according to the students' interests. Before directing the students' attention to the dialogue, help them to construct a possible conversation between the young woman and the shop assistant. Suggest that the woman ask for two things, one of which is not available. Ask one or two students to roleplay their dialogue.

 DIALOGUE

> **BACKGROUND NOTES**
> *Pink Floyd*: a world-famous rock band who enjoyed great success in the 1970s and again in the 1990s.
> *U2*: a world-famous Irish rock band whose hit albums include 'The Unforgettable Fire', 'Achtung Baby' and 'Zooropa'.

Students listen with books closed to compare the dialogue with their roleplay versions. They then open their books and listen again. Ask what questions the woman asked the assistant. Comment on any new words or expressions, e.g. *sold out*, *in stock*, *one moment*, *pity* (short for *What a pity!*), *receipt* /rɪsiːt/. In pairs, students ask and answer the questions under the dialogue. Finally, they listen to and repeat the dialogue, and read it in pairs.

UNIT 3

KEY
1 The latest Pink Floyd album and *Zooropa* by U2
2 *Zooropa*.
3 £13.99
4 Because it wasn't in stock/it was completely sold out.

FOCUS

Go through the sentences, practising chorally and individually using the back-chaining technique. The students then substitute other items in the section 'Asking for things'. Point out that a fall rise intonation indicates politeness and that in the 'Deciding to buy' sections, *have* and *take* are interchangeable. The verb *buy* is less common.

PRACTICE

Exercise 1

> BACKGROUND NOTES
> **Stationery shops**: Big stationery stores and shops in Britain, such as W. H. Smith's, also sell books, magazines, tapes, records and videos.
> **Tina Turner**: A famous female black American singer and entertainer.
> **James Herbert**: A best-selling British author of horror books.
> **Vogue**: A women's fashion magazine.
> **Arena**: A men's magazine.

Before starting, ask students to suggest some things you might buy in a stationery shop and build up a word field on the board, e.g. *writing paper* and *envelopes*, *pens*, *pencils*, *paper clips*, *computer discs*, *files*, *notebooks*. (See Unit 1, Extra activity 3.) Discuss places to buy stationery in the locality. Go through the instructions carefully so that the students know exactly what they have to do. Choose one student to work T–S and go through the shopping list to give an example of the conversation. Students then work in pairs, changing parts after the request for the writing paper, so that each students practises both sides of the conversation. Refer students back to the dialogue to use as a model.

Exercise 2

Ask students to write down as many items of clothing as they know in one minute. Collect the words on the board. Refer the students to the pictures of the clothes in the Student's Book. Ask different students to read out the prices, e.g. *The jacket costs £125.50*. Prepare the alternative conversations by working T-S with two students. Teach any other shopping expressions the students might find useful e.g. *I don't think it suits me. It doesn't fit me. It's too tight/loose. I need a larger/smaller size.*

For a follow-up activity, use mail-order catalogue pictures to shop for more items.

LISTENING

 Before you listen

Collect the answers to the questions in three lists, e.g. *Types of music, Things to buy in music stores, Ways of paying for goods*.

Listen

Play the tape as far as: *I think I'll leave it* and ask students to note down the first two pieces of information. Play the rest of the tape for students to complete the task. Play the tape a third time, pausing to check each piece of information as it occurs and to explain any new vocabulary.

KEY
1 The new recording of Beethoven's Fifth Symphony by the London Symphony Orchestra and a video of the Wimbledon Tennis Final, *Wimbledon Highlights*.
2 The first item was not in stock, the second item was too expensive.
3 Three blank video cassettes.
4 £12.50: by cheque.

TAPESCRIPT
Listen to the conversation in the record shop. Look at your Students' Book and follow the instructions.

ASSISTANT: Can I help you?
CUSTOMER: Yes, which is the classical music section, please?
ASSISTANT: It's over there to the right. Do you want anything special?
CUSTOMER: Yes, I wanted the new recording of Beethoven's Fifth Symphony by the London Symphony Orchestra.
ASSISTANT: Beethoven's Fifth by the London Symphony Orchestra? I'm afraid it's not in stock yet.
CUSTOMER: Do you know when you'll get in it?
ASSISTANT: It'll be in by Saturday I should think.
CUSTOMER: Oh, well, I'll come in then.
ASSISTANT: Anything else?
CUSTOMER: Yes, I'd like the video cassette of last year's Wimbledon tennis finals.
ASSISTANT: Wimbledon Highlights you mean?
CUSTOMER: Yes, how much is it?
ASSISTANT: It's £29.95.
CUSTOMER: Oh, that's rather expensive. I think I'll leave it. Thanks anyway. Oh, but I'll take three blank video cassettes, please. How much are they?
ASSISTANT: There's a special offer on blank cassettes. Only £12.50 for a pack of three.
CUSTOMER: O.K. Do you take cheques?
ASSISTANT: Yes, but only with a banker's card.
CUSTOMER: That's O.K. Can I borrow a pen?

UNITS 3/4

WRITING

The dialogue writing can be set for homework. Tell students to refer back to the original dialogue as a model.

EXTRA ACTIVITIES

1 Correct and act (shopping dialogues)

As an alternative way of correcting the dialogue writing, ask each student to pass their uncorrected dialogues along two places. Students correct the dialogue they have received and pass it on again two places. Students act the corrected dialogues in pairs. Ask one or two pairs to perform their dialogues for the whole group.

2 Sale time! (Classroom shop)

Students organise a classroom sale, with proceeds going to a charity or school fund. Students bring to class the items which they want to sell. They then price and display them. All the shopping must be carried out in English. Set a maximum price for any article, e.g. £1 (or equivalent).

 Workbook tapescript

Unit 3

Exercise 2

Listen and write the prices.

Example: It was really cheap, only £5.50.

1 Only £9.90.
2 £110 … Do I hear any more? Gone at £110.
3 On Mondays and Wednesdays, only £2 for senior citizens!
4 And in our foyer you can buy a selection of drinks and ice-creams starting at fifty pence.
5 The new minister will be paid £43,000 a year.

Unit 3

Speechwork: Stress and intonation
Asking for things

Exercise 3

A

Listen to these questions.
Have you got the LATest Pink FLOYD album?
Have you got any ALbums by Pink FLOYD?
Now listen and repeat.
Have you got the LATest Pink FLOYD album? [bleep]
Have your got any ALbums by Pink FLOYD? [bleep]

B

Now you ask questions. Listen to the example.
the latest Tina Turner album [bleep]
Have you got the latest Tina Turner album?
any writing paper [bleep]
Have you got any writing paper?
any books by Agatha Christie [bleep]
Have you got any books by Agatha Christie?
the latest Beat magazine [bleep]
Have you got the latest Beat magazine?

UNIT 4 GRAMMAR
Not allowed to and *not supposed to*

Photograph

Ask: *Where are the people? Who is the man and what's his job? What do you think the man is saying?* Ask students why people often wait outside stage doors after theatre performances.

 DIALOGUE

> BACKGROUND NOTES
> *Theatre Royal, Windsor*: This is a real theatre at Windsor where plays and shows are often performed before opening in a London theatre.
> *Saturday afternoon*: As well as evening performances, there are two afternoon performances (matinées) at a theatre, one mid-week, and one on Saturday.
> *Timothy Dalton*: An actor who played the name part in some James Bond films.

Students listen to the dialogue on tape with books closed. While they listen, ask them to find out what the girl wants and if she gets what she wants. Play the tape again, pausing to explain *you lot*, *block*, *at least* and *revise*. Students ask and answer the questions after the dialogue. Students listen to and repeat the dialogue, and then read it in pairs.

KEY
1 Because they're waiting to see Timothy Dalton. They want to get his autograph.
2 Because they're not allowed to.
3 Because they're not supposed to block the street. He tells them to move on.
4 She invites him to come and have a coffee.
5 Because he's supposed to be revising.

FOCUS

Draw the students' attention to the use of *not allowed to* and *not supposed to* in the dialogue. Ask what the difference is in meaning between them. Explain that *not supposed to* is not as strong as *not allowed to*. Explain also that, although the negative forms of *allowed to* and *supposed to* are quite similar in meaning, the positive forms are very different in meaning.

I'm allowed to means *I have permission to*,
e.g. *I'm allowed to stay out until ten.*
I'm supposed to means *I have a duty/responsibility to*.
e.g. *I'm supposed to be back at six.*

UNITS 4/5

PRACTICE

Exercise 1

Divide the class into six groups and give each group a situation from the list. One person in each group acts as a reporter. Help with any difficult or unusual vocabulary. After two or three minutes, ask the reporters to report their lists. Accept rules using the positive *supposed to* as well.

Exercise 2

Read each sign. Ask where students might see it. Ask if it is a definite rule, or simply a polite request. Students explain the notices to each other, using *not allowed to* or *not supposed to*.

KEY

1 You're not allowed to turn right on this road.
2 You're not allowed to drop litter in the street.
3 You're not supposed to smoke in this office.
4 You're not allowed to travel without a ticket on the bus/tube/train.
5 You're not supposed to drop litter in the street.
6 You're not allowed to park here between 8.00 and 18.30.
7 You're not supposed to talk to the driver of this bus/coach.

 ### Exercise 3

Pause after *Ann Douglas* for the students to answer the first part. Discuss the clues which show that the announcement is taking place in a theatre. Ask what is usually not allowed in a theatre. Then play the rest of the announcement.

KEY
– In a theatre.
– You are not allowed to take photographs and you are not allowed to record anything.

TAPESCRIPT
Listen to the announcement and note down where the announcement is taking place and what two things are not allowed.

Good evening, ladies and gentlemen, and welcome to this evening's performance of 'Follies' at the Theatre Royal. We regret to announce that Miss Dolores Crane is unwell and the part of Carlotta will be played by Ann Douglas. Members of the audience are kindly reminded that the taking of photographs is not allowed, nor is the recording of any part of the performance. Thank your for your attention. We hope you enjoy the show.

EXTRA ACTIVITIES

1 How to play it

Students form groups and choose a game or sport which they know well. They must try to explain the rules of the game as simply as possible, using *must*, *have to* and *not allowed to/allowed to*.

2 Rules and regulations

On the board, list the following areas of life to which rules and regulations apply:

Customs and excise   Pollution
Energy conservation   Road safety
Currency regulations Traffic regulations

In pairs, students have five minutes to write as many rules and regulations as they can. The winning pair is the one which can think of most rules.

UNIT 5 READING
Understanding boys

Pictures

Ask students to describe what the pictures show and what point they are trying to make.

Before you read

Use the questions as a way of raising the issues which occur in the text. In Question 2, ask the students if they ever played with toys which were specially designed for the opposite sex.

Text: Understanding boys

Students read the text silently, using the Comprehension questions as a focus.

COMPREHENSION

KEY

1 They dress girls in pink and boys in blue and they often give guns to boys and dolls to girls.
2 They're supposed to be good at sport, to stand up for themselves in fights and to suffer pain without crying.
3 Often other boys will tease and bully them.
4 By assuring boys that it is all right to be a swot as well as a sports star, a conformist as well as a rebel, shy as well as a girl chaser.

Re-read the text with the students. Check the meaning of any difficult words, especially those in the 'Guess the meaning' section by asking for synonyms, explanations or translations.

THINK ABOUT IT

1 Use the first question to revise the gerund with *good at*, e.g. *good at sewing/cooking/nursing people/doing housework*, etc.

2 SUGGESTED ANSWERS
Some girls think that getting married, setting up home and having children is their only goal in life. They don't think that they can be strong, intelligent, rebellious and good at sport, etc.

Guide the discussion back to the students' own lives, so that those who found the text difficult, or who have not contributed very much to the discussion, can provide some information about themselves.

WRITING

Write these sentences on the board: *I like going to the cinema./I like going to the theatre.* Ask a student to join the two sentences with *and*. Ask if any students can think of another way of joining the sentences. Elicit or present *as well as* and *both ... and* show how they are used.

Repeat with the negative sentences: *I'm not very good at English./I'm not very good at Maths.* Ask a student to link these sentences with *or*, and then ask if any of them can link the sentences with *neither ... nor*.

Students read the examples in the book and write some sentences about themselves. They can say what they like or don't like doing, or what they're good at doing or not good at doing. Each sentences must use a different linking device.

VOCABULARY

Explain that *macho* and *wimp* are common colloquial expressions. Students copy the words into their notebooks and see how quickly they can complete the list of opposites, using a bilingual dictionary. If the exercise is too difficult, or time is short, write the words and their opposites on separate pieces of paper and distribute them at random round the class. Students then have to find their right 'partner', i.e. the person who holds the opposite to their word.

KEY
big	small
brave	cowardly
extrovert	introvert
hard	soft/easy
hardworking	lazy
noisy	quiet
strong	weak
tall	short

EXTRA ACTIVITIES

1 The perfect woman/man

In groups, students discuss what society expects the ideal woman or man to be like, look like and behave like, e.g. *Women are supposed to be kind, slim and beautiful. They are supposed to be good at cooking, etc.*

2 Sentence openings

Write sentence openings on the board (see below). Students finish the sentences to make statements about the discipline they had in their own childhood. Students first discuss these sentences in pairs, then combine with another pair to discuss them in fours, and finally in groups of eight.

I wasn't allowed to ... until I was ...
I was allowed to ... when ...
I remember I wasn't/we weren't supposed to ...
My sister/brothers ... but I ...
When I was a small child, I ...
When I was a teenager, I ...

UNIT 6 GRAMMAR
Past simple and continuous

PRESENTATION

With books closed, write on the board a timetable of your daily routine, e.g.

My daily timetable	
6.30	Get up.
6.30–6.45	Have shower and get dressed.
6.45	Put on coffee.
6.45–7.10	Have breakfast and listen to news.
7.15	Leave home.
7.15–7.45	Drive/Walk to school.
8.15–11.30	Teach.

Use the timetable to practise the following three types of question and answer:

QUESTIONS	ANSWERS
1 *What did you do at 6.30 yesterday morning?*	*I got up.*
2 *What time did you get up?*	*I got up at 6.30.*
3 *Did you get up at 6.30?*	*Yes. I did.*
Did you get up at 7.00?	*No, I didn't.*

Continue with the other points of time, *6.45* and *7.15*. Then get students to ask you about what you were doing at other times during the morning, e.g. *What were you doing at 7 o'clock yesterday morning? I was having breakfast and listening to the news.*

As you give all your answers, write them on the board in the form of a table and add other pronouns.

I (He) (She)	was	having getting having listening	a shower. dressed. breakfast. to the news.
(You) (We) (They)	were	driving walking teaching	to school. to class. Class 4.

Ask the students to name the two tenses they have been using.

UNIT 6

Illustration

With books open, students describe what they can see and what is happening. Ask them to read the text beneath the picture. If necessary, explain that Sue took some money from her wallet to go and pay for the petrol and unwisely left her wallet in the car. (See a fuller version of this story in Exercise 3.) Point out the use of *garage* for *petrol station* and the preposition *for* in *pay for*. Check that students know the infinitive of the verbs *drove* and *stole*.

FOCUS

Students refer back to the text beneath the picture. They match the use of tenses with the different categories in the Focus section.

In the first sentence, the past simple is used to talk about a complete action or event in the past. In the second sentence, the past continuous is used to talk about an interrupted event in the past. Go through the other used of the tenses in the Focus section, eliciting or giving more examples of each use.

What's the difference in meaning?

In Sentence 1, the phone rang after she woke up, whereas in Sentence 2, it was already ringing when she woke up, i.e. it had started to ring some time before. Demonstrate the two sentences with *time lines*.

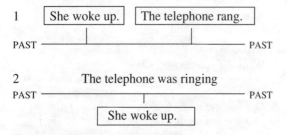

PRACTICE

> **BACKGROUND NOTES**
> **Pasadena**: A suburb of Los Angeles.
> **NBC – National Broadcasting Company**: An American broadcasting company.
> **motel**: A hotel for travelling motorists, usually on a single floor or two floors, i.e not a tall building.

Exercise 1

Use a map of the USA to set the situation of Sue Barnes in California. Students take turns to ask the questions. Explain that they must use connectors like: *then, after that, after she had lunch*, etc.

KEY

1 Before lunch
First she arrived at NBC studios. Then she had breakfast with the producer of Musical Box. After that she left the studio and drove to the concert hall in Pasadena and interviewed the jazz singer called Dee Dee Bridgewater.

2 After lunch
After she had had lunch with Dee Dee's manager, Sue took some photographs of Dee Dee Bridgewater. Then she left the concert hall and returned to the motel.

3 In the evening
In the evening Sue attended a party in Hollywood. She returned to the motel at half past twelve at night.

Exercise 2

KEY
1 She was having breakfast with the producer of Musical Box.
2 She was driving to a concert hall in Pasadena.
3 She was interviewing a jazz singer called Dee Dee Bridgewater.
4 She was having lunch with Dee Dee's manager.
5 She was taking photographs of Dee Dee Bridgewater.
6 She was attending a party in Hollywood.

Bring the class together and ask students mixed questions about Sue's timetable, e.g. *Who did she have lunch with? How was she travelling?* etc.

Exercise 3

Help the students with any new words. At the end, ask one or two students to tell the story without looking at their books. Allow time for students to talk about similar experiences which they have had or know about.

KEY
While Sue Barnes, a reporter for the New Musical Express, was travelling round the USA last year, she had an unpleasant experience. She had interviewed a jazz singer and had recorded the interview on a cassette which was on the front seat of her car together with other personal belongings.

She was driving back to her motel after a party in Hollywood on her last night when she realised that she was running out of petrol. She stopped at an all-night petrol station just off the main highway. She filled the petrol tank, took 20 dollars from her wallet and went to the kiosk to pay. While she was paying, a boy suddenly appeared from the shadows, opened her car door and took her wallet, passport and return air ticket – and her cassette!

LISTENING

Explain that the mistakes are to do with details, e.g. what time of day it was, or how much money Sue was carrying, etc. Students use Sue Barnes's notes and the text from Exercise 3 for comparison. Before students begin, explain that the tape says the singer's concert was in Los Angeles. Strictly speaking, this is not an error, since Pasadena (see the Travel Schedule in the Students' Book) is a suburb of Los Angeles. Play the tape twice. Discuss each mistake and how it should be corrected.

KEY

1 The interview was with Dee Dee Bridgewater, not Big Mama Robinson.
2 The cassette was on the front seat, not the back.
3 The incident didn't happen during her first week, it happened on her last night.
4 It was late at night, not early in the evening.
5 She wasn't driving back to the studios, she was driving back to her motel.
6 It wasn't a girl who stole her belongings, it was a boy.

TAPESCRIPT

Listen to a friend of Sue's retelling the story at a party. Note five details which he get wrong.

MAN: Did you hear what happened to poor Sue in the States last year? It was really shocking – it was her first trip, too. Um, she was travelling in California at the time and she'd got a marvellous interview on tape with Big Mama Robinson, the jazz singer. Apparently Big Mama was doing a concert in Los Angeles, and, er, Sue had managed to get an, an interview with her. Well, anyway Sue had the interview on the cassette and, er, the cassette was on the back seat of the car. Well, early one evening – um, I think it was some time during her first week there – she was driving back to the studios, but she needed to fill up with petrol, so she stopped at a petrol station and just as she was paying, a girl pulled opened the car door and took the cassette and Sue's passport and her wallet and her return air ticket!
WOMAN: Goodness! Whatever did she do? Poor thing!

WRITING

Students can invent an incident if they wish. They should use some of the remaining class time preparing for this by making notes, asking for help and writing the first few lines. They can complete the paragraph for homework.

EXTRA ACTIVITIES

1 Guess the job: a miming game

One person mimes an action which is typical of a particular job; e.g. if the person was pretending to be a waiter, he/she might mime walking over to a table and taking an order. The others must first guess what the person was doing, e.g. *Were you writing something?*, and then the name of the job.

2 Past simple and past continuous consequences

Ask each student to take a good-sized sheet of paper to use for a chain of consequences. Write the outline for the consequences on the board as follows:

1 While (Man's name) was (verb)ing this morning,
2 (Woman's name) came in to (infinitive).
3 He said ...
4 She said ...
5 And then they ... (past simple).

Start the chain by writing a sentence after the first cue, e.g. *While John was having breakfast this morning*, ... Students copy this. They then fold the paper over backwards and pass it on to the next person who writes the next cue, folds it over and passes it on, and so on until all the cues are finished. The complete set of 'consequences' is then unfolded and read aloud. The simplest way to play the game is for the teacher to call out the instructions, and to check that everyone is keeping up.

3 Alibi

Two 'suspects' have to account for their movements during a certain period of time when a 'crime' was committed. They leave the room and think of activities to establish an 'alibi', proving that they were together during the time. Each suspect is then questioned alone by the rest of the group about their activities. The questions should be in the past simple or the past continuous tenses. Alternatively, the class divides into two halves. Each half interviews one student at opposite ends of the room. Then each group ask the same questions to the other student. Any differences between the alibis will show if the suspects are telling the truth or not.

Workbook tapescript

Unit 6

Exercise 2

Listen to the scenes and write what happened.

Example:

A series of sounds in a park: birds singing, children playing, people playing tennis. Then it starts to rain. There's a muffled shout of: 'Ohhh, look at that rain' followed by the sound of running footsteps. Then a voice in a room says: 'Phew, that's better.'

1 There's the sound of a television, interrupted by the sound of the doorbell. A man says: 'Is that the doorbell?' A woman responds: 'Er, I think so – I'll get it.' We hear her open the front door and exclaim: 'Oh!' in surprise.

UNITS 6/7

2 There's the sound of a man sleeping and snoring slightly, then a large but muffled crash from next door. The man wakes up with a grunt. We can hear a man and a woman having an argument next door. The woman throws something, or hits the man. The man shouts 'Ow!' and then throws something or hits the woman. She screams.

Unit 6

Speechwork: Pronunciation
Past simple question forms

Exercise 4

A

Listen to these questions.
What did you do?
Where did they go?

Now listen and repeat.
did [bleep] did you [bleep]
What did you do? [bleep]
did [bleep] did they [bleep]
Where did they go?

B

Now you make questions. Listen to the example.

Where did they go?
You
Where did you go?

Now you do it.
Where did they go?
You [bleep]
Where did you go?
She [bleep]
Where did she go?
He [bleep]
Where did he go?
They [bleep]
Where did they go?

Unit 6

Exercise 5

Listen and circle the word which you hear.

Example: Did you like it?

1 Do you agree?
2 Were they waiting for you?
3 Is she sitting outside?
4 Do they want to stay long?
5 Was it raining?
6 Did you always stay there?
7 Are they going out?

UNIT 7 TOPIC
A career in films

Before you read

1 Ask the students if they know any films in which Antonio Banderas has acted. The ones mentioned in the text are: *Philadelphia*, *The House of the Spirits*, *Interview with a Vampire*, *The Mambo Kings*. Write any ones they mention on the board and ask if they can name one or two other stars in each of the films, e.g. Tom Hanks, Jeremy Irons, Meryl Streep, Tom Cruise.
2 Ask the students' opinion of Antonio Banderas as an actor and why they think he has become popular.
3 Refer to the list of films and ask the students which they think can be called 'major Hollywood films'. Ask what difficulties Antonio Banderas might have had in Hollywood.
4 Ask students to work in pairs listing words and phrases to do with films, e.g. *film/movie* (American English.), *film actor/actress/star*, *film role/part*, *to star in*, *to co-star in*, *(film) studio*, *(on) location*, *director*, *producer*, *to film*, *to make/shoot a film*, *a close-up*.

Text: Banderas – International filmstar

> BACKGROUND NOTES
> *Málaga*: a large city in the southern part of the Mediterranean coast of Spain.
> *Pedro Almodóvar*: a well-known Spanish writer-director who gained an international reputation through many startling and controversial films. He is noted for working with a regular team of actors.

Ask students to skim read the text and find:

1 the titles of 4 films (if these have not already been mentioned)
2 the names of 5 film stars, a film director, a novelist and an actress.

Ask students to look at Exercise 1 and note the information they need to find.

Words to learn

As students read the text, they should try to work out the meaning of the 'Words to learn'.

Exercise 1

Allow about five minutes for students to read the text and note the information. Ask questions for individual students to answer. As you work through the information, check comprehension of the words to learn.

28

SUGGESTED ANSWERS
1 He studied there between the ages of 13 and 18.
2 Pedro Almodóvar, a young film director, was the first person who asked him if he would like to make a film/movie.
3 *The Mambo Kings* was Antonio Banderas' first Hollywood film.
4 Tom Hanks, the star of *Philadelphia*, subsequently won an Oscar for Best Actor for his performance in the film.
5 Antonio Banderas became well-known as the person who said 'No' to Madonna because he was married.

Exercise 2

In pairs, students work out questions which could have been asked during the interview. Explain that they should produce at least one question for each paragraph of the text.

SAMPLE QUESTIONS
When/Where were you born?
Where did you go to school?/Where were you educated?
What acting experience did you get/have at drama school?
When did you go to Madrid?
How did you start you acting career?
Why did you decide to go into films?
How long did you work with the director, Pedro Almodóvar?
What was your first Hollywood film?
Did you have any difficulty with English?
What (Hollywood) films have you made?
Are you married? Who are you married to?
Where do you live?/Have you got any family?
What do you like doing in your spare time?
Do you lead the life of a typical film star?
How do you like Hollywood/Los Angeles/the USA?
How do you see the future?

Exercise 3

Discuss the questions with the whole class.

SUGGESTED ANSWERS
1 Almodóvar probably felt sad that he was going to lose such a close collaborator, but he was probably also pleased that his friend was becoming so successful.
2 Very glamorous and expensive.
3 Superficial and not sincere: they say everything is wonderful when it's not.

VOCABULARY

Exercise 1

KEY
Adjective	Adverb
dreadful	dreadfully
beautiful	beautifully
awful	awfully
hopeful	hopefully
wonderful	wonderfully
helpful	helpfully
terrible	terribly

 ### Exercise 2

Point out that the main stress falls on the first syllable of both adjective and adverb, e.g. SENsible SENsibly. Get them to say some of the words aloud, exaggerating the stress. Point out that the fully part of the adverb is often pronounced /fli/, e.g. /'dredfli/.

TAPESCRIPT
Listen and note where the main stress falls on the adjective and adverb.

sensible, sensibly, dreadful, dreadfully, beautiful, beautifully, awful, awfully, hopeful, hopefully, wonderful, wonderfully, helpful, helpfully, terrible, terribly

Exercise 3

In the following two exercises, students distinguish between gradable and non-gradable adjectives, i.e. those which can be preceded by *quite* or *very* and are therefore gradable, e.g. (*very/quite*) *beautiful*; and those which are superlatives in themselves and which are therefore non-gradable, e.g. *dreadful*.

KEY
She is very sensible/beautiful/hopeful/helpful.

Exercise 4

KEY
It's dreadfully/awfully/wonderfully/terribly hot.
(*Beautifully hot* is possible but not common.)

 ## LISTENING

Explain that the speaker is going to tell a story about an incident when he was younger and anxious to make a good impression on his girlfriend's parents. Write the following words and phrases on the board and ask students to guess what they think the story is about: *anxious to make a good impression*, *run the bath*, *turn off*, *tap*, *door locked/jammed*, *unlock*, *overflow*. Play the tape once. Students note the main events of the story. Play the tape again. Students listen more carefully for time indicators.

Students retell the story in their own words and/or tell similar stories.

KEY
Time indicators
a long time ago, when I was about 18, at that age, on the first morning, finally, eventually, finally

TAPESCRIPT
Listen to someone talking about an amusing incident. Note down the key points. Then listen

again and note down any words or phrases about time.

Well, er, I remember a story that happened to me ... oh a long time ago when I was about eighteen, I suppose, erm. I was visiting, visiting my, my girlfriend, erm. She lives up in, up in the north. It was quite a long way to go, erm, and I, I was meeting her parents for the first time. Well, as you can imagine, at that age I was, I was anxious to make a, a good impression and, er, on the, on the first morning I went into the bathroom and started to run the bath and have a shave and do all those sorts of things, and, erm, the bath was running away and, er, I went to turn it off when it had, er, got up to nearly full ... but the taps wouldn't work. I couldn't make them turn off. It was really embarrassing and, and whatever I did to them, they just wouldn't turn off, erm, and the water was getting higher and higher and higher and I simply couldn't turn the water off.

So I went to the door to, to open the door to, to, to call for some help, but I couldn't open the door either, er, the door, it was locked completely, erm, it jammed. It was quite, erm, worrying. So, erm, I finally called out very loudly.

Eventually my girlfriend came up the stairs and sort of relayed instructions through the door on how to unlock it and, er, we finally go it open and then the, there was the whole family standing outside and there was me, with this towel round my waist and nothing else, with the bath overflowing and pouring water on the floor, erm, er, well, so much for making a good impression!

WRITING

Ask students to check if any of the time phrases used in the Listening exercise appear in the summary of Antonio Banderas' life. Students reorder the events and then rewrite the sentences into their notebooks in the correct order.

Point out the following:

- the different ways of expressing age in the text: *at the age of thirteen*, *until I was eighteen*.

- that *after* and *before* can be followed by a gerund (verb + *ing*), to form the equivalent of a clause: *After graduating = After I graduated*.

- the difference between *for* and *during*. *For* is used with a period of time to say how long something went on, e.g. *He worked with Almodóvar for nine years*. *During* is used with a noun to say *when* something happened, now how long, e.g. *He worked with Pedro during the eighties*. It is used with nouns which refer to, or occupy, a period in time, e.g. *during the summer/winter/holidays/war/film/meal*.

- the difference between *eventually* and *finally*. *Eventually* means *after a time of waiting* when used with the past simple, e.g. *Eventually I went to Hollywood*. It can also mean *at some time in the future*, e.g. *We'll move to England eventually*.

- *Finally* means *at last*, e.g. *He has finally passed his exam*. (not *eventually*). It can also mean *lastly*, i.e. coming at the end of a list of things, e.g. *Finally, I'd like to mention the question of ...*

KEY
4, 6, 1, 3, 5, 2

Ask students to write sentences using *for*, *during*, *eventually* and *finally* and to use them in the paragraph which they write about themselves or a family member.

EXTRA ACTIVITIES

1 Find someone who ...

Students walk round asking questions to complete the following question sheet. They should collect information, not just Yes/No answers.

> Find someone who ...
> 1 wasn't watching TV last night at 9 p.m. (What was he/she doing instead?)
> 2 wasn't living in this area three years ago. (Where were they living?)
> 3 wasn't studying English two years ago.
> 4 didn't have a cup of coffee for breakfast this morning. (What did they have?)
> 5 went to church last Sunday. (Which church did they go to?)
> 6 went to the cinema last week. (What film did they see?)
> 7 visited another country last winter or summer. (Where did he/she go?)
> 8 did their homework on the way to school/college.

2 'Star' interviews

Students work in pairs. One student pretends he/she is an imaginary film star and invents a background and career for this person. The other student interviews the 'star' based on the questions from Exercise 2 (*Write questions*).

3 Film survey

Students do a survey in the class of the five most popular films, film actors and film actresses of the moment.

UNIT 8 COMMUNICATION
Apologies

PRESENTATION

With books closed, students suggest ways of apologising and responding to apologies. Note these on the board.

Illustration

With books open, but with the Dialogue covered, ask students what gives them the impression that the man is angry. Ask about the background to the scene: *What is their relationship? Where is the girl going? Why is she dressed in outdoor clothes?*

 ### DIALOGUE

With books open, get students to cover the dialogue and to look at Exercise 1 beneath it. Play the tape. Students note the answers to the questions. Students then discuss whether the father is being fair or not, and justify their reasons.

Exercise 1

KEY
1 Because she has come home very late. It is two o'clock in the morning.
2 To let him know if she is going to be late back.
3 Three times (I'm sorry/I really am sorry/Sorry, Dad.)
4 So you should be/O.K./That's O.K.

Exercise 2

Play the dialogue again. Go through it with the students, stopping at the idiomatic expressions. See how many the students can explain or paraphrase without your help. Take the opportunity to show them how to find an idiomatic expression in a dictionary.

KEY
1 What sort of a time do you call this?	Do you realise how late it is? (It is obvious that the father is angry. The question is mildly sarcastic.)
2 So you should be!	It's right that you should be sorry.
3 It's up to me.	It's my business/my decision.
4 worried stiff	extremely worried (c.f. bored stiff/frozen stiff)
5 let me know	tell me/inform me
6 give me a ring	telephone me

FOCUS

Explain that *Sorry* and *I'm sorry* are neutral apologies, whereas the following three are usually stronger. Point out that this is indicated not only in the addition of words like *terribly* but also by the way these words are emphatically stressed. Ask students to name situations in which the different apologies are appropriate. Explain that *So you should be!* is not included here as it is considered familiar and rather rude. It is used mostly by parents and teachers to children.

Point out the main stress and intonation pattern of the two expressions: *I'm sorry* and *I'm terribly sorry*. Although both expressions have a fall-rise intonation, they sound very different because of the stress shift.

PRACTICE

Exercise 1

Ask the students first to look at the pictures and say what is going on in each. Go through the explanations and explain *strike*. When they have matched the pictures with the explanations, students can practise roleplaying each scene. Encourage them to choose different apologies and responses each time.

KEY
1b 2d 3e 4c 5a

Exercise 2

> BACKGROUND NOTE
> *Ibiza*: A Spanish island in the Balearics, south west of Majorca. A popular holiday island.

Point out that there is no right answer. People get annoyed in different situations. When students have agreed on an order, ask them to select a suitable apology to match the seriousness of the situation. Explain that the 'offender' should offer to make amends where appropriate. This is clearly not possible in all situations, e.g. Situation 3.

EXAMPLE CONVERSATIONS
1 A: I'm terribly sorry. I'm afraid I left your flippers in Ibiza.
   B: Never mind. I can buy another pair.
   A: Oh no, I'll get another pair for you.
2 A: I'm awfully sorry but I forgot to buy the bread for the party.
   B: Oh never mind. It doesn't matter. I'll get it myself.
   A: No, no. I'll go out and get it now.
3 A: Is that 67744?
   B: No, this is 67743.
   A: Oh. Sorry, I've got the wrong number.
   B: That's O.K.

4 A: Oh, no. I really am sorry. I don't know how it happened.
   B: It doesn't matter. Don't worry about it.
   A: Look, you must let me pay for the cleaning.

LISTENING

You may like to ask the discussion question first, i.e *Can you remember an incident at a party where you had to apologise?* This can lead on to a general conversation about embarrassing things that can happen at parties. Elicit incidents like, e.g. *break/glass, spill/drink, arrive too early/arrive on the wrong day*, etc.

Tell the students that they are going to listen to an incident at a party. The first time they listen they should note what the woman did wrong and how she offered to make amends (Questions 1 and 4). The second time they listen, they should note down the other details (Questions 2, 3 and 5).

KEY
1 She broke a vase.
2 She said: 'I'm terribly sorry. I've broken your lovely vase. (There are bits everywhere, I'm afraid.) Oh, I am sorry!'
3 He said: 'Listen, don't worry about it. It's all right.'
4 She offered to mop up the water and to buy him a new vase.
5 He didn't accept. He said he never like it anyway.

TAPESCRIPT
Listen to an incident at a party. Look at your Students' Book and follow the instructions.

TIM: Suddenly he came up to me and said ...
ALISON: Who came up to you?
TIM: The man in the shop. Hey, mind that vase of flowers, Alison. You're ...
ALISON: Oh no! I bet it's valuable. And there's water everywhere.
TIM: Let's pick up the bits.
ALISON: Mind the flowers, Tim. You're treading on them. I'd better tell Paul.
PAUL: What's up, Alison?
ALISON: Paul. I'm dreadfully sorry. I've broken your lovely vase. There are bits everywhere, I'm afraid. Oh I am sorry!
PAUL: Listen. Don't worry about it. It's all right.
ALISON: But there's water all over the floor and all over the sofa. I'll go and get a cloth.
PAUL: Leave it Alison. Don't worry. It'll dry. It's only water.
ALISON: Look, I'll buy you another vase if you tell me where you got it.
PAUL: I haven't a clue, Alison. My aunt gave it to me and I never liked it anyway. Forget about it. Come on and have a drink.
ALISON: I really am frightfully sorry. I can't think how I ...

WRITING

Go through the expressions in the book and get the students to suggest different ways of finishing each expression. The letter can be done as a combined class effort on the board, or it can be started in class and set for homework.

SUGGESTED LETTER
Dear Paul,

Just a quick note to say thank you so much for your lovely party last Saturday. I had a wonderful time and met some really interesting people. I just wanted to say again that I'm terribly sorry about breaking your vase. I know you said it didn't matter but I'd really like to replace it with another vase if you can find something you like. Please let me know if you do.

Many thanks again and hope to see you soon.

Best wishes/Love,

Alison

EXTRA ACTIVITIES

1 Expanding apologies in a chain

One students starts with the word *Sorry* and the other students in turn have to add a word or phrase to expand the apology, each time repeating what has gone before, e.g. *Sorry ... I'm sorry ... I'm terribly sorry ... I'm terribly sorry I broke your vase ... I'm terribly sorry I broke your beautiful vase ...*

2 Chinese whispers

Think of a sentence of apology – the more complicated the better – and write it on a piece of paper, e.g. *I'm terribly sorry, but I am afraid I left your mask and your flippers in a hotel in Ibiza.* Ask all the players to form a circle. Whisper the apology to one person in the circle, who then has to pass the whispered message on to the next person, and so on, round the group. Compare the last person's sentence with the original and note the difference!

3 Embarrassing apologies

In groups of three, students discuss their 'most embarrassing apology'. When they have decided on three, they should put these in rank order from the least to the most embarrassing. Bring all the groups together for a general discussion to decide on the 'Top 10' embarrassing moments.

Workbook tapescript

Unit 8

Speechwork: Stress and intonation
Apologies

Exercise 3

Listen to these apologies.

SOrry.
I'm SOrry.
I'm TERRibly SOrry.
I'm AWfully SOrry.
I REAlly AM SOrry.

Now listen and repeat.

SOrry. [bleep]
I'm SOrry. [bleep]
I'm TERRibly SOrry. [bleep]
I'm AWfully SOrry. [bleep]
I REAlly AM SOrry. [bleep]

Exercise 4

Listen to the apologies and write which person sounds more sorry: a or b.

Example: a) Sorry. [polite] b) Sorry. [impolite]

1a I'm sorry. [polite]   1b I'm sorry. [impolite]
2a I'm terribly sorry. [impolite]
2b I'm terribly sorry. [polite]
3a I'm awfully sorry. [impolite]
3b I'm awfully sorry. [polite]
4a I really am sorry. [polite]
4b I really am sorry. [impolite]

UNIT 9 GRAMMAR
Used to and *be used to*

What's the difference in meaning?

Sentence 1 means that the person ate red meat in the past but doesn't any more, i.e. it was a past habit. Sentence 2 means that the person is accustomed to eating red meat, i.e. it is a present custom. Make sure the students notice the structural differences between the two sentences and point out that many students forget the *-ing* form of the verb when producing *I am used to* sentences. Ask the students for the different question forms of *used to* and *be used to* to elicit *Did you/she use to …?* and *Are you/Is she used to …?*

Text

Read the presentation text aloud. As you read, elicit or explain the meaning of: *masses of, dairy products, red meat, conscious of* and *diet*. Then ask these questions around the class:

Where did Sue grow up?
(She grew up on a farm.)
What sort of food did she use to eat a lot of?
(She used to eat a lot of/masses of meat and dairy products.)
How often did she use to eat red meat?
(She used to eat red meat nearly every day of the week.)
What happened a few years ago?
(She became more conscious of her diet.)
What food does she avoid now?
(She avoids red meat.)
What sort of diet is she used to now?
(She is used to a much lighter diet.)

FOCUS

Read the *be used to* sentences aloud to point out that *be used to* can be followed by either a verb in the *-ing* form, or a noun. Check the pronunciation of *used to*: /ˈjuːstə/ not /ˈjuːztə/.

Students may then like to discuss the following questions: *What sort of diet are you used to? What do you think your parents'/grandparents' diet was like? In what ways was it different from yours?*

PRACTICE

Exercise 1

> BACKGROUND NOTES
> **Manchester**: A big industrial city in the north west of England.
> **Fiat Uno**: A small Italian car.

KEY
1 Sue used to eat a lot of meat but now she is mainly vegetarian.
2 She used to have milk and cream with everything but now she drinks tea and coffee without milk.
3 She used to go on holidays with her family but now she goes abroad.
4 She used to live on a farm but now she lives in a flat in Manchester.
5 She used to drive a Fiat Uno but now she cycles everywhere.

Exercise 2

Introduce a few more examples of changes in your life. Revise how to form questions and negative statements using *used to*. Prompt with questions, e.g. *Did you use to go on holidays with your parents? What did you use to do at weekends? How much homework did you use to get when you were at primary school?*

When they have answered the questions, ask the students to make full sentences, e.g. *When I was at primary school, I didn't use to get any homework at all.*

Exercise 3

Ask students if they remember from Unit 6 what Sue's job is and where she was travelling when her cassette was stolen. Ask them to suggest what aspects of life in the United States they might find

UNIT 9

unusual and difficult. Students then compare their suggestions with Sue's notes. Go through the notes to make sure that they are all understood. Students should summarise and interpret the notes as if Sue is actually speaking. e.g. *I'm not used to driving everywhere*. With a good class this would be a chance to introduce the additional structure: *get used to*, meaning to become used to, e.g. *I can't get used to driving on the right*.

KEY

Driving:
I'm not used to driving everywhere.
(I can't get used to driving everywhere.)
I'm not used to a speed limit of 55 mph.
I'm not used to driving so slowly.
I'm not used to driving on the right.
I'm not used to driving without ever passing a traffic light.

Shopping:
I'm not used to being able to shop at any time of the day or night.

Weather:
I'm not used to so much sunny weather/the weather being sunny all the time.
I'm not used to sunbathing any time I like.

Exercise 4
On the board, write the heading: *What David isn't used to* and add under this: *living away from home*. Students read the paragraph, then work in pairs and make a list under the heading. Collect the students' notes and write them on the board.

Exercise 5
Students should write full sentence in their books.

KEY
1 He's not used to living away from home.
2 He's not used to doing things like cooking, washing and ironing for himself.
4 He's not used to choosing which lectures to go to.
4 He's not used to planning his own timetable.
5 He's not used to having so much freedom.
5 He's not used to working right through the night.

ACT IT OUT
Students use the sentences from Exercise 5 to prepare and act out a conversation. First read the opening sentences T–S, with you taking Sue's part and a student taking the part of the friend. Help the students to make questions for the friend, e.g. *How is he getting on with his studies?/How about his studies?* Then give students a few minutes to prepare their conversations. If there's time, one pairs acts out their conversation for the group.

EXAMPLE CONVERSATION
FRIEND: How's your brother settling down at university?
SUE: O.K., but it's a bit hard for him because he's not used to living away from home.
FRIEND: Really?
SUE: No, he's not used to doing things like cooking, washing and ironing for himself.
FRIEND: What about his studies?
SUE: I think he's getting on fine but it's very different from school.
FRIEND: How do you mean?
SUE: Well, he's not used to having so much freedom. You know, he can choose which lectures to go to and he can plan his own timetable.
FRIEND: That sounds all right to me.
SUE: Yes, but he has to work harder and he's not used to that either!

 LISTENING

Before you listen
Set a time limit of two to three minutes for the group discussion. Write on the board any suggestions which are not in the book.

Listen
Pause after each speaker on the tape to discuss what they say. When the students report back, explain that you can also say: *I'm not used to (noun) (verb)ing* where the subject of *used to* is different from the subject of the following verb, e.g. *I'm not used to people eating so quickly*.

KEY
Student 1: She's not used to speaking English all the time
Student 2: He's not used to the traffic/to (cars) driving on the left.
Student 3: He's not used to how quickly the English eat their meals/not used to people eating so quickly.
Student 4: She wasn't used to the noise of the traffic at first but now it's all right. She's not used to so much pollution. She's not used to people being so polite all the time.

TAPESCRIPT
Listen to some foreign students who are studying in Britain. Note what features of British life they aren't used to.

Mainly I find difficult to speak English all the time, er, it was, erm, a pressure, but, yes it's the only way to, really, kn... get to know the culture and a language.

I had a lot of troubles with the traffic. Because they drive on the, on the left. When I crossed the road, I looked always in the wrong direction. And it was so, sometimes so difficult.

I had to get used to how quickly the English eat their meals, We, we build relations at the table and spend more time.

I am living in a school building and my, my room faces the street and there is a lot of noise and in the beginning it was really awful. I couldn't sleep in the night and it took me actually three days to get used to it. And then I was so tired. I found the pollution was really striking. I'm not used to so much pollution and when I was visiting the city of London I feel it was so difficult to breathe. I, you could feel the pollution. I found people here are very polite and sometimes it seems like they are too polite to me, I'm not used to to it. It seems like it's printed in them to say 'Oh I'm sorry', 'Excuse me' and so all the time. I'm not used to that.

WRITING

Students may prefer to write about their own experiences.

EXTRA ACTIVITIES

1 Memories

Students discuss hobbies they used to have as children, family holidays they used to go on, pets they used to have and any unusual habits they had.

2 Settling down

Arrange students in small groups and ask: *What problems do you think these people have?*

1 A family who have just moved from a cold to a hot climate (or vice versa).
2 A couple who have moved from the city to the country (or vice versa).
3 People who become self-employed after working for a large organisation.

 Workbook tapescript

Unit 9
Speechwork: Pronunciation
Used to

Exercise 4

A
Listen to these sentences.
I used to have a car.
I used to enjoy school.

Now listen and repeat.
used [bleep] used to [bleep]
I used to have a car. [bleep]
used [bleep] used to [bleep]
I used to enjoy school. [bleep]

B
Now you make sentences. Listen to the example.

have short hair
I used to have short hair.

Now you do it.
have short hair [bleep]
I used to have short hair.
eat a lot of sweets [bleep]
I used to eat a lot of sweets.
play football [bleep]
I used to play football.
walk to school [bleep]
I used to walk to school.
go to bed at eight o'clock [bleep]
I used to go to bed at eight o'clock.

UNIT 10 READING
Cider with Rosie

> BACKGROUND NOTES
> **The Cotswolds**: The Cotswold Hills are a range of low-lying hills and valleys in the 'West Country' (south-west England). In Laurie Lee's day it was a very isolated area. Today it is considered one of the prettiest parts of the country.
> **Laurie Lee**: A 20th century writer and poet. His best known work is probably 'Cider with Rosie'. This is a beautiful and personal account of his childhood in a remote Cotswold village. A later book 'As I walked out one midsummer morning' tells how he left his village at nineteen and set out

PRESENTATION

With books closed, introduce the text using a map of England to show the position of the West Country and the Cotswolds. Present the content of the introductory paragraph in your own words. Check that the students know the dates of the First World War (1914-18).

Before you read

With books open, discuss the illustration of the room. Elicit words connected with furniture, fixtures and fittings and list them on the board. Alternatively, students do 'word maps' or 'spidergrams' of rooms and their furniture and fittings, e.g.

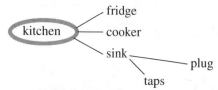

Games to exploit the picture are suggested in 'Extra activities'.

UNIT 10

COMPREHENSION AND

 Text: Cider with Rosie

Students read through the comprehension questions and the text silently. Ask them to notice how many of the 'furniture' words which they originally suggested actually occur in the text. Go through the text in detail, glossing and paraphrasing where necessary.

Guess the meaning

Ask students to define the words in the 'Guess the meaning' section, or to use them in sentences of their own.

Exercise 1

KEY
1 Eight, including Laurie's mother.
2 In the kitchen.
3 A piano and an organ.

Exercise 2

KEY
1 No, Laurie Lee grew up in a large cottage.
2 No, the girls all slept together in the attic.
3 No, the kitchen had a very low ceiling.
4 No, there were mats on the floor.
4 No, there were mats on the floor.
5 No, there were six tables of different sizes.
6 No, there were books on every chair.
7 No, the newspapers were in shapeless piles all round everything.

Ask more detailed questions about the text, e.g. about the furniture in the room, the tables, the potatoes, the armchairs, the clocks and the sofa.

THINK ABOUT IT

SUGGESTED ANSWERS
1 He didn't come from a wealthy family, but his family wasn't poor either. They had books, musical instruments and 'fine china'.
2 Because there was no privacy and nothing to do in the cottage because it was so far away from a town.
3 She was kind and loving but rather careless and untidy. She certainly wasn't 'house proud'. Perhaps she was quite cultured.

ABOUT YOU

Remind students how to use *used to* for talking about memories. Bring any interesting experiences to the attention of the whole class.

STYLE

Exercise 1

Ask different students to read the similes from the text and to think about how they are expressed in their own language. Then students work in pairs making similes. They can translate similes from their own language if they like, but you might like to mention the conventional similes below.

SUGGESTED SIMILES
as white as snow/a sheet/a ghost
as strong as iron/an ox/a horse
as tall as the sky/a tree/a mountain/a giraffe
(s)he sang like an angel/a nightingale/a bird/a lark
(s)he swam like a fish/a dolphin
(s)he ran like lightning/a deer/a gazelle/an arrow/the wind

Exercise 2

Ask the students why the phrases are strange. (Because they suggest that the objects are being used for unusual purposes. You would not normally say *a piano for playing*.) The phrases suggest that life in the cottage was untidy and carefree and that nobody bothered very much to keep the place clean.

TALKING POINT

Students first list their ideas to use in discussion with the whole group.

VOCABULARY

KEY
armchair, housework, tablecloth, candlestick, windowsill, washbasin, bookcase, dining room

Point out that *dining room* is written in two words (whereas *bedroom* is one word).

TAPESCRIPT AND KEY
Listen to the words and copy them, writing the main stress in capital letters. On which half of the noun does the stress fall?

ARMchair, HOUSEwork, TABlecloth, CANdlestick, WINdow sill, WASHbasin, BOOKcase, DIning room

The reverse stress for *armchair* is also possible, i.e. *armCHAIR*.

WRITING

Read the example paragraphs aloud, pointing out the order of the topics – size, description of colours, etc, and atmosphere. Show how the example paragraphs relate to the instructions. Point out how the last sentence describes how the writer feels about the room.

If students cannot think of a room of their own, they can write about the room in the illustration.

EXTRA ACTIVITIES

1 Picture exploitation

1 KIM'S GAME
Students look at the picture of the cottage kitchen for one minute to memorise as many details as

possible. They then have two minutes to write down all the objects they can remember.

2 WHO AM I?
One student takes the identity of a piece of furniture in the room and describes it so as to give clues to its identity, e.g.
I am old. I have four legs. I am comfortable. The cat likes to sit on me. My insides are falling out.
(Answer: I am the armchair.)

2 Listen and draw
Students draw as you read the passage below describing Laurie Lee's arrival at the cottage. Read once for the students to get the gist without drawing. Check the words: *path, doorstep, slope, lake, cellar, pump, bush.*

Read the passage again, pausing for students to sketch the details. Read it a third time for students to check their drawings for detail.

'My eldest sister lifted me into her long brown hair, and ran with me down the path and through the steep garden with all the roses. She set me down on the doorstep of the cottage which was our new home – although I couldn't believe it.
    The cottage stood in a large garden on a steep slope above a lake. It had rooms on three floors as well as a cellar; it had a pump to bring up water from a well; and apple trees, great masses of flowers and fruit bushes; and birds in the chimneys, all for a rent of three shillings and sixpence a week.'

CHECK Units 1–10

It should be possible for the students to complete the Check exercises without any help. Ideally, they should complete the whole section in one lesson. Before the lesson, you might like to photocopy the key so that students can exchange their exercises and correct each other's answers. When the students have finished and have had their answers corrected, give them time to look through he exercises again and assess their difficulties. Ask individual students which exercises they found easy and which difficult. Encourage them to make a list of their most important mistakes. Students should be asked to correct all mistakes (including spelling) and should study any Grammar or Communication focus points again if necessary.

KEY

Exercise 1
1 he's doing
2 She cycles
3 The children are starting
4 He doesn't like
5 I never work
6 They are travelling
7 she's saying
8 Do you speak
9 I'm trying
10 She hates working

Exercise 2
buy/bought, go/went, win/won, run/ran, take/took, give/gave, come/came, tell/told, say/said, lose/lost, do/did, make/made, see/saw, bring/brought, speak/spoke, read/read, know/knew, forget/forgot, steal/stole, find/found

Exercise 3
1 While I was having breakfast
2 When I saw ... I realised
3 It was raining ... I woke up.
4 I wrote
5 I took ... it was raining
6 It was snowing ... I wanted

Exercise 4
1 I'm not used to
2 Did you use to
3 I'm used to
4 Did you use to
5 I wasn't used to
6 She's used to
7 She didn't use to
8 He's used to
9 Didn't they use to
10 She isn't used to

Exercise 5
We have to
we didn't have to
I was allowed to
We're not allowed to
Anyone ... has to
We're not supposed to

Exercise 6
(Example answers)
1 I enjoy swimming.
2 I have a shower./I have breakfast.
3 I'm wearing a white T-shirt and blue jeans.
4 I went to school./I bought a magazine./I watched television.
5 I was having supper.
6 I used to like playing on the street with my friends.
7 We weren't allowed to chew gum.
8 We're not supposed to speak (Italian) be we sometimes do.

Exercise 7
1b 2a 3a

Exercise 8
1B 2E 3C 4G 5A 6F 7D

Exercise 9
1 So do I. 2 Nor do I. 3 I do. 4 So do I. 5 I don't.
6 I do.

Exercise 10
(Example responses)
1 Have you got any tickets (left) for (the performance of) Romeo and Juliet tonight?
2 I'm (terribly) sorry I'm late but my alarm clock didn't go off so I missed the bus.
3 I think I'll leave it (thank you). It's not quite what I want. (But thank you for showing it to me.)
4 Don't worry about it. It wasn't valuable (expensive).
5 Excuse me, you're not supposed to smoke here.

USE YOUR ENGLISH
Units 1–10

Exercise 1
Establish round the class who is going to take the part of Student A and Student B, and tell them to keep their A or B roles for Exercise 2 as well. Instruct the B students to find the relevant page at the back of their Students' Books. Ask students to look at their respective pictures. Explain that their pictures are similar but there are several small differences. Emphasise that they must not cheat by looking at each other's pictures. Try to get the pairs to sit back to back or facing each other squarely so that they cannot see each other's picture. Focus their attention on the picture by asking a few general questions like: *How many people can you see in your picture? Where are they sitting or standing? What are they doing?* Now tell the A students to describe their picture to the B students, saying what each person is wearing and doing. Tell the B students that they must say after each description if their picture is different, e.g.:

A: There's a man standing on a table. I think he's singing.
B: No, the man who's singing isn't standing on a table, he's standing on a chair. *etc.*

KEY
The differences:

Picture A	Picture B
1 The man who is singing is standing on a table.	The man who is singing is standing on a chair.
2 The woman on the sofa is sleeping.	The woman on the sofa is reading a book.
3 The man on the sofa is eating a hot dog.	The man on the sofa is drinking Coca-Cola.
4 The person who is playing the piano is wearing a clown costume.	The person who is playing the piano is wearing a gorilla costume.
5 Tarzan is swinging from the chandelier.	Tarzan is standing on the piano eating a banana.
6 A woman is playing a guitar.	A woman is playing a trumpet.
7 A girl is throwing a drink at her boyfriend.	A girl is slapping her boyfriend's face.
8 A couple are dancing a tango.	A couple are dancing rock and roll.

Exercise 2
As in the previous exercise, students should be seated in pairs so that they cannot see each others' instructions. Give the students time to read through their sentence openings and endings and assist with any unfamiliar vocabulary, e.g. *ran out, collapsed, bicycle chain*. Let students complete the exercise in pairs and check with the whole class afterwards. Students who finish early can be encouraged to draw one of the scenes depicted in the completed sentences.

KEY
1 The reason I was late was because my mother phoned just as I was leaving.
2 I was cycling along the other day when suddenly my jeans got caught in the bicycle chain.
3 When I opened the door of the fridge, a carton of milk fell out onto the kitchen floor.
4 A burglar broke into my flat while I was lying in the bath.
5 While I was washing my hair this morning, the hot water ran out.
6 A student got up and started shouting while the lecturer was still speaking.
7 The audience were laughing and enjoying themselves when suddenly the stage collapsed.
8 When I asked him who he was, he turned round and walked off.

Exercise 3
Students work individually to complete the exercise. Then check the answers by asking pairs of students to read the completed exchanges. Emphasise that there may be different ways of wording the answers.

KEY
1 I'd better not. It's nearly 6.30 and I'm supposed to be punctual for meals.
2 I'd better not. I'm supposed to keep my room tidy.
3 No, you'd better not. I'm not supposed to play/have/listen to loud music after ten o'clock.
4 I'd better not. I'm supposed to be in by midnight.

Exercise 4

Go through the pictures with the students first, asking them to describe what they see. Give an example of how to convert the first picture into a statement with *be used to* and then ask the students to work individually or in pairs to make sentences for the other pictures. Tell them to make two different sentences for 2, 3, 5 and 6, one with *not used to* and one with *used to*.

KEY
1 He's not used to speaking in public.
2 She's not used to getting 'A' grades in her exams./She's used to getting low grades in her exams.
3 He's not used to sleeping in a hard bed/sleeping in a prison bed./He's used to sleeping in a soft bed.
4 He's not used to cooking/making cakes.
5 He's not used to driving on the right/driving on the continent./He's used to driving on the left/on the other side of the road.
6 She's not used to eating with a knife and fork./She's used to eating with a spoon.

Exercise 5

Ask the students to imagine the person writing the poem. Who is 'he'? How old is he? What has happened in his life? What is his situation now? Then ask the students to think of the most common situations where people have wishes and dreams that are not always fulfilled, e.g. love and personal relationships, money, career, home, lifestyle. Ask the students to try and create a new poem on either the same theme but with different 'dreams', or on a different theme. Explain that the sentences in between *I used to dream* can be any length they wish, within reason. It is important to emphasise that there is no right answer, and to encourage the students to be as creative as possible. When they are ready, ask students individually to read out their new poem. If there are too many students to do this, collect the poems and pin up a selection on the classroom wall if possible.

PROGRESS TEST Units 1–10

For the rationale behind the Progress tests, see under 'Special Features of New Blueprint Intermediate' in the Introduction.

Set students a time limit to complete the test, e.g. 30 minutes, and tell them that they may use a dictionary if they wish for the Vocabulary exercise. The key can be photocopied for students to correct each other's tests, or you may like to collect in the work to mark yourself. Each student's total can be expressed in percentage form by dividing it by the total number of possible marks and multiplying by a hundred.

When going through the correct answers with the students, get them to consider all the alternatives in the Grammar and Vocabulary exercises, and to explain why the other options are not correct. In the Vocabulary exercise, students can be asked to make sentences to contextualise the other three words in each group.

KEY

Exercise 1
1a 2b 3b 4a 5c 6b 7b 8c 9a 10b

Exercise 2
1a 2d 3b 4c 5b 6a 7d 8c 9c 10a

Exercise 3
1 hundred 2 which 3 way 4 very 5 praying
6 take 7 my 8 landed 9 to 10 asked 11 still
12 up

Angie

UNIT 11
Angie, a motorcycle courier

BACKGROUND NOTES
East End: The terms *East End* and *West End* have special meaning for Londoners. The East End covers the whole area of East London where people live and work. It was once a traditional working class area based on the London docks. The closeness of the East End to the City of London – the business and financial centre of London – has made it an attractive and profitable place for development. (See the 'About Britain' text on the modern development of Docklands.) The West End refers specifically to the theatre, entertainment and shopping area of central London. The other geographical areas of London are referred to as North London, South London

Text about Angie

Students read the text to find out more information about Angie, e.g. her age, where she was born, where she lives and what she does. Refer the students to the Glossary and explain that *yuppy* often has a negative meaning. Find out if they have a similar term in their own language for people like this and what their lifestyle is like. Comment on the effect which the arrival of yuppies can have on an area. Read the text in detail, checking the meaning of the words from the 'Words to learn' section as you go along. Get students to answer the comprehension questions in Exercise 1.

Exercise 1

KEY
1 It involves delivering important packages and letters to different parts of London.
2 She likes the day-to-day battle with the London traffic and getting somewhere fast.
3 She's going to ask for a rise.
4 She lives in the East End of London.
5 She belongs/goes to a health club.
6 She dreams of being a sports photographer.
7 She wants to buy a house for her mother in the country.
8 She wants to get out/leave the East End and do something with her life.

Exercise 2

SUGGESTED ANSWERS
1 It is dangerous and dirty. It's hard work to ride a heavy motorbike. Some people also think is it 'unladylike' to ride a motorbike.
2 They can move quickly in and out of traffic, especially in traffic jams.
3 Because rich people who are moving into the area can afford to spend a lot of money on housing, cars and leisure.
4 She probably thinks that it isn't a proper career/that the money will never be very good/that it involves doing the same thing all the time/that there is not enough challenge in the job/that she wants to get out and do something with her life/that she would like to be a sports photographer or a journalist.

Exercise 3

Students suggest how they could improve traffic congestion and discuss some of the positive effects of developing areas and economic growth.

VOCABULARY

Exercise 1

When students have completed the exercise, check that they know what the words mean and what the jobs involve. If there is time, develop the topic of jobs and professions to include a discussion of the qualifications, skills and personal qualities required for certain jobs; what the salaries are like and how beneficial the jobs are to society.

KEY

–er	–or	–ist
painter	solicitor	telephonist
plumber	doctor	receptionist
butcher	inspector	scientist
carpenter	surveyor	typist
dancer		pharmacist
waiter		physicist
jeweller		dentist

 ### Exercise 2

After checking the exercise, ask students to notice what happens to the stress in four-syllable words.

TAPESCRIPT AND KEY
Listen and copy the words, writing the stressed syllable in capital letters.

PAINter, teLEphonist, PLUMBer, reCEptionist, soLIcitor, DOCtor, SCIentist, inSPEctor, BUTCHer, surVEYor, TYpist, CARpenter, PHArmacist, DANcer, PHYsicist, WAIter, JEWeller, DENtist

TALKING POINT

Ask if the students agree with the statement in the example. Students practise the example expressions, paying special attention to the intonation. Students then think of other examples of jobs. They should give reasons for their opinions.

ABOUT BRITAIN

The development of London's Docklands

This text gives important background information to the Listening exercise. Before students read the text, explain that the area was once a port and a mainly working class area. Use a map of Greater London to show the location of Docklands next to the City of London. Ask the students if they know, or can guess, what has happened to the shipping industry in the last twenty years and why it has declined. Steer the discussion to predict the information in the text and some of its vocabulary.

Go through the text with the students, rephrasing and explaining any difficult words and expressions.

 LISTENING

Introduce the context by asking questions such as: *Do people always like to see their local area changing? How do people sometimes feel when rich people come to live in their neighbourhood? What problems can be caused by building and redevelopment?*

Play the tape once for gist and then play it again, pausing after each 'complaint' for students to write down their answers.

KEY
She makes five complaints:
1 Docklands is all changed and now it's full of rich people.
2 There are so many BMWs (smart cars) roaring down the High Street that it's not safe to cross the road.
3 Rich people are buying all the houses and pushing up the prices so that people can't afford to live there any more.
4 There is a lot of noise, lorries and dirt from the new building.
5 The pubs have all been modernised and local people don't feel welcome.

TAPESCRIPT
Listen to Doris, a fruit and vegetable stall-holder in Docklands, talking about the changes she sees around her. Note the complaints she makes.

I was born and brought up in the East End and I can tell you it's not like it used to be any more. It's all changed. Now it's called 'Docklands' and it's full of rich people with more money than they know what to do with. There are so many BMWs roaring down the High Street that it's not safe to cross the road any more.

But it's not only the traffic. They're buying all the property and pushing all the prices up so that people like me can't afford to live here any more. But we belong here and they don't.

Then there's all the building, the noise, the lorries, the dirt. It seems to go on and on. I don't know when it's going to stop. The first thing you hear when you wake up is the noise of a road drill.

Then there are the pubs. They're not like they used to be. They're all modernised now and called 'cocktail bars' or 'wine bars'. Local people aren't welcome any more – you get the feeling you're in the way.

EXTRA ACTIVITIES

1 Who uses what?

Students say which of the tools below are used in which occupations, e.g. *A painter uses a paintbrush.* They can use dictionaries if they like.

spanner	measuring scales	microscope
chopping block	power drill	plane
stethoscope	headphones	word processor
pliers	compass	spirit level
hammer	test-tube	saw
syringe	screwdriver	tweezers

2 What's my job?

One person chooses a job or occupation and mimes an action connected with it. The other students try to guess what the occupation or job is by asking twenty Yes/No questions, e.g. *Do you work with other people?*

3 Give us a clue

Students work in pairs. They select one of the occupations from the unit and write five sentences, each containing a clue to the occupation. Explain that the clues should range from the general to the specific. The students in each pair take turns to read out one clue at a time and see how long it takes (i.e. how many clues) for the others in the class to guess the occupation.

UNIT 12 GRAMMAR
Future tenses: *going to* and *will*

What's the difference in meaning?

With books closed, write the two sentences on the board and ask students what they think is the difference between them. Elicit that Sentence 1 is a planned decision or intention because the speaker has already decided to phone. Sentence 2 is a spontaneous decision: the speaker is making a sudden decision (at the time of speaking) to phone.

41

UNIT 12

With books open, students note where and how *will* and *going to* are used in the Unit 11 text about Angie. Ask students to group the sentences according to type or use.

FOCUS

Students read the Focus section to see if there are any other uses which they haven't mentioned.

Point out the difference between the use of the present continuous and the *going to* future. The present continuous is used for definite 'diary arrangements and usually occurs with time phrases, e.g. *tomorrow, on Tuesday, on 15th December*, etc. The *going to* future is more of an intention or planned decision than an arrangement. Compare:

I'm taking my driving test tomorrow. (fixed arrangement)
I'm going to learn how to drive as soon as I'm eighteen. (intention/planned decision)

Illustration

Discuss the scenery, the weather, what the people are doing and what they are wearing.

PRACTICE

Exercise 1

Make sure that students understand what the items of clothing are in the last section. Give an example of a possible A–B conversation showing how to choose items from each section.

Exercise 2

Students work in small groups for Questions 1 and 3, and report back to the class in the 3rd person about the other group members. For Question 2, get a student to ask you the question. Ask Question 4 of the whole class. If possible, refer to a real weather forecast from a daily newspaper.

Exercise 3

To check the answers, set up a question and answer session about weekend arrangements across the class.

Exercise 4

On the board write: *Things to do. Saturday – buy some plants for my windowbox.* Explain the rubric by working T–S with your example on the board. Show how the verb tense differs between *going to* for plans and arrangements (as in Exercise 3), and *will* for a spontaneous decision. Students exchange lists and choose activities to ask and answer about.

 ## LISTENING

> **BACKGROUND NOTE**
> *Crystal Palace*: A major sports stadium in South London.

Exercise 1

Make sure that students close their books so that they cannot read the dialogue in Exercise 2. Write the instructions for Exercise 1 on the board and play the tape for students to note the answers.

KEY
Angie phones Colin to ask him if he wants a ticket for the athletics meeting at Crystal Palace. He can't come because he's playing in a football match. He suggests asking Mike, who is very keen on athletics, instead. He promises to tell Mike to phone Angie in the evening.

TAPESCRIPT
Listen to Angie talking to a friend of hers, Colin. Look at your Students' Book and follow the instructions.

COLIN: Hello.
ANGIE: Colin? It's Angie.
COLIN: Oh, hi, Angie. How are things?
ANGIE: O.K., thanks. Listen, are you doing anything on Saturday?
COLIN: Saturday? I'm not sure. Why?
ANGIE: Well, it's the international athletics meeting at Crystal Palace. I've got two tickets. I think it'll be good. Do you want to come?
COLIN: It sounds fun. I'll just get my diary. Hang on.
ANGIE: O.K.
COLIN: Right, let's see. Oh, that's a pity!
ANGIE: What's wrong?
COLIN: I'm playing in a college football match that afternoon, I'm afraid.
ANGIE: Oh, that's a shame! Who else can I ask?
COLIN: You could ask Mike. He's quite keen on athletics.
ANGIE: Yes, O.K. What's his number?
COLIN: I can't remember. But I know he's going to be at college this afternoon. I'll get him to phone you.
ANGIE: Fine. I'll be at home about nine.
COLIN: O.K.
ANGIE: Thanks. Look, I'd better go. I'll be late for work if I'm not careful. Bye for now.
COLIN: Bye, Angie.

Exercise 2
Now listen again, and complete the dialogue in your book.

Exercise 2

With books open, ask students to predict the missing words in the dialogue from the context and from their memory of the tape. Then play the tape again for them to write down the correct words. Replay parts which students find difficult to hear. Students can compare their answers with each other before reading the completed dialogue in pairs.

KEY
1 Are you doing 2 'll be 3 I'll just get
4 I'm playing 5 going to be 6 I'll get 7 'll be
8 'll be

WRITING

Students refer to the dialogue for the information to use in the note. Point out that a past tense will be necessary after *she wondered if* ... (Reported speech is introduced and practised in Unit 42.) Remind students of the difference between *come* and *go* (*Would you like to come/go?*) which depends on the point of view of the speaker.

EXAMPLE NOTE
Dear Mike,
Sorry I missed you but I've got a message from Angie. She's got two tickets for the international athletics meeting at Crystal Palace on Saturday. I can't go myself because I'm playing in a college football match so she wondered if you were doing anything on Saturday. If not, would you like to go? Can you telephone Angie this evening and let her know? She'll be home about nine. Hope you can go.
Colin

EXTRA ACTIVITIES

1 Plans

In this version of *20 Questions*, one person chooses a place to go to for a holiday. Others try to guess where it is by asking Yes/No questions, e.g. *Are you going somewhere hot? Are you going to swim/take sunglasses?* etc. Alternatively, students work in groups to plan a weekend trip. A reporter summarises the discussion and reports the plans.

2 Resolutions

Write on the board a selection of subjects such as *Health, Lifestyle, Family, Job, Possessions, Appearance, Qualifications,* etc. In pairs, students choose among these to talk about their resolutions, e.g. (*Health*) *I'm definitely going to give up smoking.*

3 Predictions

Students use the same topics to discuss changes they think will occur within the next five to ten years in relation to themselves, their children or grandchildren, their home town and country, world affairs, e.g. *I think I'll move away from because I can't afford to live here any more.*

 Workbook tapescript

Unit 12

Speechwork: Pronunciation
Going to and *will*

Exercise 4

Going to

A
Listen to these sentences.
They're going to arrive on Saturday.
They're going to come on Saturday.

Now listen and repeat.
going [bleep] going to [bleep]
going to arrive [bleep]
They're going to arrive on Saturday. [bleep]
going [bleep] going to [bleep]
going to come [bleep]
They're going to come on Saturday. [bleep]

B
Now you make sentences. Listen to the example.
I/see her tomorrow [bleep]
I'm going to see her tomorrow.

Now you do it.
I/see her tomorrow [bleep]
I'm going to see her tomorrow.
We/have a party soon [bleep]
We're going to have a party soon.
She/leave her job [bleep]
She's going to leave her job.
You/meet him tonight [bleep]
You're going to meet him tonight.
He/phone back [bleep]
He's going to phone back.

Exercise 5

Will

Listen and tick the sentences which you hear.
Example: I'll go to that school.

1 You'll sleep in this room.
2 She'll be here tomorrow.
3 They arrive at three.
4 We'll stay in a hotel.
5 They live with her parents.

UNIT 13 COMMUNICATION
Requests

Photograph

Students say where they think Angie is and if she is in a big or small office building. Ask the questions in the book and try to elicit from the students

UNIT 13

different ways of making polite requests. List these on the board. (Note that some students may mention the more formal structure *Would/Will you* + verb, which are not practised in this unit.)

KEY
1 The receptionist is giving Angie a packet/parcel/package/letter.
2 She is going to deliver it to the address on the packet.
3 Could/Can/Would you take/deliver this packet as quickly as possible, please?

🔊 DIALOGUE

Explain: *receipt*, *urgent*, *rush hour*. Students cover the text and read the questions after the dialogue. Play the tape and elicit the answers.

KEY
1 She wants her to deliver a package to the Computer Centre in Allington Street.
2 She gives Angie £15.
3 She asks her for a receipt.
4 It is either between 7–10 a.m. or 4–7 p.m.
5 Four:
Could you take this to the Computer Centre?
Could I have a receipt?
Do you think you could hurry?
Would you mind asking them to call me as soon as they get it?

Students now uncover the text and point out (or underline) the requests in the dialogue. Comment on:
– the expression *off* in directions, usually indicating a smaller road leading off a larger one.
– the spelling and pronunciation of *receipt*, which rhymes with *deceit*.
– the expression *I'll do my best*.
– the stress on *is* in *It is rather urgent* and *It is the rush hour*.
– the pronouns *them* and *they* which refer to the people at the Computer Centre.

FOCUS

Students listen and repeat after you. Point out that the most useful form of request is *Could you/ I ... ?* The indirect form *Do you think you/I could ... ?* is more polite. Stress the importance of sounding polite and friendly when making requests. Point out that *please* alone is not sufficient and that if said with a falling intonation it can sound rude.

PRACTICE

Exercise 1

Students identify the people in the pictures and their roles and describe the situation. Explain that in Picture 3, the man is writing out a cheque and is pointing to the pen on the cash till. Students should vary the form of request each time.

KEY
1 Could you/Do you think you could post this letter for me (please)?
2 Could you/Do you think you could open the door for me (please)?
3 Do you think I could borrow your pen? Would you mind lending me your pen (please)?
4 Could you/Do you think you could take a photo of us (please)? Would you mind taking a photo of us (please)?

Exercise 2

Introduce the exercise by asking the students what sort of requests you might make while staying as a guest in someone else's house. Either ask the students to work through all the situations in pairs, or, if short of time, divide the situations between the two halves of the class. Ask one or two pairs at random to act out their situation, giving the request and the reply each time.

SUGGESTED REQUESTS
1 Could I have/Do you think I could have an extra pillow on my bed?
2 Could you/Do you think you could post/Would you mind posting these letters for me?
3 I'm afraid I don't like coffee. Could I have/Do you think I could have tea without milk for breakfast?
4 Could I/Do you think I could use your phone?
5 Could you/Do you think you could sign/Would you mind signing this application form for a student travel card?

WRITING

This can be started in class and finished for homework. Alternatively, it can be used as a 'Letter consequences' activity in which each student writes a sentence of the letter according to the instructions in the Students' Book and passes the letter on until it is completed. There are six sentences to write. Ask one or two students to read aloud their completed letters. For homework, each student takes home and corrects the letter they have received at the end of the activity.

SUGGESTED NOTE
Dear ...,
I'm afraid I won't be in class this week because I'm ill in bed with flu. I would like to do some homework while I am away. Do you think you could tell Lydia what I should do? I am also enclosing an application form for a student travel card. Would you mind signing it/Do you think you could sign it for me? I hope to be back in class next week.
Yours sincerely,
...

UNIT 13

 **LISTENING**

Before you listen

KEY
They are all words for types of roads, e.g. *Baker Street, Leicester Square, Burlington Gardens, King's Road, Park Lane, Northumberland Avenue.*

If there is time, photocopy a page from a London street directory and ask students to find as many different names as possible for streets and roads.

Listen

Check that students understand the meaning of *client*. After completing the task, students can listen again to note down the wording of the different requests. Afterwards students can roleplay the conversation using the notes.

KEY
Name of client:	Ms Carter
Address of client:	15, Queens Road Bromley, Kent
The delivery address:	86, Oxford Street, London, W.1.
Cost:	£20.50

TAPESCRIPT
A client calls Lightning Dispatch Courier Service with a request. Listen and note the name and address of the client, the delivery address and the cost.

MAN: Hello, Lightning Dispatch. Can I help you?
CLIENT: Oh hello, yes. I need to get a package to the West End urgently.
MAN: Right. Where are you?
CLIENT: In Bromley. The address is 15, Queens Road.
MAN: Sorry. I didn't quite catch that. Would you mind repeating it?
CLIENT: Certainly. It's 15, Queens Road, Bromley, Kent.
MAN: ... Bromley ... Kent. And what's the delivery address?
CLIENT: It's in Oxford Street. Number 86, Oxford Street, W1. It's a photographic studio.
MAN: 86, Oxford Street, West One. Fine. And your name, madam?
CLIENT: Carter. C.A.R.T.E.R.
MAN: Right. Let me just check those details again. Your address is 15, Queens Road, Bromley, and the name is Carter. You want us to deliver a package to 86, Oxford Street.
CLIENT: That's it. Could you tell me how much it'll be?
MAN: Bromley to Oxford Street. I'd say about £20.50.
CLIENT: Right. I'll pay the courier when he comes. Do you think you could send one along as quickly as possible? It's urgent.
MAN: We'll do our best, but we're rather busy at the moment. I imagine it'll be there in about an hour, depending on the traffic.
CLIENT: That's fine. Thank you very much.
MAN: Goodbye.

ACT IT OUT

> BACKGROUND NOTE
> After a taxi journey, it is not normal to get a receipt unless you specifically ask for one. It is customary in Britain to tip taxi drivers between ten and fifteen percent of the fare.

Show a picture of a London taxi if you have one. Go through the addresses, making sure students can pronounce the street names correctly. Choose one of the destinations to work T–S, with you taking the part of the taxi-driver. To add realism, students use two chairs, one in front of the other, so that the taxi-driver is slightly turning his head and leaning back when talking to the 'passenger'. Encourage students to chat during the journey before asking the coast.

SUGGESTED ROLEPLAY
YOU: Could you take me to ...
TAXI DRIVER: Where's that?
YOU: It's in ...
TAXI DRIVER: Oh yes, I know it.
YOU: Do you think you could hurry, please? I'm late for an appointment.
TAXI DRIVER: O.K. I'll do my best, but it is the rush hour.
YOU: Just look at the weather! Do you think it'll stop raining soon?
TAXI DRIVER: I don't know. It's often like this in July.
YOU: How much is that, please?
TAXI DRIVER: It's £5.40.
YOU: Here you are. And could I have a receipt, please?
TAXI DRIVER: Yes, sure.
YOU: Thank you. Oh, would you mind helping me with my suitcase?
TAXI DRIVER: Yes, of course.
YOU: Thanks very much.

EXTRA ACTIVITY

What can I do for you?

Prepare small 'situation' cards with labels as follows:

Hotel Reception, Tourist Information Office, Theatre Box Office, Railway Lost Property Office, Airport Check-in Desk, School Secretary's Office, Newspaper Kiosk, Foreign Currency counter (in a bank). Post Office Enquiry Counter, Police Station. On a Train, Petrol Station, Restaurant, An English Friend's House.

45

UNITS 13/14

Place all the cards in a box. In turn, students pick a card and make a request appropriate to the situation on the card, choosing someone in the class to respond, e.g. (At the Foreign Currency counter in a bank):
S1: Do you think you could change these travellers' cheques for me, please?
S2: Certainly. How many travellers' cheques/How much would you like to change?

The student who responds is the next person to pick a card from the box. Make sure that every student has a turn and that no request is repeated.

Note that these cards can be used for other communication topics such as checking and confirming facts (Unit 18), complaints (Unit 23), polite requests for information (Unit 33); and for general revision of directions. The settings can be adapted to suit the local environment.

 Workbook tapescript

Unit 13

Speechwork: Stress and intonation
Asking people to do things.

Exercise 3

A
Listen to these requests.

Could you TAKE this to the comPUTer Centre, please?
Do you think you could HURRY?
Would you MIND asking them to CALL me?

Now listen and repeat.
to the comPUTer centre, PLEASE [bleep]
Could you TAKE this to the ComPUTer Centre, PLEASE? [bleep]
you could HURRY [bleep]
Do you think you could HURRY? [bleep]
to CALL me [bleep]
asking them to CALL me [bleep]
Would you MIND asking them to CALL me? [bleep]

B
Now you make requests. Listen to the example.

Could you post this letter, please?
this parcel
Could you post this parcel, please?
would you mind
Would you mind posting this parcel, please?

Now you do it.
Could you post this letter, please?
this parcel
Could you post this parcel, please?
would you mind [bleep]
Would you mind posting this parcel, please?

closing the door [bleep]
Would you mind closing the door, please?
opening the window [bleep]
Would you mind opening the window, please?
do you think you could [bleep]
Do you think you could open the window, please?

UNIT 14 GRAMMAR
Ability and possibility: *can, could* and *be able to*

PRESENTATION

With books closed, ask students questions about different skills, e.g. *Is there anybody here who can*:
- *say goodbye in Japanese?*
- *say three words in Russian?*
- *say the alphabet backwards?*
- *sing the first few bars of the American national anthem?*
- *play the violin?*
- *do a handstand or cartwheel?*

After the last question, try to elicit, or say yourself: *I used to be able to do a handstand, but I can't any more.* Explain or revise the fact that *to be able to* is the infinitive of *can*. *Can* has several 'missing tenses', e.g. the infinitive, the future, the present perfect and the conditional. To use one of these tenses, you often have to use the verb *to be able to*, e.g. *won't/wouldn't be able to, might be able to, haven't been able to*, etc.

The cartoons

> BACKGROUND NOTE
> These are all drawn by Thelwell, a cartoonist famous for portraying children and ponies.

Ask the students to describe the situation in each picture and to read the captions. Explain: *joy* and *control*. Explain that *was able to* means *managed to*. Here, *could* would be wrong. Although *could* is the past tense of *can* and is used to talk about general ability, in the positive it is not used to talk about ability to do something on one occasion in the past. Instead we have to use *was able to* (or *managed to*).

Write these two sentences on the board: *I'm afraid he couldn't come. I'm afraid he wasn't able to come.*

Explain that both are grammatically possible but the second is more emphatic.

FOCUS

Students read the Focus section. Ask them to give other example sentences using *can, could* and *be able to* in the ways listed in the Focus section.

Students suggest one or two further examples for each use of *be able to*.

PRACTICE

Exercise 1

Explain that in the response, the main verb phrase does not need to be repeated, i.e. *I'm afraid I can't (help you with your project) this week but I might be able to help you next week.* Students should produce the response as fluently as possible. Use the example to demonstrate the correct stress and intonation, e.g.

A: Could you help me with my project SOME TIME THIS WEEK?
B: I'm afraid I can't THIS week but I might be able to help you NEXT week.

(The key below shows where the emphatic stress falls in each sentence.)

KEY
1 A: Could you help me with my project SOME TIME THIS WEEK?
  B: I'm afraid I can't THIS week but I MIGHT be able to help you NEXT week.
2 A: Could you come to lunch on TUESday?
  B: I'm afraid I can't on TUESday but I might be able to come on WEDNesday.
3 A: Could you help me to buy a new suit NEXT WEEK?
  B: I'm afraid I can't NEXT week but I might be able to help you the WEEK AFTer.
4 A: Could you look at my computer THIS WEEKend?
  B: I'm afraid I can't THIS weekend but I might be able to look at it NEXT weekend.
5 A: Could you translate a letter THIS EVEning?
  B: I'm afraid I can't THIS evening but I might be able to translate it toMORROW evening.

Exercise 2

KEY
1 Oh dear, I can't remember her address.
2 I used to be able to wiggle my ears but I can't any more.
3 Where are the keys? I couldn't find them last night.
4 She's moved to York so she will be able to see her parents more often.
5 The theatre seats were awful. We couldn't/weren't able to see the stage.
6 The show is very popular but luckily I was able to get two seats for Saturday.
7 My car broke down and I haven't been able to drive it for a week.
8 The exam was easy. I could/was able to do all the questions.
9 It's nice to be able to sleep late on Sundays.
10 My sister couldn't/wasn't able to swim until she was eleven.
11 After the accident he couldn't/wasn't able to smell or taste anything.
12 I lost all my money but fortunately I was able to borrow some from friends.

ACT IT OUT

Assign the A and B role in each pair. Then get all the A students to prepare their roles together in pairs and all the B students to prepare their roles. Suggest some sentences to include in the roleplay, e.g.

for A:
I'm going to spend a year travelling round Europe.
Do you think I could borrow ...?
Do you think you could lend me ...?
I promise I'll write to you every week.
I'm going to look for a job while I'm away, so I'll be able to pay you back quite soon.

for B:
Where are you going?
How much do you want to borrow?
When/How are you going to pay it back?

EXAMPLE ROLEPLAY
A: Mum/Dad, I've decided that I'm going to spend next year abroad.
B: Really?
A: Yes, I've got some savings in the bank but it's not enough and I'd like to borrow some money from you.
B: How much?
A: Well, do you think you can lend me £500?
B: £500! That's a lot of money. Where are you going?
A: I'm going to spend a year travelling round Europe.
B: Where are you going to live? What are you going to do?
A: I'm going to live in youth hostels.
B: How and when will you be able to pay this money back?
A: I'm going to look for a job so I'll be able to pay you back quite soon.
B: What sort of job?
A: I can speak English, French and Italian and I can type, so I think I'll be able to find a job. Maybe in an office. Or I can work in a restaurant.
B: But how will we know where you are? How will we know if you're all right?
A: I'll write to you every week, I promise.

WRITING

Ask students to name some current popular shows or events for which it is difficult to get tickets, and to name suitable hotels for visitors to their town or city.

KEY

(Your address)

(the date)

Dear ...,

After our conversation last week, I telephoned the theatre and luckily I was able to get some tickets for 'The Phantom of the Opera' on Friday, 23rd April. I hope you can come. The performance starts at 7.30.

I'm afraid I won't be able to meet you at your hotel because I have to work late that evening so do you think you could meet me at the theatre instead at 7.15?

Could you telephone me to say if you can come or not? I'll be in the office all this week so you can phone me any time during the day, or you can phone me at home in the evening.

With best wishes,

(Your name)

EXTRA ACTIVITIES

1 Coffee-potting

Players ask questions using *do, did, can, could* or *be able to*. One person chooses a skill. The others have to guess it by asking Yes/No questions with the verb replaced by the word *coffee-pot*, e.g. *Can you coffee-pot in the sitting-room? Were you able to coffee-pot when you were six? Did you coffee-pot this morning?*

2 Things I'd like to be able to do

Write on the board the sentences:

There are many things I'd like to be able to do.
There are certain things I'll never be able to do.

Students consider the sentences according to their own lives. Set a five-minute time limit for a 'snowball' discussion in which students first work in pairs, then join up in fours, then eights, etc.

 Workbook tapescript

Unit 14

Speechwork: Pronunciation
Can/can't

Exercise 3

A
Listen to these sentences.
She can sing very well.
She can't read music.
Can you come on Monday?
Yes, I can.

Now listen and repeat.
can [bleep] She can sing very well. [bleep]
can't [bleep] She can't read music. [bleep]
can [bleep] Can you come on Monday? [bleep]
can [bleep] Yes, I can. [bleep]

B
Now you make sentences. Listen to the example.
speak five languages
She can speak five languages.

Now you do it.
speak five languages [bleep]
She can speak five languages
play the guitar [bleep]
She can play the guitar.
fly a plane [bleep]
She can fly a plane.
ride a horse [bleep]
She can ride a horse.
do everything [bleep]
She can do everything.

UNIT 15 READING
Blackberries

Before you read

Ask students to look at the illustration and before asking the questions in the book, ask some general background questions, e.g.:
Where are the people? What time of year do you think it is? Have you ever eaten any blackberries? Where do they grow in your country? Why are blackberries difficult to pick?

In this way, try and elicit some of the words in the text, e.g. *stain, scratch, juice*.

Now direct students to the questions in their book and use the suggested answers below to give the context of the story and build up atmosphere. Elicit words and phrases which occur in the text like: *cap, peak, blackberry bush*.

SUGGESTED ANSWERS
The setting is somewhere in the country, probably in England sometime in the 1930s. The illustration shows a man in his late 30s. He is wearing old-fashioned looking clothes and a cloth cap. He is with a fair-haired boy aged about five, who is probably his son. The boy is also wearing old-fashioned clothes and a peaked cap. They are standing quite close to each other picking blackberries from a bush. The man is putting a blackberry into the boy's mouth. By the look of their clothes they are country people and quite poor.

UNIT 15

> BACKGROUND NOTES
> **Blackberries**: the extract is from a story in *The Girl from Cardigan*, a collection of short stories by the Welsh writer, Leslie Norris. Cardigan is a town in Wales.
> **Fletcher's Woods**: the name of a certain piece of woodland.

COMPREHENSION AND

 Text: Blackberries

Divide the text into sections:
1 to '… the house himself.' (end of the seventh paragraph)
2 to '… filled it with berries.' (end of the seventeenth paragraph)
3 to the end of the passage

Students read the text section by section, completing the comprehension exercise. Ask them to explain the words listed in 'Guess the meaning'.

KEY
1 a) 2 c) 3 b) 4 c) 5 a)

Exercise 2

Allow students time to work individually or in pairs to reconstruct the story.

SUGGESTED STORY
One day a mother and her young son went to the hairdresser's to have the boy's hair cut. Afterwards, his mother bought him a beautiful new cap with a peak and a button on top. Unfortunately the cap was a little too big and rather expensive, but the mother bought it because the boy liked it so much. When he got home, the boy showed his new cap to his father. The father promised to take his son out for a walk on Sunday so he could wear his new cap. On the walk, his father showed him lots of wild blackberry bushes. They picked and ate lots of blackberries. They decided to take some blackberries home to the boy's mother so they put them in the boy's cap to carry them home. When they got home the mother was very angry because the blackberry juice had stained the boy's new cap. She then accused her husband of not earning enough money. The little boy was very upset when his parents started to quarrel and he began to cry. As he cried he began to realise that he was growing up and that sometimes in life he would have to learn to be alone.

THINK ABOUT IT

SUGGESTED ANSWERS
1 It is a very good one. They are both proud of one another. He promises to take him out for a walk on Sunday.
2 Partly it is to do with money. But the wife seems also to be deeply dissatisfied with her life and her husband's inability to provide extras for his family.
3 He was crying from emotional rather than physical pain. Perhaps he had never seen his parents quarrel before. He had begun to understand that the relationship between his parents was not as happy as he had always thought.
4 That his childhood innocence is over; that his parents are not a unit but separate people with separate desires and ambitions; he realises too he will have to learn how to be separate and independent.

ABOUT YOU

Students work in groups and then reform as a whole class to share their discussion and any interesting childhood experiences.

VOCABULARY

Ask students to do the exercise in their notebooks. Students can work on this in class individually or in pairs. If preferred, the exercise can be completed as part of their written homework. When checking the exercise allow students time to discuss the variations. Finally ask students to write four or five sentences using the verbs and nouns

KEY
mark: cup, clothes, mirror, armchair
scratch: hands, cup, mirror, armchair
spoil: clothes, performance, evening
stain: hands, cup, clothes, armchair
soak: hands, clothes, armchair
crack: hands, cup, mirror
tear: clothes, armchair
ruin: clothes, armchair, performance, evening

WRITING

Students work in pairs thinking up ideas for their quarrel. Say that it should be quite short – not more than 10–15 lines. They can start it in class and finish it for homework.

SUGGESTED QUARREL
BROTHER: By the way, have you seen my jeans jacket?
SISTER: Um … yes … I borrowed it last night.
BROTHER: You what!
SISTER: Sorry, but I wanted to wear it to go out with Matt on his motorbike. Here it is…
BROTHER: But look! You've torn the sleeve, and there are stains all over it.
SISTER: I know. We had a breakdown.
BROTHER: It's ruined!
SISTER: Don't be so silly. It's not ruined. Put it in the washing machine.
BROTHER: What about the tear! Look, here, on the sleeve.
SISTER: It's only a little tear. I'll sew it back for you if you want but …

UNITS 15/16

BROTHER: But what!
SISTER: I think torn jeans jackets look great. Everyone at college is wearing torn jeans jackets.

EXTRA ACTIVITIES

1 Accusations!

Write a list of 'spoiling' verbs on the blackboard. Ask students individually to write a list of ten mixed items of value, personal clothing, furniture, special ornaments, crockery or household fittings (e.g.: *a silk shirt, the sofa, the carpet, Grandmother's Chinese vase, the curtains*, etc.) Give help where necessary. Students work in pairs. One student reads out an item of value and the partner responds by making an accusation using a suitable 'spoiling' verb, e.g.
A: *a white silk shirt*
B: *You've stained my white silk shirt!*

2 Modern times

Students make notes for an illustrator to draw the same scene from *Blackberries* but in a contemporary setting. Help students with words to describe modern leisure clothing and accessories. The class choose the best three descriptions.

3 Food for free

As homework, ask students to research a recipe which has wild berries or wild mushrooms as the main ingredient.

4 The day I grew up ...

This activity will work best with a class of students who know each other well and are not afraid to reveal personal memories. Ask them to try and remember a point in their childhood or teenage years when they felt as if they grew up.

UNIT 16 GRAMMAR
First conditional and time clauses

PRESENTATION

Find several entry forms for competitions, e.g. to win a foreign holiday, a car and a cash prize. With books closed, show one form to the class and say:

T: I'm going to enter this competition. What will I get if I win?
S: You'll get a car.
T: If I win this competition, I'll get a car.

Give a form to the student and say:

T: What will you get if you win your competition?
S: I'll get two weeks' holiday in Thailand.
T: Now ask each other about the things you might win.

Students use the other entry forms to ask and answer in pairs. Then draw the class together again.

T: Will I win?
S: Maybe yes, maybe no.
T: I've already got a car so if I win, I'll give it to my father. What will I do if I win?
S: You'll give the car to your father.

Write on the board:

| If I win a car, | I'll give it to my father. |
| | I won't keep it. |

Explain or revise the fact that this is a first conditional and that one of its uses is to describe a possible future event and its consequence.

The illustrations

With books open, students look at the speech bubbles in the pictures and answer the questions.

KEY
1 They'll play inside.
2 She'll keep her balance better.
3 He won't be in the team.

KEY
– giving advice: Sentence 2
– talking about a possible future event: Sentence 1
– giving a warning: Sentence 3

KEY
The verb in the *if* clause is in the present tense; the verb in the main clause is in the simple future tense with *will/won't*.

Give alternative ways of saying each sentence, using a negative in the *if* clause, e.g.
If it doesn't rain we'll play outside
If you don't bend your knees, you'll fall over.
If you're not on time in future, you won't be in the team!

FOCUS

Pay special attention to the 'Points to note' section. Spend time on the second point, giving more examples of sentences with *unless*. Also point out that in most sentences containing first conditional and time clauses, the main clause and subordinate clause can be reversed in order. Get students to do this with some of the sentences in the Focus section.

What's the difference in meaning?

In Sentence 1, there is only a possibility that the person will see Jan.
In Sentence 2, the person will definitely see her.

PRACTICE

Exercise 1

Explain *afford a holiday* and *residence permit*.

UNIT 16

KEY
1 If you don't work hard, you won't pass your exams.
2 If you don't go to the market early, you won't get any fresh fish.
3 If you don't hurry, you won't catch the bus/you'll miss the bus.
4 If I don't sell my car, I won't be able to afford a holiday.
5 If it isn't sunny, we won't go to the beach.
6 If I don't get a residence permit, I won't be able to stay in the USA.

Exercise 2

Do the first few sentences in class and ask the students to complete the remainder for homework.

KEY
1 You won't pass your exams unless you work hard.
2 You won't get any fresh fish unless you go to the market early.
3 You won't catch the bus/you'll miss the bus unless you hurry.
4 I won't be able to afford a holiday unless I sell my car.
5 We won't go to the beach unless it's sunny.
6 I won't be able to stay in the USA unless I get a residence permit.

Note that these sentences can also be reversed.

Exercise 3

KEY
1b 2d 3f 4a 5c 6e

Exercise 4

Students read the completed dialogues in pairs.

KEY
ANGIE: ... But I'll ring you if there are any problems.
MOTHER: ... Well, if you're back before me, you'll have to get something for supper.
ANGIE: ...I'll decide on something when I get to the supermarket.
MOTHER: If I pass a greengrocer's, I'll buy some strawberries for us.
ANGIE: He didn't say but if he gets in touch, I'll invite him to supper.
MOTHER: Look at the time. I'll miss the bus unless I go now.
ANGIE: O.K. Bye. I'll see you when I get home.

Exercise 5

Point out that statements of general truths do not need *will* in the main clause, e.g. *House plants die if you don't water them.*

Suggested tips

1 Your T-shirts won't shrink if you dry them naturally/if you wash them in warm water.
2 You'll get a smoother shave if you use shaving soap and hot water.
3 If you use suntan lotion/go on a sunbed first, you'll tan more quickly.
4 If you lie in the sun too long/wash your face with soap and water, your skin may go dry.
5 Your roses will last longer if you crush/bash/cut the end of the stems/put them in a bucket of water overnight.
6 Your house plants will die unless you water them/feed them/put them near the light.
7 Your car won't use so much petrol if you drive more slowly.

Exercise 6

Suggest some other areas for handy tips: diet, health, home maintenance, pet care and training, cooking, parking, driving, etc.

 LISTENING

Before you listen

Revise other parts of the body. Get students to predict what the trainer might say about the correct position of the back, etc. Write on the board the following words and discuss their meaning: *amateur, take it seriously, posture, loosely, swing*.

Listen

KEY
Correct position of:
– the back: straight.
– the body: leaning forward slightly.
– the head: head up, looking ahead.
– the arms: loosely relaxed at your sides.

How to breathe: naturally (through the mouth is easiest)

TAPESCRIPT
Listen to an interview with a trainer who gives advice on how to run properly. Note down what advice he gives about the correct position of your back, your body, your head and your arms, and how to breathe.

INTERVIEWER: Welcome to Sportsline. Our first guest this afternoon needs no introduction from me. He's the marathon runner and trainer, John Haines. John, thank you for coming.
JOHN: My pleasure.
INTERVIEWER: John, I believe you're going to tell us how to run?
JOHN: That's right. Well, er, just a few tips for the amateur runner. If you want to start running to keep fit, it's worth taking it seriously. You see, how you run does make a difference. Whether you're running a race or just for the fun of it, you've got to do it the right way.

UNITS 16/17

INTERVIEWER: So, um, what do you advise John?
JOHN: Well, first of all you must make sure you've got the correct body posture. You should run with your back straight and with your body leaning forward slightly.
INTERVIEWER: I've, I've seen a lot of people running with their head down. Is that all right or …?
JOHN: No, no, no, you should keep your head up and er, look ahead. If you're looking down at your feet all the time, your back won't be straight, and, er, it's just not comfortable to run like that.
INTERVIEWER: I see. Er, what about the arms, John? Is there a correct way of holding them?
JOHN: Er, yes, the best way is to hold them loosely and relaxed at your sides. If you run with your arms too high, you'll only tire your shoulders and back. And you shouldn't clench your fists or swing your arms strongly either. Both of these use up energy unnecessarily.
INTERVIEWER: And lastly, what about breathing? Some people seem to breathe through their nose only, some through their mouth. Does it matter?
JOHN: Well, you should breathe naturally, that's the main thing. You can keep your mouth open or closed, but you'll probably find that you can only get enough air if you breathe through your mouth.
INTERVIEWER: I see. Good. Er, anything else important do you think?
JOHN: Erm, that's the lot, I think.
INTERVIEWER: Well, thanks for the good advice, John. I think I'll start running too!
JOHN: What a good idea!
INTERVIEWER: Thank you John Haines. Our next guest …

WRITING

Preparation

Ask students for advice about another sport and write their ideas on the board, e.g.

SKIING
DO   DON'T
make sure your boots   overdo it on the first day
are comfortable

Encourage students to make an *if* sentence to accompany each *Do* or *Don't*. Alternatively, write a *Do* or a *Don't* on a strip of paper and give one to each student. Students then read it aloud and follow it with an appropriate *if* sentence.

EXTRA ACTIVITIES

1 Magazine letters

Students choose one of the following situations and write a letter to an advice column, asking for advice. They should use sentences with *if/unless* in their letters.

1 JOB CHANGE
A married man/woman with young children is offered a job in another country. The partner has just got a well-paid job with good career prospects in this country.

2 RELATIONSHIPS
A man/woman wants to know how to break up a steady relationship with their partner who is unstable and depressive.

A teenager hates his/her stepparent and wants to know what to do. Students give their letter to another student who then has to answer, giving appropriate advice.

2 Discussion

Before the discussion, students write sentences using the first conditional about *either*:

Terrorism: dealing with terrorists in hijacking, bomb attacks or kidnapping incidents; *or*

Drug abuse: educating young people about drug and alcohol abuse and dealing with offenders.

Encourage students to introduce their sentences into the discussion.

3 For or against

A pop concert promoter wants to hold a big open-air concert for charity in a nature conservation area near a picturesque village. The promoters argue that the area is not heavily populated and is an economically run-down farming area. The villagers are against the idea.

Students form groups of four and take sides for and against the siting of the festival in the village. Remind students to include sentences with *if/unless*.

UNIT 17 TOPIC
Sport

Ask a student to draw the symbol of the Olympic Games on the board. Ask if they know what the guiding principle of the Olympic Games is (*'The important thing is not winning but taking part.'*) and if they agree with it.

Before you read

Without looking at the text, students discuss the first four 'Before you read' questions. Ask the students if they can recall any scandals concerning the Olympic Games in the past. List these on the board and if possible put dates to them. Guide the discussion towards the ice-skating scandal involving the US skating athletes, Tonya Harding and Nancy Kerrigan. Use the photograph to jog their memories for details of the incident.

Text: Winning at all costs?

Ask students to scan the text to note the scandals which are mentioned in the text. Check the meaning of the 'Words to learn'.

Exercise 1

Students first copy the chart then read the text again to complete the information about the three people.

KEY
1

Name	Zola Budd	Ben Johnson	Tonya Harding
Nationality	South African	Canadian	American
Sporting event	5,000m	100 m final	Figure skating
City	Los Angeles	Tokyo	Lillehammer
Year	1984	1988	1994
Scandal	Tripped her rival, Mary Decker	Used steroids	Conspired to attack her rival, Nancy Kerrigan

2 She was fined £100,000 and given 500 hours of community service. Her career was also destroyed.

3 She earned a lot of money from a TV interview. She was offered $2 million to become a wrestler in Japan.

Exercise 2

Students discuss the various explanations as a class.

Exercise 3

Ask the students to work in groups and then come together for a reporting session. At the end of the discussion find out by a show of hands what opinions the class have about the two questions.

VOCABULARY

Exercise 1

KEY
Types of sport
Water: swimming, windsurfing
Team: football, volleyball
Winter: skiing, ice skating
Indoor: wrestling, boxing, table tennis, gymnastics
Motor: scrambling, motor racing

Exercise 2

KEY
ski slope, swimming pool, athletics track, boxing ring, skating rink, tennis court, golf course, football pitch

Ask students to tell you about any sports locations in the area, e.g. *There's a good swimming pool with a water slide at Richmond.*

LISTENING

Find out from the students what clues in each commentary helped them to make their guesses. Do not bother to explain in detail the technical terms mentioned in the ice skating and gymnastics.

KEY
1 ice skating
2 cycling
3 gymnastics

TAPESCRIPT
Listen to the sports commentaries and note which sports are taking place.

1 At last, the one that everyone is waiting for! There is a hush throughout this vast Olympic Stadium as the audience waits expectantly for the British number-one title holder, Joanne Rodway, to take up her position on the ice for her free programme.

With a new coach, Robbie Cousins, Joanne is tonight hoping to defend her European Championship title. At present she is lying in second place, only a few points behind the German girl, Elke Kreiss. Joanne will have to pull out all the stops tonight. So this is it! Will Joanne Rodway be able to hold on to her number one position?

Oh. Oh, I say, what a magnificent start! A triple salko, followed by a lutz and a perfect landing. What a breathtaking beginning to her free programme. This girl is clearly out on the ice to win!

2 They're coming round the track now in the final round with the computer showing the Polish man, Lech Piasecki, a close two seconds behind the Irish champion. Hodge's five minutes twenty-three point four six (23.46). Can the Pole rally enough on the last circuit to gain those vital seconds? Can he pedal fast enough to repeat his last year's burst to victory in the great French amateur road race?

3 MIKE: And now it's the little Russian girl, Natalia Zvereva's turn on the beam. She must be one of the youngest competitors here, isn't that right, Hayley?

UNITS 17/18

HAYLEY: Yes, Mike, she's just turned fourteen and this is only her second international competition.

MIKE: And at the moment she's in third place as they start the beam final. Nine point two three five (9.235) she carries through from the last round. She really is elfin-like on the beam. Flic flic free back walkover. Lovely fluency. The judges here are looking for fluency. Any big hesitation while the gymnast is setting up for a combination could mean a deduction. Every hand and head movement practised. There her variation on the Yorchenko move. Double pike back, just a little step backwards, a superb routine.

TALKING POINT

Help with vocabulary such as: *invest money in*, *sponsor*, *train* and *coach*. Write up students' ideas from Question 2 on the board to use in the following writing activity.

WRITING

Students should copy out the letter in full.

EXAMPLE LETTER
Dear Sir,

It has recently been announced that the next Olympics are going to be held in (Birmingham). As a resident of (Birmingham), I am very worried about this decision. If we hold the Games here, we will not only have to build a new (stadium and an Olympic village) but also (build) several new (hotels) for the (tourists).

The amount of extra traffic will be enormous and, as well as building (new car parks), they will also have to improve (the roads, the transport system and the shopping facilities).

What I would like to know is, how (are we going to raise the money to pay for all of this)?

Yours faithfully,
...

EXTRA ACTIVITIES

1 Guess the sport

In pairs, students choose a sport or athletic event and write ten descriptive statements about it. The statements must range from the general, e.g. *You can play this outside*, to the specific, e.g. *You play this game on a court*. In this way, the sport is gradually revealed. Each pair reads a sentence in turn, while the rest of the group try to guess the name of the sport as quickly as possible.

2 Olympic hall of fame

Students find out about athletes who have achieved, or who may be about to achieve, fame in the Olympic Games. They then write about an athlete and his or her sporting event, illustrating their work with magazine pictures and newspaper cuttings.

Workbook tapescript

Unit 17

Exercise 3

Look at your book, listen to the holiday advertisements and complete the table.

Example:

And what about The Gambia if you want to go somewhere different this year? After lazing in the sun, there are lots of sports for those who are feeling energetic. There's windsurfing and waterskiing for the water lovers, as well as swimming. Most hotels provide tennis courts and, if you like, you can try an unusual round of golf – on a sand course.

1 The glorious beach at Agadir is perfect for watersports. You can have a go at windsurfing, sailing or waterskiing. If you prefer getting you exercise on land, there are some good tennis courts. Or how about seeing the Moroccan countryside on horseback? There are horse-riding facilities for beginners as well as for those with experience.

2 Sports enthusiasts will love Gran Canaria, it has so much to offer. There are good quality tennis courts at several of the hotels. Or maybe you fancy a round of golf? There's a golf course by the spectacular dunes of Maspalomas. If you want to cool off, go for a swim or have a go at windsurfing. And if that's not enough, then there's horse-riding, or, if you're feeling really adventurous, camel-riding.

UNIT 18 COMMUNICATION
Checking information

Photograph

> BACKGROUND NOTE
> It is compulsory to wear a crash helmet when riding a motorbike in Britain.

Discuss with the class how old the boy is and if he's still at school, how Angie knows him, what Angie is holding in her hand and what the boy wants.

DIALOGUE

Play the tape while students listen first for general gist with books closed. Ask why Angie calls Carl *lazy bones*.

With books open, refer to the questions and ask students to note the answers. Play the tape a second time.

Explain *afternoon off*, *shallow*, *kids*, *grab* and *jump on*.

KEY
1 Because he has got the afternoon off.
2 Because the pool is closed all this week.
3 Because it's very shallow and all the kids go there.
4 Because it takes too long.
5 She offers to take him there on her motorbike.

FOCUS

Play the tape a third time. Ask students to note down all Angie's questions. Write the questions on the board in two separate columns headed *negative questions* and *tag questions*.

Refer to the Focus section and explain that these are used to check information that you are fairly sure of, or to show surprise.

Practise the sentence chorally. Use a rising intonation for the tag question as the speaker is not quite sure of the information. Mention the difference in meaning between tag questions with a rising intonation and tag questions with a falling intonation. The falling intonation is used when the speaker is very sure of the answer, e.g. *You're French, aren't you?* or is making a remark, e.g. *Nice day, isn't it?* With a rising intonation, the sentence is more like a real question.

The distinction between the two intonation patterns is difficult for learners of English. So as not to discourage the students, it may be wise not to spend too long practising the different patterns.

PRACTICE

Exercise 1

To clarify the construction of tag questions, build a diagram on the board to show the positive/negative relationship in tag questions, i.e. when one half is positive, the other half is negative, and vice versa:

POSITIVE	NEGATIVE
You're French,	aren't you?
You live in Paris,	don't you?
You were here yesterday,	weren't you?

NEGATIVE	POSITIVE
You aren't English,	are you?
You don't live in London,	do you?
You weren't here yesterday,	were you?

Practise these with both falling and rising intonation patterns.

KEY
There's a pool in Lansbury Park, isn't there?
Doesn't the 49 bus go there?
You're supposed to be at school, aren't you?

Exercise 2

Leave the diagram on the board while students build up a fact file about their partner. Suggest areas for the questions, e.g. nationality, age, where they live, what sort of car they drive, what newspaper they read, how many children they've got, what TV programmes they like, etc. Students work in pairs to check the information, using tag questions.

For the second part of the exercise, ask a student to tell you one or two of his/her questions. Show how to convert these into negative questions. Students interview each other again, using negative questions in place of the tag questions which they used previously.

Exercise 3

Refer back to Angie's first question in the dialogue: *Aren't you supposed to be at school?* Explain that Angie is very surprised that Carl is not at school. Stress the importance of the fall-rise intonation pattern.

KEY
1 Aren't you going to get up?
2 Aren't you going to finish them?/Aren't you feeling hungry/well?/Aren't the chips nice?/Don't you like chips?
3 Aren't you feeling well?/Didn't you sleep well?
4 Can't you swim?
5 Didn't you put it in your bag/pocket/leave it on your bed?
6 Aren't you …?/Isn't your name …?/Didn't you go to school with me?/Weren't you in the same class as me at school?

🔊 LISTENING

Students read the questions. Play the tape and check the answers.

Exercise 1

KEY
1 Mike and Helen.
2 He's American.
3 At Jeff's party last Saturday.
4 He had to meet someone at the airport.
5 He asks her to come and have a cup of coffee with him.

Exercise 2

Play the tape again. Pause for students to write down the questions.

KEY
Haven't we met somewhere before?
It's Helen, isn't it?
You're Glenn from New York, aren't you?
Wasn't it a good party?
Didn't you have to met someone at the airport?
Are you very busy right now?
Can't you spare ten minutes for a coffee with me?

UNIT 18

TAPESCRIPT

Listen to two people who meet in the street and answer the questions in your Students' Book.

GLENN: Oh, hello. Haven't we met somewhere before?
HELEN: Er, yes, now you mention it, I think we have. It was at Jeff's party last Saturday, wasn't it?
GLENN: That's right. Jeff introduced us and then I had to leave early. It's, er, Helen, isn't it?
HELEN: Yes. And you're Glenn from New York, aren't you?
GLENN: Correct.
HELEN: Yes, I remember now. Wasn't it a good party?
GLENN: Yeah, it certainly was.
HELEN: Didn't you have to meet someone at the airport?
GLENN: You got it. That's why I had to leave so quickly. Anyway, are you very busy right now?
HELEN: Well, I was just going to the dry cleaners.
GLENN: Couldn't you spare ten minutes for a coffee with me?
HELEN: Yes, O.K. Why not. Thanks.

ACT IT OUT

Students should refer to the questions which they copied down from the listening activity. Use the listening tapescript as a model for the roleplay.

READING

Explain that English-speakers always seem to be asking questions when they are not really doing so. Give an example, e.g. *How do you do?* Students skim read the text to answer the questions. Explain difficult words or expressions, e.g. *inappropriate, state of health, wrapped in bandages* (see cartoon).

KEY
1 Four.
2 How do you do? = a (formal) greeting
  How are you? = an (informal) greeting
  Could you pass the milk? Could you go and fetch them? = requests for action

WRITING

This would be a good opportunity to pause and get feedback on how the students think they are progressing. Collect their ideas to use in their writing.

EXAMPLE PARAGRAPH
I think English is quite a difficult language to learn. For example, the grammar is very different from my language. In my language there are no question tags. Another thing is the vocabulary. There are so many words in English to describe the same thing. Also, English spelling is difficult because it is hardly every the same as the pronunciation. And finally, there are too many idioms and phrasal verbs to learn!

EXTRA ACTIVITIES

1 The Yes/No game

This game involves answering questions without using the words *yes* or *no*. Players who do so are eliminated immediately. To avoid using *yes* or *no*, the one who answers must rephrase the question as a statement, e.g.:

QUESTION: *Your name's John, isn't it?*
ANSWER: *That's right. My name's John.*

VERSION 1
Prepare five cards, each with variations of ten questions, which may be tag, negative or Yes/No questions, e.g.

You're in Class Five, aren't you?
Are you learning English?
Isn't your name ...?
The weather's ... today, isn't it?

Two students come to the front of the class. One chooses a question card and the other is the 'victim'.

VERSION 2
Students use the questions they prepared in Practice Exercise 2 to make their own cards of ten questions. They exchange these round the class. Students choose their own 'victim' to question.

2 Who's got the tag?

Write a selection of statements on separate cards, e.g.

You're Italian.
You live in London.
They don't like tea

and an equivalent number of tag endings on other cards, e.g.

aren't you?
don't you?
do they?

Make sure that a) you use a variety of familiar tenses; b) you use a variety of positive and negative statements and c) there is a matching tag to each statement. Divide the class into two halves. Students in one half pick a statement each and students in the other half pick a tag each. One student reads out a statement and the one who has the corresponding tag has to complete it. The class must see if all the sentences can be completed correctly the first time.

Workbook tapescript

Unit 18

Speechwork: Stress and intonation
Checking information

Exercise 6

A

Listen to this question.
ISn't there a POOL in Lansbury PARK?

Now listen and repeat.
Lansbury PARK? [bleep]
a POOL in Lansbury PARK? [bleep]
ISn't there a POOL in Lansbury PARK? [bleep]

B

Now make negative questions. Listen to the example.
I've met you before.
Haven't I met you before?

Now you do it.
I've met you before. [bleep]
Haven't I met you before?
You were at Sarah's party. [bleep]
Weren't you at Sarah's party?
You're Sarah's sister. [bleep]
Aren't you Sarah's sister?
You came with that actor. [bleep]
Didn't you come with that actor?

C

Listen to this question.
THIS BUS goes there, DOESn't it?

Now listen and repeat.
DOESn't it [bleep]
THIS BUS goes there, DOESn't it? [bleep]

D

Now you make tag questions.
Listen to the example.
You're coming to the party.
You're coming to the party, aren't you?

Now you do it.
You're coming to the party. [bleep]
You're coming to the party, aren't you?
David's coming with you. [bleep]
David's coming with you, isn't he?
He knows my address. [bleep]
He knows my address, doesn't he?
You can remember where is it. [bleep]
You can remember where it is, can't you?

UNIT 19 GRAMMAR
In case

PRESENTATION

Bring to the class some fresh fruit and a small bottle of soft drink like orange juice.

Show these and say:

T: I've got this fruit with me in case I get hungry during the day. Why have I got the bottle of orange juice?

S: In case you get thirsty.
T: That's right. But if I get hungry again on the way home, I'll buy some crisps.

FOCUS

With books open, read the quotation at the top of the page. Go through the Focus section paying particular attention to the points to note.

What's the difference in meaning?

In Sentence 1 you will only buy the apples if and when you feel hungry. If you don't feel hungry, you won't buy the apples. In Sentence 2 you are definitely going to buy the apples as a precaution against being hungry.

PRACTICE

Exercise 1

KEY
You need:
- a spare can of petrol in case you run out (of petrol).
- a road map in case you get lost.
- a red triangle in case you break down in the dark.
- a spare wheel in case you have a puncture.
- a first aid kit in case you have an accident.

Students discuss any similar incidents where they have got lost, broken down, or had a puncture.

Exercise 2

KEY
1 I'll take an umbrella in case it rains.
2 Here's my address in case you come to my country (again)/in case you ever pass through my home town.

Exercise 3

Refer again to 'What's the difference in meaning?' to emphasise the difference in meaning between *if* and *in case*.

KEY
1 I'll take a plastic bottle of water in case I get thirsty.
2 Can you buy me a newspaper if you pass a kiosk on your way home?
3 We'll have a swim if we see a nice place by the river.
4 I'll change a travellers' cheque if the bank is open.
5 He took some extra travellers' cheques in case he ran out of money.
6 If the post office is open, can you buy me some stamps?
7 When you drive to the mountains this winter, put chains on your wheels in case/if the roads are icy.

UNIT 19

TALKING POINT

Ask students about the geographical location and climate of the places listed. With a time limit of two or three minutes, students discuss their lists in pairs or groups. Collect their ideas on the board under each place name and ask students to explain their precautions using *in case*.

LISTENING

Students try to predict what advice the speaker is going to give about each of the topics, and then compare their ideas with what the speaker says. Write on the board and explain the meaning of: *chilly*, *bargain* and *fares*. Play the tape. Ask if anything the speaker said surprised them.

KEY
LUGGAGE: Take as little as possible and take light bags.
CLOTHES: Take something warm in case it gets chilly (a bit cold) in the evening.
MONEY: Take a range of money – travellers' cheques, credit cards and cash in case you need to take a taxi when you arrive.
LEARNING THE LANGUAGE: Learn numbers in case you need to bargain over your fare. It is also useful to learn the words for 'please' and 'thank you' and 'How do I get to …?'

TAPESCRIPT
Listen to someone giving advice about a trip to Thailand. Note the advice she gives about luggage, clothes, money and learning the language.

> I think what's really important … to carry as little as possible, so that maybe your actual travel bags should weigh very little in themselves. So travel light, both the bags but also what you take in the sense of taking the minimum, erm.

Q: So you don't need any warm clothes or anything?

> Well, you have to be careful because it might be, for example where I was, it was very warm during the day, but then in the evenings it could really – particularly during the winter period – get quite chilly. So you do want to have it's … I would always suggest take something warm, erm.

Q: And what about money?

> Well, there I'd say take a range of money with you. I think it's always useful to have travellers' cheques and if you've got a credit card for some expensive item you might not know about in advance, and also cash, erm, because, just in case you arrive and you suddenly need to take a taxi or something it's useful to have that bit of cash with you.

Q: And what about learning the language, erm. Do you reckon it's useful to, to, to try and learn some before you go?

> Well, I think it is really, just the minimum, because it's really well worthwhile, in fact maybe essential, to have … just learn the numbers. Because, well that sounds quite a big thing, but if you just learn what the, the price is in advance of what your fares are going to be because you're going to want to bargain those fares for travelling around. And then just the normal 'please' and 'thank you' and 'How do I get to …?' and even though you won't understand the Thai response, at least you can see what direction they're pointing in.

WRITING

Discuss briefly the reasons for leaving the particular items listed in the rubric, eliminating sentences with *in case*.

EXAMPLE LETTER
Dear Mark and Jenny,

Welcome to the flat! You will find some extra blankets in the airing cupboard in case it gets cold. There is a spare key on the kitchen table in case you have a friend to stay. You will find our phone number pinned to the notice-board in case you need to call us, and the doctor's phone number is in the address book by the phone under 'D' for doctor! Hope you have a lovely time and please treat the place as your own. See you when we come back.
Love from
Tessa and Mike

EXTRA ACTIVITIES

1 Luxury villa
Students write a note for guests coming to stay at their luxury villa. They should use their imaginations to explain what and where things are in the villa, e.g. the champagne and caviar, 'in case' their guests need them.

2 Cloze letter
Give the Example letter from the writing activity above as a 'cloze' gapped writing activity.

3 Dictation
Use the same letter or a similar note as the basis for a dictation.

UNIT 20 READING
Fever Pitch

Before you read
These questions can be treated either superficially or in depth depending on the level of interest in football among the students. Be careful in question 4 not to go into too much detail at this stage. Many of the key football words appear later in the vocabulary exercise.

 Text: Fever Pitch

> BACKGROUND NOTES
> *Highbury*: an area in north London where the Arsenal football ground is situated
> *fish and chip shop*: fish and chips are a favourite takeaway food to eat before or after football matches.

COMPREHENSION
Give the context to the text. Explain that the writer is describing from memory what an ideal Arsenal match was like. It may be worth pointing out that Arsenal have a reputation for being rather a boring and disappointing team, and the writer often wonders himself why he is such a keen supporter of the team.

Ask the students to read the two comprehension questions before reading the text.

KEY
1 1 He had to go with his dad. 2 They had to eat lunch in the fish and chip shop sitting down at a table. 3 They had to have seats in the Upper West Stand. 4 Arsenal had to win by two clear goals. 5 The stadium had to be full. 6 The game had to be filmed on TV. 7 His dad had to be wearing warm clothes.
2 Because Arsenal were too good, Charlie George's goal was too spectacular and the crowd was too big and appreciative.

THINK ABOUT IT
SUGGESTED ANSWER
They probably shout insults when the team are playing badly, and boo if one of their players misses a goal.

VOCABULARY

Exercise 1
KEY
1 truly 2 tunnel 3 superb 4 entire 5 fixation
6 spectacular 7 appreciative

Exercise 2
KEY
pitch/ground: a pitch is the actual playing area with a goal at each end; the ground includes the pitch and the area around it where people stand or sit.
player/team: a player is a single person in a team of eleven players.
stand/stadium: the stand is where the spectators sit or stand to watch the match; the stadium includes the stand and the pitch.
fans/crowd: fans follow one particular team enthusiastically; a crowd is the whole group of people who watch a match.
free kick/penalty: a free kick is awarded against a player during a match for a minor offence. It is taken where the offence occurred on the pitch; a penalty is awarded to the opposing team for a serious offence committed in the goal area. One player is allowed to kick the ball directly at the goal mouth from a marked position in the centre of the goal area.
to beat/to win: in sport you beat an opponent or a team; you win a match or a tournament.
to shoot/to score: you shoot the ball at the goal but the ball may miss. You score when you shoot and the ball goes into the net.
to kick/to head: in football a player may use his feet to kick the ball and his head to head the ball.

 LISTENING

> BACKGROUND NOTES
> *The Cup Final*: the final match of the English football season, which usually takes place in early May. It is always held in Wembley Stadium and is a major event in the sporting calendar.

Explain to the students that the commentary is quite fast and that they should not try to understand every word that is spoken. Play the tape a couple of times through for the students to catch the relevant information.

KEY
Chelsea versus Manchester United; Manchester United won 4–0.

TAPESCRIPT
Listen to the extract from the end of a football match and say which two teams are playing, who won, and what the final score was.

Here come United, or Chelsea, again, moving forward towards the Manchester penalty area. Good cross in. Cascarino heads it down. Francis shoots. And it's another good save by Schmeichel. they can't beat them now. Can't beat them now. That's three or four chances they've had in the last ten minutes.

Corner again to Chelsea. Wise takes it quickly, almost fooling the referee. Gives it to Hoddle. Back to Wise. The cross is low and scooped away by Parker. And away to Cantona. Now United counter-attack. Cantona in field to Hughes. Is there a fourth goal? Ince is through. Ince is on side. This is the fourth, is it? Around Kharine. He must score. He taps it back, and it's knocked in in the end by Brian McClair. McClair gets the fourth goal. Deep into added time. Reward for him; great reward; a flattering reward for Manchester United. Salute the Champions. They're also the Cup winners. They've won the Double.

And the referee puts his whistle to his mouth. And that's the end of a dramatic second half in this 113th FA Cup Final. Salute Manchester United. Salute Alex Ferguson: his team the outstanding side of the season. No question of that. And they finished it in outstanding sy, style, winning this cup by four goals to nil.

TALKING POINT

Students can choose one or more of the topics and discuss in pairs or in groups. Tell them to close their eyes and imagine the answer to certain questions, e.g. (a summer picnic): *What month of the year is it? What is the weather like? Where are you sitting? What is the surrounding scenery like? Who are you with? What are you eating? What are you talking about? What are you wearing?* Suggest that students use the present tense in their descriptions. e.g. The conditions for a summer picnic:

It has to take place preferably in June or July when the leaves are still very green; it has got to be warm and sunny but not too warm; ...

For homework students can choose one of the events to write about for a composition.

EXTRA ACTIVITIES

1 Project: Footballer/Football team of the year

With students who are interested in football, suggest that they decide who they want to feature as 'footballer of the year' or 'football team of the year'. They collect information as well as magazine and newspaper photographs to produce an illustrated project to display in the classroom.

2 Football story

Write the following words on the board and ask students to see how quickly they can write a paragraph in the past tense which includes all the words.

beat score win shoot kick pitch play match team

Ask different students to read out their finished paragraphs.

Workbook tapescript

Unit 20

Exercise 1

Look at your book, listen to the commentary and complete the chart.

And we're getting near to the end of the route now. But it's still by no means certain who's going to make it to first place. Number 182, that's John Stevens from Bristol, is in the lead at the moment but 218 is very close behind him. There are a lot of people cheering 218. He's raising money for the Children's Hospital and there are a lot of people here to support him.

Hang on, there's someone coming up from behind. It's, er, 81 – he was way behind a few minutes ago. The Old People's Home will be pleased about him; let's hope he's collected lots of money for them. That's, er, Tim Hunter from Brighton, and he's doing very well.

Just behind him is the first woman to come in, Clare Andrews from Cambridge. Clare is collecting money for a local hostel for the homeless. I think she's sure to be the first woman to complete the race. That's number 128, Clare Andrews.

First place now seems to be between John Stevens and Alec Jones, who's still got lots of supporters along the way. John's supporting the Animal Rescue Society, so I suppose they couldn't really come along to cheer. And of course Alec is from London so he's got plenty of local support. And now they're approaching the finishing line. Ah yes, Alec has made it to first place, 182 is close behind him and third place goes to a woman this year.

CHECK Units 11–20

(See notes for Check Units 1–10.)

KEY

Exercise 1

1 I'm going to do
2 is leaving
3 you're going to like
4 We're going to be
5 Sue and Alan are getting married
6 it's going to snow
7 I'm taking
8 The twins are arriving
9 I'm going to be
10 The new boutique is opening

Exercise 2

1 I'll answer
2 what are you going to do ...?
3 I'll get
4 I'll send
5 When are you going to ...?/I'll do
6 I'll turn on
7 I'll have
8 I'm going to/I'll take

Exercise 3

1 she hears/she'll be
2 I won't phone/something important happens.
3 he doesn't come/will you be upset?
4 They'll laugh/they realise
5 you'll like/you meet
6 I'll send/I reach
7 I'll get/they have
8 Will she go/she gets

Exercise 4

1b 2e 3f *or* i 4a 5c 6h 7i *or* f 8d 9j 10g

Exercise 5

1 we can/'ll be able to
2 she can't/she's not able to
3 be able to
4 couldn't/wasn't able to
5 were able to
6 I couldn't/wasn't able to

Exercise 6

1 does she
2 isn't it
3 am I
4 could you
5 are they
6 hasn't he
7 didn't it
8 did we

Exercise 7

1 solicitor
2 pull
3 heel
4 tree
5 golf
6 score

Exercise 8

1 She's not only the director of the company but also the mother of two young children.
2 I like neither cooking nor washing up.
3 I like both giving presents and receiving them.
4 I enjoy going to concerts as well as listening to jazz.
5 I suggest either hiring a video for the evening or going to the cinema.

Exercise 9

1b 2b 3c 4c 5a

Exercise 10

(Example responses)
1 Do you think I could leave a message?
  Could you give him/her a message?
  Would you mind taking a message?
2 Could I have/Can I have/Could you give me/Do you think I could have a receipt, please?
3 Didn't we go to the same school?
  Didn't you go to school with me?
  Weren't you at school with me?
  You went to the same school as me, didn't you?
4 Don't you like ice cream?
5 Do you think you could give me extra grammar lessons? Would you mind giving me extra grammar lessons?
6 Aren't you/Weren't you supposed to be at a meeting? You're supposed to be at a meeting, aren't you? You were supposed to be at a meeting, weren't you?

USE YOUR ENGLISH
Units 11–20

Exercise 1

Ask students who took Student A and B roles in the last Use your English section to reverse their roles. The B students turn to their page at the back of the book. Give the students time to read through their sentence prompts, and tell the A students to start. Do the first example aloud with the whole class so they can see how the exercise works.

KEY

A: give a party on Saturday – B: help you with the food
B: paint my bedroom a different colour – A: choose a colour for you
A: see the latest James Bond film this evening – B: come with you to see it
B: do the washing up – A: dry the dishes
A: spend the evening at home – B: bring over some CDs and join you
B: catch the six o'clock bus – A: drive you to the bus station
A: find a holiday job this summer – B: lend you my book called *Summer Jobs*
B: learn Italian this year – A: come to classes with you
A: make some lunch – B lay the table
B: buy a second-hand bicycle – A: give you my old one

Exercise 2

Students continue to work in pairs. Remind them first of the different ways in which they can start a polite request. Go through the six 'situations' making sure the students understand them and then set them to work in pairs. Go round and listen as they work through the exercise, noting any errors as you go along. These can be taken up with the class as a whole afterwards.

SUGGESTED CONVERSATIONS

1. A: Could you give me change for a £5 note, please?
   B: I'm sorry but we're not allowed to give change.

2. A: Would you mind emptying this ashtray, please?
   B: Yes, certainly.

3. A: Do you think you could buy me a video cassette/a set of three video cassettes when you go into town? I'll give you the money.
   B: Well, actually, I'm not going anywhere near the video shop. Sorry.

4. A: Could I record your Sting CD on to a cassette?
   B: Yes, O.K.

5. A: I bought this sweater this morning and the colour doesn't suit me. Would you mind exchanging it for a blue one please?
   B: Yes, of course. But I need to see your receipt.

6. A: Do you think you could turn the sound up a little?
   B: O.K.

Exercise 3

BACKGROUND NOTES
Lerici: A medium-sized resort near the city of La Spezia on the Italian Riviera.
Scottish Highlands: Mountainous areas of north Scotland.
Ullapool: A small village on Loch (Lake) Broom in the North West Highlands.
self-catering: You provide and cook your own food.
highland estate: A large piece of land.
SAE: Stamped addressed envelope.

Go through the holiday advertisements explaining any small print of interest. Students work in pairs matching the holiday to the person.

SUGGESTED ANSWERS
Mr Wood: Scottish Highlands
Mrs Wood: Lerici or 'Sail or Windsurf'
Cara Wood: Lerici
Jeff Wood: 'Sail or Windsurf'

The students should imagine that they are talking directly to each member of the family when they make their suggestions. Finally, ask them to see if they can come to an agreement on which of the three holidays would please most of the family.

PROGRESS TEST Units 11–20

(See notes for Progress test Units 1–10.)

KEY

Exercise 1
1b 2c 3a 4b 5b 6a 7c 8b 9a 10c

Exercise 2
1c 2b 3a 4a 5b 6c 7c 8b 9a 10a

Exercise 3
1 also 2 of 3 taking 4 able 5 for 6 If 7 best
8 pool 9 swim 10 alone

Glenn

UNIT 21
Glenn, an American in Britain

Ask students to look at the photo of Glenn and to describe what he looks like and what he is wearing and doing. Ask if the students think he looks American. Direct them to the address at the top of Glenn's letter and use a map to show where Stratford-upon-Avon is situated. Ask if any students have been there and why it is a famous town (Shakespeare's birthplace).

> BACKGROUND NOTES
> *Hamlet*: One of Shakespeare's best known plays.
> *the theater*: (The British English spelling is *theatre*.) The Shakespeare Memorial Theatre, the home of the Royal Shakespeare Company (RSC), is devoted almost exclusively to the performance of Shakespeare's plays.
> *favor*: The British English spelling is *favour*, c.f. *color/colour*.

Students read Glenn's letter silently and answer the questions in Exercise 1.

Exercise 1

KEY
1 He's in Stratford.
2 He's pleased because he's got a ticket to see 'Hamlet'.
3 He's got a job as a waiter in a small hotel.
4 He doesn't want to lose it because he really needs the money

Ask any students who have been to Britain to comment on the British habit of queuing and whether people queue as much in their country.

Exercise 2

Check that students understand: *reason*, *incident*, *enquiry* and *description*. Ask questions around each topic, e.g. *Tell me about Glenn's job/travels.* Encourage students to produce connected sentences.

KEY
1 an apology and a reason for not writing earlier.
2 his recent travels
3 where Glenn is at the moment
4 his opinion of Stratford
5 a description of his job
6 a description of the chef in his job
7 an incident which occurred at work
8 an inquiry about life back in the USA

At this point you may like to introduce the first question from Exercise 4, 'About you'.

Exercise 3

Depending on interest and time, elicit more 'Americanisms', including current popular slang.

KEY

American English	British English
standing in line	queuing
guess	think
movie	film
mad	angry
vacation	holiday
Hi!	Hello!

Exercise 4

Introduce vocabulary like: *legal/illegal*, *work permit*, *residence permit*, *job agency* and *immigration laws* where necessary.

VOCABULARY

Exercise 1

Before reading the note in the book, get students to suggest sentences to show some of the meanings of *get*, e.g. *He got the letter. You must get permission to go. We got to London at five o'clock.*

Refer to the two uses of *get* in Glenn's letter, e.g. *got mad at me* and *get fired*.

KEY
1 Ann has been very ill but at last she's getting better.
2 Barry and Amy have just announced that they're going to get married.
3 The reason they were late was because they got lost.
4 I made a lot of spelling mistakes because I was getting/I got tired.
5 When she can't find a parking space, she always gets angry.
6 If you're late again, you'll get fired.
7 They're coming in ten minutes. Please hurry up and get ready.
8 Have a good time at the party but don't get drunk.

Exercise 2

Give an example of the *ea* sound in each sound group.

 ### Exercise 3

Students may like to group the words before listening. Ask if they can think of any other *ea*

UNIT 21

words and say which group they belong to.

KEY

Group 1 /iː/	Group 2 /e/	Group 3 /eɪ/	Group 4 /ɪə/
tea	dead	steak	real
speak	ready		year
read	head		theatre
mean			dear
pleased			Shakespeare
leave			

Point out that there is a difference in pronunciation between the infinitive *to read* /riːd/ and the past tense read /red/.

TAPESCRIPT
Listen and write the following words in the correct sound group /iː/ /e/ /eɪ/ /ɪə/.

tea, real, year, speak, theatre, read, dead, mean, dear, ready, steak, pleased, head, leave, Shakespeare

 LISTENING

> BACKGROUND NOTES
> *Tom Stoppard*: A modern British playwright. One of his most famous plays is *Rosencrantz and Guildenstern are dead*.

Write on the board and explain: *Tom Stoppard*, *the British voice/accent*, *intriguing*, *twilight* and *thatched roof*.

TAPESCRIPT
Listen to an American student who has just visited Stratford-upon-Avon and note why she's in Britain, what she thinks of the British theatre and her impressions of Stratford.

INTERVIEWER: Barbara, you're from the United States, aren't you? Where are you from exactly?
BARBARA: I'm from Santa Barbara, California.
INTERVIEWER: Ah ... and you've just come over to Britain, have you?
BARBARA: Ah, yes, er, let's see, a couple of weeks ago.
INTERVIEWER: Mmm. Why, er, why have you come? Is it just a holiday or ...?
BARBARA: No, I've come to study drama.
INTERVIEWER: Why particularly British theatre?
BARBARA: Well, erm, the English have been known to have good theatre and you know you have such, er, writers as Shakespeare and, erm, Tom Stoppard. You know, the very old to the very new. The British voice is quite intriguing too, erm, I think Americans, erm, especially when the theatre ... when it comes to theatre, we sort of have, erm, a fascination for the British accent, and so it's wonderful to come here and, erm, see British theatre and ...
INTERVIEWER: What does your visit involve now? You're here, as you say, two weeks. Erm, or is it ... longer?
BARBARA: Five.
INTERVIEWER: Five weeks.
BARBARA: Erm, we're in Britain for five weeks.
INTERVIEWER: Right. What does that, er, entail? What're you doing?
BARBARA: Well, we spent the first five or six days here in London and then we went to Stratford-upon-Avon, erm.
INTERVIEWER: What did you think of the place?
BARBARA: It's beautiful. It's ah, the river Avon, it, is it Avon? Yes.
INTERVIEWER: Yes.
BARBARA: The river Avon is ah, oh, beautiful, especially in the twilight, with the sun shining on it and ... It was quite touristy.
INTERVIEWER: Did you get to, to see the, the birthplace of Shakespeare?
BARBARA: I saw it from the outside.
INTERVIEWER: Yes.
BARBARA: And that was, that was really neat ... was to see the Elizabethan homes with the thatched roofs and, erm, how uneven the levels are. It's, er, wonderful.

KEY
1 She's come to Britain to study drama.
2 She thinks the British have good writers, both old and new, like Shakespeare and Tom Stoppard. The British theatre is supposed to be very good. Like most Americans she find the British voice/accent intriguing.
3 She thinks it's beautiful, especially the River Avon in twilight with the sun shining on it. She thought is was quite touristy. She has seen the outside of Shakespeare's birthplace and thought it was great to see the Elizabethan homes with the thatched roofs.

TALKING POINT

Before starting, ask students to suggest one positive and one negative aspect of tourism. Practise the sentence openers. Show how to complete the sentence with a noun phrase or a gerund, e.g. *The worst thing must be the crowds in places like banks and post offices/finding your favourite restaurant full of tourists.*

EXTRA ACTIVITIES

1 Time capsule

In groups, students choose ten small items to put into a sealed 'time capsule'. When the capsule is opened in the future, it will give some idea of what life was like at the end of the 20th century.

2 Famous birthplaces

Students write descriptions of two other famous birthplaces of great literary, artistic, religious or political figures. The following names may help students choose places to write about: El Greco, Tito, Napoleon, Hans Christian Andersen, Queen Christina, Saint Bernadette, Joan of Arc, the Goddess Aphrodite, Christopher Columbus.

3 Horror sounds and spellings

Ask students to look through their notebooks or text book and find words which they think have a strange pronunciation or a strange spelling, e.g. the numbers: *one*, *two* and *eight*. You can make a 'rogues' gallery' of these on the board.

 ## Workbook tapescript

Unit 21

Exercise 1

Before you listen, look at your book and read the breakfast menu. Then listen to the conversation and find the mistakes in Glenn's order. After listening, rewrite the order correctly.

GLENN: Are you ready to order now?
A: Er, yes. What kind of fruit juice do you have?
GLENN: Orange, grapefruit, or tomato.
A: Right, I'll have a tomato juice to start with, please.
B: And I'll have cereal. Do you have cornflakes?
GLENN: Yes, we do.
B: Fine. Some cornflakes for me. And I think I'll have the mushrooms after that, please.
A: Me too. No, on second thoughts, I'll have scrambled eggs.
GLENN: Er, yes. Would you like toast to follow?
A: Yes, please.
GLENN: Tea or coffee?
A: I'd prefer tea, please.
B: Coffee for me, please.
GLENN: That's one tea and one coffee.
B: No, actually I think I'll have tea as well.
GLENN: Sure.

UNIT 22 GRAMMAR
Present perfect simple and continuous

PRESENTATION

With books closed, ask:

T: What time is it now?
S: It's 8.40.
T: When did I start teaching?
S: At 8.00.
T: Am I still teaching now?
S: Yes, you are.
T: So how long have I been teaching this morning?
S: For forty minutes.
T: That's right. I've been teaching for forty minutes. I've been teaching since 8.00.

Write the last two sentences on the board, including the question form: *How long have you been teaching?* Then draw a 'time line' to show the duration of time.

I've been teaching since 8 o'clock.
            for forty minutes.
→→→→→→→→→→→→→→→ . . . .
PAST   NOW   FUTURE
(8.00)   (8.40)

Ask:
T: How long have you been sitting here?
S: We've been sitting here for …/since…

Remind students how both the present perfect and the present perfect continuous are contracted in their spoken form, e.g. ***He's** just bought a ticket to see Hamlet.*

What's the difference in meaning?

In Sentence 1, the person is no longer working in Stratford; in Sentence 2, the person is either still working there, or has just finished.

Students refer to Glenn's letter in Unit 21 to identify examples of the two tenses and say which are simple and which are continuous.

Some of the uses of the present perfect in the letter are more common in British English than in American English, e.g. *I've already done it/I've just done it.* (Br Eng) but *I already did it/I just did it* (Am Eng). Whether you wish to mention this may depend on the level of the class.

FOCUS

Students supply similar example sentences for each point. Prompt them if necessary, e.g. *Tell me if you've seen any films with Robert Redford in them. Tell me a city you've never been to.*

Explain that the present perfect continuous is not used with expressions of quantity. Compare: *I've been driving all morning* **and** *I've driven 100 miles.*

KEY TO THE SHORT CONVERSATIONS
A: What did you do last night? (past simple)
B: I read a book. (past simple)
A: Why are your eyes sore? (present simple)
B: I've been reading. (present perfect continuous)
A: Do you way to borrow this book? (present simple)
B: No thanks, I've read it. (present perfect simple)

UNIT 22

Before starting the practice on the next page, ask rapid questions about Glenn's adventures in Europe, using the present perfect simple and the present perfect continuous. Alternatively, dictate the questions or duplicate them for students to answer for homework, e.g.

1 What's Glenn been doing for the last few months?
2 Which countries do you think he's been to?
3 Has he been in Stratford (for) long?
4 What job has he just started?
5 What play has he managed to buy a ticket for?
6 What sort of weather have they been having on the east coast of the USA?

PRACTICE

Exercise 1

Before starting the exercise, revise the past simple and present perfect forms of the verbs: *go*, *break*, *see*, *write*, *win*, *find*. After completing the exercise, students report back items of general interest about their partner's experiences.

KEY
1 Have you ever been to the USA?
2 Have you ever broken an arm or leg?
3 Have you ever seen a famous person in real life?
4 Have you ever written to a magazine or newspaper?
5 Have you ever won a competition?
6 Have you ever found anything valuable?

Exercise 2

KEY
1 What have you been reading?
  I've been reading a romantic novel.
2 What have you been doing/eating?
  I've been eating chocolate. *or*
  I've been playing with my toys.
3 What have you been watching?
  I've been watching a sad/romantic film.
4 What have you been cooking/making?
  I've been making dinner/a cake/a curry …
5 Who have you been talking to?
  I've been talking to my girlfriend.

Exercise 3

Students take notes so that they can report the information about each other.

Exercise 4

SUGGESTED ANSWERS
1 I've been playing a lot of (tennis).
  I've been doing a lot of (gardening).
2 I haven't been (swimming) for ages.
  I haven't done any (jogging) for a long time.
  I haven't played (squash) for weeks.
3 I've been reading ('Gone with the Wind').
  I've been reading (a detective story).
4 I've always wanted to visit (Thailand).

LISTENING

Ask if any of the students have ever sent a letter-cassette and if it was more difficult or easier than writing a letter. What are the advantages of letter-cassettes? Write on the board and explain: *to joke*, *cabin*, *waves*, *ruined*, *cheer you up*.

TAPESCRIPT
Listen to Lori's letter-cassette to Glenn, look at your Students' Book and follow the instructions.

Hi, Glenn. Lori here. Do you recognise my voice? Well, I thought I'd send you a cassette rather than write you. I don't have too much time right now and I guess this'll be quicker. It was good to hear your news, Glenn. You sound as if you've been having a great time. I've never been to Britain but you're making it sound like I have to go!

Here it's been a weird summer. We've, er, just had the Midsummer Festival. We've been preparing for it for days. It was a good evening, even though it rained most of the time. The weather's been really bad this summer. You've obviously heard about the storms from the newspapers. You joked about our boat but last week our summer cabin was washed away. Really! The waves were over ten feet high. Most of the cabins round here were ruined.

Oh, by the way, did you know that I've been taking driving lessons? I've already had five and I'm doing just fine.

Well, I guess I'd better stop now. Here's a bit of music to cheer you up. I really like it. What do you think? Write me soon, Glenn, and don't annoy the chef again.

KEY
The Midsummer Festival.
The weather has been really bad.
They've been having a lot of storms.
The summer cabin got washed away.
She's been taking driving lessons.

WRITING

Before you write

Write the headings on the board. Call out each expression and ask a student to tell you which heading to write it under. Students may like to suggest other expressions.

KEY
1 **To start a letter**
   Thanks very much for your last letter.
   Sorry I haven't written before but …
   It was great to get your letter.

2 **To introduce a new topic**
   By the way …
   Did you know that …
   Have you heard …

3 To close a letter
Well, that's enough for now,
Give my regards/love to …
Anyway, I'd better stop now.
Best wishes, …
Say hello to …
Love from …

Write a letter

Tell students that they must use at least on expression from each group.

EXAMPLE LETTER

Dear Julie,

Sorry I haven't written before but I've been studying very hard for my exams and I've also been working part-time in a wine bar. Did you know that I've started to learn Spanish? We've already had six lessons but I can't say very much yet. But the way, I've just passed my driving test – third time lucky! I've now bought an old Ford Fiesta which I've called 'Lucky'.

The weather has been marvellous here over the last few days. I've been sunbathing in my lunch hour in the park and I've got quite brown. What have you been doing recently? Are you still seeing Jeremy or is it all over? Write and tell me all your news.

Anyway, I'd better stop now and catch the post. Give my love to your parents and say hello to Domino.

Love from
Kim

EXTRA ACTIVITY

Find someone who …

Duplicate questionnaire cards (see below) for each student, or each pair of students. Set a time limit of three to four minutes and ask students to walk round the class questioning people. When they find someone who answers *yes* to their question, they should write down the name of that student and move on to the next question. The questions can be adapted according to circumstances.

Find someone who …

1 has been living in the same home for less than two years.
2 has had an ice cream today.
3 has been studying another language this week.
4 has been taking driving lessons.
5 hasn't seen a horror film.
6 hasn't read a newspaper today.
7 has been in a jacuzzi.
8 has been sleeping badly.
9 has never heard of Julio Iglesias.
10 has been cycling recently.

 Workbook tapescript

Unit 22

Speechwork: Pronunciation
The present perfect

Exercise 5

A

Listen to these sentences.

I've already done my homework.
She's had a baby girl.

Now listen and repeat.
I've [bleep]
I've already done my homework. [bleep]
She's [bleep] She's had a baby girl. [bleep]

B

Now you make sentences. Listen to the example.
I've been here before.
She
She's been here before.

Now you do it.
I've been here before.
She [bleep]
She's been here before.
They [bleep]
They've been here before.
You [bleep]
You've been here before.
He [bleep]
He's been here before.

C

Listen to these questions.

Have you finished that book yet?
Has she left school?

Now listen and repeat.
Have [bleep]
Have you finished that book yet? [bleep]
Has [bleep] Has she left school? [bleep]

Listen to these short answers.
Yes, I have.
No, I haven't.
Yes, she has.
No, she hasn't.

Now listen and repeat.
have [bleep] Yes, I have. [bleep]
haven't [bleep] No, I haven't.
has [bleep] Yes, she has. [bleep]
hasn't [bleep] No, she hasn't. [bleep]

UNIT 23 COMMUNICATION
Making complaints

Before you read

Ask the students to describe the scene in the restaurant and to guess what they think the woman is complaining about. Broaden out the discussion to cover other types of complaints that may arise in a restaurant. Check if any students have complained about anything and if so, what.

DIALOGUE

With books closed, play the tape and ask the students to say what the two complaints are about. Then play the tape again with books open so that the students can follow it. Ask students to guess the meaning of *pot*, *rushed off our feet* and *charged*. Students ask and answer the questions in pairs. Check the answers with the whole class.

KEY
1 She asks the waiter to bring a fresh pot of coffee because it was almost cold.
2 He says there's a problem in the kitchen and they're rushed off their feet.
3 He asks the waiter to check the bill again as they have been charged for two bottles of mineral water instead of one.
4 The manager doesn't charge them for the coffee.

Ask the students to read the dialogue in pairs, changing parts between the two sections of the dialogue. Then choose three students to act it out from memory in front of the class, using a desk as the restaurant table.

FOCUS

Ask students to find the complaints in the dialogue and notice how both speakers start their complaint with an apology. Practise the sentences chorally, making sure that students make their voices rise at the end of the request, otherwise it may sound rude.

PRACTICE

Exercise 1

Write up the categories on the board before you start. Fill in the lists as the students give you the words.

KEY

Food	*Hotel rooms*
overdone	noisy
underdone	dark
salty	small
cold	damp (cold)

Clothes	*Vending machines*
zip broken	gone wrong
button missing	broken down
sweater shrunk	doesn't work
lining torn	doesn't return coin

Students use the vocabulary to make their own complaints, e.g. *I'm afraid this pie is too/rather salty. I'm sorry but there's a button missing on this jacket and it's brand new.*

You may wish to use the occasion to revise food and clothes vocabulary with the students.

Exercise 2

Ask check questions for each situation to make sure that students understand what they involve. Divide the four situations between the students and help with vocabulary. When students have practised them, one pair from each group should perform their conversations. Record the conversations for later playback and correction.

SUGGESTED CONVERSATIONS

1 A: Excuse me. I'm afraid I can't eat this hamburger. It's very dry and overdone. Could you bring me another one, please?
  B: Yes, of course. I'm sorry about that.
  A: That's all right. Thank you.

2 A: Excuse me, do you think you could give me another room? I'm in Room 301 overlooking the car park and it's extremely noisy. I didn't get any sleep last night.
  B: I'll see if there's another room free. One moment.
  A: Thank you.

3 A: Excuse me. I bought this pair of jeans last week from this shop and the first time I wore them the zip broke.
  B: Let me have a look at them. The zip broke when you put them on, did it?
  A: That's right. I didn't wear them at all. Could you give me another pair in exchange?
  B: One moment and I'll get the manager.

4 A: Excuse me, this machine doesn't work.
  B: What do you mean?
  A: I've just put in 50p to get a Coca-Cola and nothing happened. Could I have my money back?
  B: Have you pressed the Coin Return?
  A: Yes, but I didn't get it back.
  B: O.K. Here's a 50p. Try the other machine over there.

LISTENING

Preparation

Before you play the first conversation, ask if anyone has had noisy neighbours and what they did about it. Ask what other things neighbours can do that are annoying.

Before the second conversation, ask if anyone has ever complained about a service bill, e.g. for heating or electricity, and if so, why. What happened?

TAPESCRIPT

Listen to the telephone conversations. Note what the callers are complaining about and what action they are requesting.

1
GIRL: Hello, 776 2235.
WOMAN: Oh good evening. It's Mrs Richards here. I'm phoning from Number 65 next door.
GIRL: Yes?
WOMAN: Well, I've been trying to get to sleep since eleven o'clock, but I'm afraid the noise from your house is so loud it's quite impossible.
GIRL: Oh, sorry.
WOMAN: Would you mind asking your friends to be a little quieter and turn the music down? I'm sorry but it's absolutely deafening.
GIRL: Sorry. Yes, I will.
WOMAN: Thank you.

2
WOMAN: Accounts. Can I help you?
MAN: Oh good morning. I'm ringing up about my telephone bill.
WOMAN: Yes?
MAN: Well, it seems to be ridiculously high. £176.50. That's about twice what it normally is. I was wondering, could you check it for me?
WOMAN: Could you give me your name, address and telephone number, please?
MAN: Yes. It's Mr Alan Weeks, 76 Alderton Road, Staines. And the number is 8155673.
WOMAN: Let me just check this. One moment. Hello? Mr Weeks?
MAN: Yes.
WOMAN: Well, I'm afraid there must have been a fault with the computer at the time. Your bill should read £76.50, not £176.50. I'm very sorry about that. I'll get the bill revised and send you a new one.
MAN: Thank you. Goodbye.

KEY

Caller	Complaint	Action requested
1 Mrs Richards	music too loud	turn music down, ask friends to be quieter
2 Mr Alan Weeks	telephone bill wrong, too high	check bill, send a new one

READING

> BACKGROUND NOTE
> *mail order*: Shopping by post. The customer selects goods from a catalogue, places the order by post and the goods are delivered to the customer's house.

Introduce the subject of mail order catalogues, preferably using a real one. Find out if any students regularly buy by mail order. Ask what advantages there are in shopping by mail order.

Exercise 1

KEY
– a radio cassette player and an alarm clock
– the cassette player
– the alarm clock
– the cassette player costs £34.99
– the alarm clock costs £17.99

Find out if any students own similar items and what sort of things can go wrong with them.

Exercise 2

KEY
– The customer bought a Braun alarm clock.
– The alarms keeps on buzzing when he shouts at it. (It is supposed to stop when you shout at it.)
– He wants the company to send him a new one or to refund the money.

The letter

Go through the layout notes in detail. Other points to mention:
– Do not put your name above the address in the top right-hand corner.
– In letters where you know the name of the person you are writing to, you write *Dear Mr/Mrs/Ms* and their name, and end the letter *Yours sincerely*.
– Contractions are not normally used in formal letters.

WRITING

SUGGESTED LETTER
Dear Sir/Madam,

I ordered a radio cassette player from your mail order company recently and am pleased to say that it arrived safely last week. It worked very well until I went on holiday with it. Now I find that the fast forward button doesn't work when I press it. I am returning the radio-cassette player with this letter and I would be grateful if you could either refund the money or send me a new one.

Yours faithfully,
…

UNITS 23/24

EXTRA ACTIVITIES

1 Jigsaw letters

Write a similar letter of complaint, make copies and cut them up sentence by sentence into about seven or eight different strips. Each group gets a letter in the form of a jumbled assortment of sentences which they have to sort into the correct order to make a complete letter.

2 What's the problem?

One student thinks of a complaint, e.g. the jacket he/she has bought has a torn lining. The other students must ask Yes/No questions to guess exactly what the complaint is.

3 Video recordings

Teachers with access to portable video equipment can video students' performances in the situations in Exercise 2 of the Students' Book. These can be played back for correction and feedback.

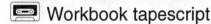
Workbook tapescript

Unit 23

Speechwork: Stress and intonation
Making complaints and requesting action

Exercise 6

A

Listen to this complaint and request for action.

I'm afRAID I can't EAT this STEAK.
Could you CHANGE it, PLEASE?

Now listen and repeat.
can't EAT this STEAK [bleep]
I'm afRAID I can't EAT this STEAK. [bleep]
Could you CHANGE it, PLEASE? [bleep]

B

Now you make complaints and request action.
Listen to the example.
You are in a hotel.
The shower's broken/fix it.
I'm afraid the shower's broken. Could you fix it, please?

Now you do it.
The shower's broken/fix it. [bleep]
I'm afraid the shower's broken. Could you fix it, please?
My room's cold/turn on the heating. [bleep]
I'm afraid my room's cold. Could you turn on the heating, please?
The towels are dirty/change them. [bleep]
I'm afraid the towels are dirty. Could you change them, please?

UNIT 24 GRAMMAR
Make and *do*

PRESENTATION

With books closed, recap Glenn's story so far, including his problems with the chef and the restaurant customers.

(Glenn said in his letter in Unit 21 that the chef, Mr Partridge, was 'really strange' and was 'persecuting' him because he made a mistake with the breakfast orders.)

Photographs

With books open, ask students to say who does the different jobs in a hotel kitchen and to suggest what mistake Glenn may have made with the breakfast orders.

FOCUS

Students with good dictionaries can look up *make* and *do* and find the meanings which are listed in the Focus section, plus one or two more meanings. Go through each meaning with the class, asking students for more example sentences.

Note

If there is time, students can make sentences in pairs using each of the fixed phrases.

PRACTICE

Exercise 1

KEY
1 I've made up my mind to leave my job.
2 They made an arrangement to meet.
3 I'd like you to make an effort to arrive on time in future.
4 You've made a mistake here.
5 You can't make me go.
6 He made a lot of money buying and selling houses.

Exercise 2

KEY
1 It only takes me a second to do my room.
2 She is doing very well at art school.
3 We do all our shopping in the new supermarket.
4 Last year he was doing business with Russia.

Exercise 3

Students exchange sentences to compare their answers.

EXAMPLE SENTENCES
1 I like doing the cooking/making the beds.
2 I hate doing the cleaning/washing-up.
3 I like making chocolate cakes.

70

4 I've made some book shelves/a dress.
5 I've made a promise to do my room every week.
6 I'm going to do my homework on the train home tonight.

EXTRA ACTIVITIES

1 *Make* and *do* tennis

You need a largish room and a tennis ball, or other soft ball. Players can remain in their seats and everyone can play. Players throw the ball to anyone they please, calling out the person's name and command of either 'Make!' or 'Do!'. The recipient of the ball must give a sentence with either *make* or *do* which has not been given before. Failure to give a correct sentence means elimination. If a player throws the ball to someone who is already eliminated, he/she too is eliminated. The last player remaining is the winner.

2 Which is it?

Write on separate cards the fixed phrases of *make* and *do* from the Students' Book, omitting the words *make* or *do*. Hand the cards out among the students, who have to put them in the correct *make* or *do* pile.

UNIT 25 READING
Theatrical anecdotes

Before you read

Elicit some titles of Shakespeare's plays (see list below). Write on the board those which any of the students have seen performed. Ask for their opinions of any plays they have seen.

A selection of well-known Shakespeare plays are:

Tragedies	**Comedies**
Hamlet	*Twelfth Night*
Othello	*As You Like It*
King Lear	*Much Ado About Nothing*
Macbeth	*A Midsummer Night's Dream*
Romeo and Juliet	

Roman plays	**Historical plays**
Julius Caesar	*Henry V*
Antony and Cleopatra	*Richard II*
Coriolanus	*Richard III*

Guess the meaning

Check the meaning of these after the students have completed the comprehension exercise.

COMPREHENSION

Exercise 1

Explain that there are four amusing anecdotes contained in the eight paragraphs. Ask the students first to skim read the eight paragraphs and work out the two halves which are connected in each case. It should be possible to guess this without close reading of the text. After a minute or two, check that all the students have the right combinations.

KEY
Anecdote 1: a and e
Anecdote 2: g and b
Anecdote 3: h and c
Anecdote 4: d and f

Now ask the students to read each anecdote in detail. Ask some comprehension questions after each one.

Exercise 2

In pairs, students match each heading and the appropriate anecdote.

KEY
1 Joint performance = Anecdote 3
2 Hamlet made simple = Anecdote 2
3 Not known in Denver = Anecdote 1
4 A timely interruption = Anecdote 4

Exercise 3

Students should try and do the summaries without looking at the original texts. In this way, they are more likely to shorten the texts and get the essence of each anecdote. These summaries can be done orally with the whole class and then written as part of a homework assignment.

SUGGESTED SUMMARIES

1 This is about a very rich man who got angry when he discovered a portrait of Shakespeare in the foyer of the theatre which was built in honour of himself. He wondered why it was not his own portrait in the theatre because Shakespeare 'had done nothing to help Colorado!'
2 This is about an amusing incident during a performance of *Julius Caesar* when a telephone rang backstage just as two conspirators were about to murder Caesar. One conspirator said loudly, 'What shall we do if it's for Caesar?'
3 This is about an unusual performance of *Hamlet* when the actor in the title role was taken ill and an understudy had to go on. The understudy was so nervous and his performance was so bad that on the second night the director asked for the play to go on without the main character of Hamlet. Many of the audience said that this version of the play was better.

UNITS 25/26

4 This is about the famous actor, John Barrymore, whose performance of Hamlet was disturbed one afternoon by a then famous film star who talked loudly all the time to her friends. When he took his curtain-call, Barrymore publicly thanked the film start for 'co-starring' with him.

VOCABULARY

Students do this exercise as a whole group. Ask individual students for explanations of the three other words in each group.

KEY
1 painter 2 box-office 3 chapter 4 programme
5 orchestra

EXTRA ACTIVITIES

1 Word puzzle

In five minutes, students make as many English words as they can out of the letters in: *William Shakespeare's Hamlet.*

2 Theatre visit

Students use the theatre entertainment section of a national newspaper to choose a classical drama, a modern play, a comedy, a musical, a thriller, an opera and a ballet.

Ask students to use each of these in turn in roleplays in which they invite a partner out for the evening.

3 Shakespeare on video

Students might enjoy one of the following contemporary filmed versions of Shakespeare's plays on video: *Hamlet* with Mel Gibson and Glenn Close, *Much Ado About Nothing* with Kenneth Branagh and Emma Thompson, and Kenneth Branagh's *Henry V.* Also available on video are the British classic films directed and acted by Laurence Olivier, *Hamlet, Richard III* and *Henry V.*

4 Panel discussion or debate

More advanced groups can discuss or debate the topic: *Should an introduction to the classics of world literature be a compulsory part of everyone's education?*

UNIT 26 GRAMMAR
The passive

PRESENTATION

With books closed, ask general knowledge questions similar to those in Exercise 2, e.g. *Where is wine produced in Europe/Latin America?* In this way elicit a selection of both singular and plural sentences in the present passive and write one of each on the board. Then elicit sentences in the past passive by asking about the students' personal background, e.g. *Where/When were you educated/ brought up?* Write and example sentence on the board. Explain that these sentences are in the passive voice.

What's the difference in style?

Sentence 1 is more informal than Sentence 2. Sentence 1 is in the active. Sentence 2 in the passive. Sentence 1 sounds like something you would say to a friend, whereas Sentence 2 sounds like a sentence you would write in a report.

FOCUS

Use the language table to explain how the passive is formed by combining the verb *to be* (in the tense required) with the past participle of the main verb.

Text about 'Cats'

> BACKGROUND NOTES
> Andrew Lloyd Webber, a famous British composer and songwriter, broke theatrical records by having three musical shows – 'Cats', 'Phantom of the Opera, and 'Starlight Express' – performed in New York and London at the same time.

To highlight the use of the passive, ask comprehension questions, e.g.
What is 'Cats' based on?
Who was it composed by?
Who was it directed by?
When and where was it first produced?
Where else has it been performed?
What reputation has it got?

PRACTICE

Exercise 1

SUGGESTED ANSWERS
Wine is produced in many parts of France.
VW cars are made in Germany.
Oil is produced in Texas/the Middle East.
Rice is grown in China.
Tea is grown in India/Sri Lanka.
Coffee is grown/coffee beans are grown in Brazil/South America/Jamaica/Africa.
Bananas are grown in the Caribbean/parts of Africa/South America.
Vodka is made in Russia.
Citroën cars are made in France.
Whisky is made in Scotland/Ireland. (In Ireland it is spelt *whiskey*.)

Exercise 2

Bring the whole class together to discuss the answers to Exercises 1 and 2.

Exercise 3

For homework, students can each devise a similar set of true/false quiz questions about inventions (using the passive).

KEY
1 True.
2 False. Ferdinand Porsche designed the Beetle, though he is better known for his sports cars. (Olivetti is known for his typewriters.)
3 True.
4 True.
5 False. He was assassinated in a theatre.
6 False. The sound is produced by its wings.

EXERCISE 4

KEY
1 The lions are being fed by the lion keeper.
2 The sports car is being chased by the police car.
3 The grapes are being picked.
4 *Cats* is being performed by Moscow City Theatre.
5 The boy is being told off by his teacher.
6 The house is being demolished.

Exercise 5

Read through the text with the students to make sure they understand the expressions: *reduce taxes*, *bring public spending under control*, *wide-ranging*, *inner city schools*, and *fulfilling our promises*.

KEY
Manifesto
- Taxes will be reduced
- Public spending will be brought under control.
- Wide-ranging educational reforms will be introduced.
- Teacher's salaries will be increased.
- The National Health Service will not/won't be destroyed.
- Our plans to improve our inner city schools will not be abandoned.
- Our promises will be fulfilled.

Exercise 6

Encourage students to talk around the subject and give additional information.

KEY TO QUESTIONS
Have you ever been:
1 stopped by the police?
2 interviewed on television?
3 given a surprise party?
4 fined for parking?
5 searched by customs?
6 asked to give a speech?
7 involved in a road accident?

 LISTENING

Discuss what usually happens at auditions and draw out any experiences the students have had. If necessary, provide the following background information. In the extract, an actor who is usually cast as upper class characters goes for an audition for a part in a musical called 'Streets of London'.

TAPESCRIPT
Listen to someone describing an audition. Look at your Students' Book and follow the instructions.

This was some time ago, and they were doing a musical, erm, called 'The Streets of London'. And, erm, at the time I was quite, erm, er, often cast as, as upper class characters, and, erm, my agent rang me up and asked me if I'd audition for this musical and there was only one part left to cast and it was a very good part but it was, er, a cockney barrow boy.

I decided that I would go into the interview and, and I'd be cockney. So, er, I'd also I'd, I'd, I'd, I w'd, I'd been told that I had to prepare a song. So I got a wonderful song which I knew nobody else would know about. I did the whole interview in a cockney accent and I made them believe that, er, I was born in Bethnal Green and my father worked at Spitalfields Market and, er, they, they, they believed my absolutely, and they believed I was a cockney and the audition went extremely well. I played the spoons and it was the best audition I've ever done in my life.

And at the end of the audition they all applauded, which is very very rare at an audition. At the end of it the producer ... one of the producers came up on the stage and put his arm round me and said that he thought I was marvellous and that I'd done a very very good audition, but unfortunately they couldn't give me the part because there was only one part left to cast and they were looking for someone to play an upper class English gentleman.

KEY
1 The audition was for the musical 'The Streets of London'.
2 He was usually cast as an 'upper class' character.
3 He thought the audition was for the part of a cockney barrow boy.
4 He was told to prepare a song.
5 The audition went very well, (He did the whole interview in a cockney accent and they thought he was cockney. After his song, everyone applauded and the producer thought he was marvellous.)
6 No, he wasn't. They were looking for someone to play the part of an upper class English gentleman.

WRITING

As an alternative, students may write a description of an audition or interview which they have had. Refer them to the informal letter-writing expressions in Unit 22 of the Students' Book.

UNITS 26/27

EXTRA ACTIVITIES

1 An observation game

Everyone is told to take a quick look at the classroom. Two people leave the room while personal possessions, objects and furniture, etc. are rearranged or hidden. Make a note of all the changes. Then ask the players to return and sport the differences in the room. They must use a present perfect passive, e.g. *The wastepaper basket has been moved. The chairs have been rearranged.* The winning pair are those who spotted the most changes.

2 Project

Using the passive, students write brief entries about certain topics for a reference book of general knowledge.

SOME POSSIBLE TOPICS
1 Christmas in Britain or their country
2 Schnapps
3 Tropical rain forests
4 Saffron
5 Petrol
6 The telephone
7 New Year in Scotland or their country
8 The early inhabitants of Australia
9 The Seventh Seal
10 Oklahoma! (The musical)
11 The first printed book
12 Silk

3 Discipline

Students discuss punishments that they were given as children. Use the questions below to open the discussion:

Were you ever:
– *kept in after school?*
– *given lines to write?*
– *punished unfairly?*
– *smacked, strapped, caned or beaten?*

 Workbook tapescript

Unit 26

Speechwork: Pronunciation
Past simple passive

Exercise 4

A
Listen to these sentences.
This car was made in Italy.
These chairs were made in England.

Now listen and repeat.
was [bleep]
This car was made in Italy. [bleep]
were [bleep]
These chairs were made in England. [bleep]

B
Now you make sentences using *was made* or *were made*.
Listen to the example.
This car / Canada
This car was made in Canada.

Now you do it.
This car / Canada [bleep]
This car was made in Canada.
These trousers / Spain [bleep]
These trousers were made in Spain.
This television / Japan [bleep]
This television was made in Japan.
This carpet / Turkey [bleep]
This carpet was made in Turkey.
These shoes / Greece [bleep]
These shoes were made in Greece.

UNIT 27 TOPIC
The USA

Before you read

With books closed, collect some of the students' ideas on the board.

Photograph and text

BACKGROUND NOTES
Midtown: (American English) a central section of a city.
downtown: (American English) the lower part or main business district of a town or city.
Fifth Avenue: Famous street in Manhattan, beginning at Washington Square and ending at the Harlem River. It is lined with fashionable shops, and landmarks such as the Empire State building, the Rockefeller Center and St Patrick's Cathedral.
The Statue of Liberty: A gift from the French people to the American people. Dedicated in 1886, the Statue is 151 feet high and stands on Liberty Island in New York Harbor. (British English *Harbour*).
Brooklyn Bridge: When completed in 1883 it was the largest suspension bridge in the world. It connects Manhattan to Brooklyn.
Art Deco: A decorative style of the 1920s and 1930s characterised by bold outlines, geometric shapes and the use of new materials.
World Trade Center: (British English: *Centre*) Completed in 1973 it has twin towers 1,350 feet high and stands on the southern tip of Manhattan.
Sears Tower: Completed in 1973, it is 1,559 feet high.

Discuss the photograph. Build on the board a group of adjectives like: *spectacular, exciting, breathtaking, amazing*. Students read the questions in Exercise 1 to focus their reading before tackling the text.

Exercise 1

KEY
1. Five boroughs.
2. It is situated on Fifth Avenue, between 33rd and 34th Street.
3. It was built in 1931.
4. It is floodlit with coloured lights.
5. It was first cleaned.
6. A giant gorilla in a film called 'King Kong'.

Exercise 2

KEY
1. No, New York State is situated at the mouth of the Hudson River.
2. No, in the downtown district of Manhattan the buildings scrape the sky/are very tall (and modern)/are skyscrapers.
3. No, the World Trade Center is the tallest building in New York.
4. No, the Empire State was built in 1931.
5. No, it was first cleaned in 1962.
6. No, the building is shaped like a pyramid.

Discuss why New York City is: 'one of the world's most loved and most hated cities.'

Exercise 3

For Question 2, illustrate the word *monument* by giving a local example.

VOCABULARY

Exercise 1

If possible, use pictures or sketches to explain and discuss these words and the categories, especially *privacy*. Find out if students have preferences for any type of dwelling, and if any buildings are characteristic of certain places.

KEY
Height: b), a), c), d)
Size: c), a), b), d)
Privacy: c), a), b), d)

Exercise 2

KEY
c)

 **LISTENING**

Preparation

Ask students who have not been to the USA what they imagine Americans and New York to be like. Collect some of their ideas on the board. Those who have been to the USA can add to or disagree with these ideas if they wish.

Write on the board and explain: *sensitive*, *rat-race*, *subway*, *trainers*, *anorak*, *scruffy*

If the points mentioned in the listening do not come up in the preliminary discussion, take the opportunity during or after the listening to discuss the students' reactions to these comments.

Listen

Play the tape, pausing at key intervals for students to make notes under the headings.

TAPESCRIPT
Listen to someone talking about how her original ideas about Americans and the USA – in particular New York – were altered by her visit. Note what she thought before her visit and what she thinks now.

INTERVIEWER: You went to the United States recently, didn't you?
WOMAN: Erm, well, it, it's not really recently. It was about three years ago, but yes, yes I did visit, for about six months.
INTERVIEWER: And how did you like it?
WOMAN: I loved it. I thought it was absolutely wonderful. I was very surprised that I did enjoy it as much as I did. I'd read a lot and I'd seen a lot of movies and people told me what to expect and I suppose I was under the impression that everybody would be loud and, erm, you know, wearing quite bright clothes and that, er, they would be interested in, talking about money only and making money.

And, I, I found none of that. I mean, I was only on, erm, on the coasts. I was in California and New York but all the people I met were, were quiet; they were intelligent; they were sensitive and they didn't seem the slightest bit interested in making money. Erm, in fact, they were more interested in getting out of the rat-race. So, it was completely different from what I'd expected. I did send most of my time, though, in New York, for about six weeks, and I rented an apartment there, and I did find that New York was completely different from what I expected.

I ... people said it would be noisy, dirty, dangerous, expensive, erm, people dressed terribly smartly and I'd feel a bit out of place but ... none of that ... I ... well, that's not true, erm, it was dirty and it was noisy. There's no doubt about it. Erm, but it wasn't dangerous. Erm, I travelled the subway all the time, erm, and at night, and did a lot of walking round the streets and I, I, I wasn't frightened at any stage – not at all.

Expensive ... yes. I mean, obviously parts of it were expensive. Going to the theatre was very expensive, eating in good restaurants was expensive and, and clothes, but you could live very cheaply if you wanted to.

And then I expected people to be very smart, erm, to be smartly dressed, but they weren't. I didn't find that very much. I, er, a lot of women used to wear trainers and, erm, anoraks and things like that, and, er, jeans and, and change when they got to the office because they used to like to walk to work. So they didn't dress up. And I found that if you looked along a street they looked pretty scruffy.

KEY

What she thought before	What she discovered
AMERICANS IN GENERAL	
Personality	
loud, wearing bright clothes	quiet, intelligent sensitive
Topic of conversation	
money	not interested in making money
NEW YORK	
The city	
1 noisy	noisy
2 dirty	dirty
3 dangerous	not dangerous
4 expensive	theatre, good restaurants and clothes were expensive but you could live cheaply
NEW YORKERS' CLOTHES	
smart	some looked pretty scruffy

TALKING POINT

> **BACKGROUND NOTES**
> **Walt Disney**: (1901-1966) A US film animator and producer who invented the cartoon character Mickey Mouse and created Disneyland, a large pleasure park which was opened in California in 1955.
> **Ronald Reagan**: A former Hollywood filmstar who became President of the USA 1980-88.
> **Marilyn Monroe**: An American filmstar who was born in 1926 and died of an overdose of sleeping tablets in 1962. She was beautiful and glamorous, and became a universal sex symbol.
> **Martin Luther King**: (1929-1968) A baptist minister and key figure in the US civil rights movement. He was assassinated by a sniper's bullet in 1968. His speech 'I had a dream' was a source of inspiration for those who were struggling to obtain political freedom for black people in the USA in the 1960s.
> **Henry Ford**: An American car manufacturer. He built the Model 'T' Ford car in 1908 and his company subsequently sold more than 15 million of them. The Model 'T' was the first 'everyman's' car, which brought motoring to the masses in the USA. His factories pioneered mass production and his company formed one of the bases for prosperity in the USA.

Students should support each opinion with an example.

WRITING

This writing activity can be conducted as a 'Writing Consequences' game (see Unit 6 'Extra Activities'). In this case, one building should be selected. It should be famous and relatively easy to describe. Write some facts about the building in note form on the board. Alternatively, set the exercise as a composition.

EXTRA ACTIVITIES

1 I went to the USA

Play a variation of the Shopping or Market game round the class or group. Start the sentence with: 'I went to the USA and I saw the Empire State building'. The list can include what the students saw, ate, did, who they met, etc., but each item must be related to the USA. Each student repeats the previous sentence and adds to the list each time. Failure to remember an item which has gone before means elimination.

2 Americanisms

Students collect 'Americanisms' in common use in their country, e.g. on signs and advertisements, in their own language, and any that they have picked up from TV and films. An on-going list can be kept in the classroom.

 Workbook tapescript

Unit 27

Exercise 1

Look at your book and listen to the guided tour of the River Thames. Write the correct number from the map next to each location.

And now on your left you can see the South Bank complex. The National Theatre is the first building you can see in the complex, just before we go under Waterloo Bridge. The theatre was opened in 1976 and thousands of people visit it every year.

Now we've gone under the bridge and on your right-hand side is the Victoria Embankment, one of the most interesting riverside walks in London. At the edge of the embankment you can see the tall, pointed statue of Cleopatra's Needle. This was brought from Egypt in 1878.

Now we're going under the Hungerford Railway Bridge. The ship you can see on your right is the Hispaniola, and coming up on your left is the enormous Shell Building. It has a tower which is 107 metres high and it is one of the largest office blocks in Europe. After the Shell Building, you can see County Hall. This housed the offices of London's local government, until the end of the Council in 1986.

This next bridge is Westminster Bridge, and, just past it, on your right, you can see one of the most famous buildings in London, the Houses of Parliament. If you want to check your watches now, have a look at Big Ben. On the other side of the river is St Thomas's Hospital. This is a teaching hospital and the centre of the Nightingale Scheme for Nurses...

UNIT 28 COMMUNICATION
Obligation and prohibition

Introduce the subject of 21st birthday parties and explain that in Britain this has always been considered to be the occasion for a large party or celebration to mark the 'coming of age'. However, more recently, the 18th birthday has become almost equally popular as an important milestone, as it coincides with a certain amount of 'legal' freedom.

Write the following two sentences on the board:

| What | are you
are the guests | expected to
supposed to | wear?
bring? |

Ask about the tradition in the students' own country or countries of dressing up and bringing presents on such occasions. Refer the students to the invitation in their books and explain *black tie* (in other words a dinner jacket and black bow tie). Then ask different students to read the sentences in the bubbles. Explain the difference between *to dress* and *to dress up* and revise the difference between *bring* and *take* if necessary.

FOCUS

Point out that, depending on the content, it is possible to use *not allowed to* instead of *not supposed to* or *shouldn't*. (See Unit 4). Explain that questions which require Yes/No answers normally have a rising intonation.

PRACTICE

Exercise 1

Make sure that students understand each context first. Check by asking random pairs to give their versions aloud. Suggest alternative sentences using other structures than *should*.

SUGGESTED CONVERSATIONS

1   A: What do you think we should do about Mrs Webster?
    B: I think we should collect some money for a present.

2   A: Jack's in hospital. Do you think we should go and visit him?
    B: Yes, and I think we should take him some magazines and fruit.

3   A: Do you think I should wear a hat?/Am I expected to wear a hat?
    B: Yes, I think you should./Yes, I think you are.

4   A: Do you think we should take something?
    B: Yes, I think maybe we should take some flowers or some chocolates.

5   A: Are we expected to go to the funeral?
    B: No, we don't have to if we don't want to. But I think we should send some flowers.

6   A: What should we give them to eat?
    B: I don't know. Maybe we should ask them what sort of things they eat and drink.

Exercise 2

Go through the example carefully and ask students to skim read the questionnaire to find out if there is anything they don't understand. If possible, pair students of different nationalities and cultures.

Exercise 3

Students join other pairs to discuss their answers and reactions to the questionnaire. End by asking students if they consider etiquette is important and, if so, which areas they consider most important.

ABOUT BRITAIN

Refer to the cartoon and ask what point it is making. Then ask if students know how to lay a table for a formal meal in England and what cutlery you use at what stage of the meal. Ask also if they know where to place the knife and fork after eating. Students read to check if they are right.

TALKING POINT

Make sure you do not offend any students by suggesting that some customs are rude. There may be quite normal and acceptable in some cultures. Let the students make the judgements.

UNIT 28

ACT IT OUT

Students form pairs or groups of three and elect a 'teacher'. The teacher must try to answer the questions as well as she/he can. As a follow-up, photocopy the following information for everyone to read, or, alternatively, gloss the main points orally. The 'guests' can decide if the advice which they were given was good or not.

BACKGROUND NOTES

Clothes: A man doesn't have to wear a suit but it's polite to wear a jacket and tie. Women are expected to dress up a bit, but should be careful not to over-dress. If you are at all worried about what to wear, phone your hosts and ask what other people will be wearing.

Forms of address: You should call your host 'Mr and Mrs' if they are married partners. Most people will ask you to call them by their first names.

Time to arrive and leave: It can be considered a little rude to arrive exactly on time. The best time to arrive is about ten minutes after the time you have been invited. The best time to leave is about half an hour after after-dinner coffee has been served. It is not polite to stay after midnight, especially midweek, unless it is made very clear by your hosts that they would like you to stay.

Gifts: It is not necessary to take a gift but flowers and chocolates are always welcome. Many people bring a bottle of wine for an informal gathering of friends.

Thanking the hosts: You are expected either to send a note or to telephone and thank your hosts. This should be done with in a week. It is not necessary to send a gift.

LISTENING

Before listening, students discuss how and when to hold a knife and fork according to polite behaviour in their own country.

KEY
1 A man is supposed to pull back the chair for the lady who is sitting on his right.
2 They hold it in their left hand to cut the food and in their right hand to eat it.
3 When they want to cut up meat (or other food).
4 They place it on the side of their plate.

TAPESCRIPT
Listen to an American explaining American etiquette on table matters. Answer the questions in your Students' Book.

Well, first of all, when you go to sit down at a table, a gentleman is supposed to pull back the chair for the lady who is sitting at his right.

Then, to eat in the proper American way, you have to cut a small bite-size piece or meat and place your knife on the side of your plate with the blade and handle across the rim. You're not supposed to rest the handle of the knife on the table, as this looks really messy. Then you have to switch your fork to your right hand and bring the food to your mouth.

WRITING

The final versions of these can be used for Extra Activity 2.

EXTRA ACTIVITIES

1 Good behaviour

In groups, students discuss and prepare a list of things a girl/woman/boy/man is expected/supposed to do either on a first date or when meeting the parents of the girl/boyfriend.

2 Useful advice for tourists

Students prepare a booklet of useful tips on behaviour, etc. for English-speaking people visiting their country for the first time. Students can produce work on separate topics.

3 The Marriage Ceremony: a cross-cultural project

Students research the marriage ceremony in different cultures. Their work can be accompanied by a visual display. This would be particularly relevant to multi-lingual classes in British-speaking countries.

Workbook tapescript

Unit 28

Speechwork: Stress and intonation
Obligation and prohibition

Exercise 3

A
Listen to this question.
Do we HAVE to stay to the end?

Now listen and repeat.
Do we HAVE to stay to the end? [bleep]

B
Now you make questions. Listen to the example.
stay to the end
Do we have to stay to the end?

Now you do it.
stay to the end [bleep]
Do we have to stay to the end?
arrive on time [bleep]
Do we have to arrive on time?
reply in writing [bleep]
Do we have to reply in writing?
shake hands [bleep]
Do we have to shake hands?

C
Listen to these sentences.
You're exPECted to make a SPEECH.
You're NOT supposed to SMOKE on the UNderground.

Now listen and repeat.
make a SPEECH [bleep]
You're exPECted to make a SPEECH. [bleep]
SMOKE on the UNderground [bleep]
You're NOT supposed to SMOKE on the UNderground. [bleep]

D
Now you make sentences. Listen to the examples.
wear a tie
You're expected to wear a tie.
not take photographs in here
You're not supposed to take photographs in here.

Now you do it.
wear a tie [bleep]
You're expected to wear a tie.
not take photographs in here [bleep]
You're not supposed to take photographs in here.
say thank you [bleep]
You're expected to say thank you.
not talk during the speeches [bleep]
You're not supposed to talk during the speeches.

UNIT 29 GRAMMAR
Defining relative pronouns

Photographs

> **BACKGROUND NOTES**
> ***The Lake District***: An area in the north west of England famous for its lakes and mountains. It is very popular for walking and climbing holidays. The poet William Wordsworth lived in the Lake District and his famous poem 'The Daffodils' was written there.
> ***South Shields***: A fishing port on the north west coast of England in the county of Northumberland.
> ***Clovelly***: A picturesque small port in the county of Devon in the south-west of England. The village is set on an extremely steep hill and no cars are allowed in the village. Consequently, everything has to be pulled up the streets on sledges (like the milk in the photograph) or alternatively on donkeys.
> ***Flower Show***: Flower shows are quite common in Britain, especially in agricultural areas. Vegetables are often included in flower shows, as here. Local people display their flowers, fruit and vegetables and compete for prizes.

Ask students to describe each photograph and to suggest what time of day some of them were taken. Ask which photo they like best.

Introduce each photograph and read the caption as if it has been taken by you.

Hold the book up and point to the photographs in a random order. Students have to identify each one by saying: *That's a photograph of some fishermen you met ….*

FOCUS
Explain that *that* can be used instead of *who* or *which* either as a subject or as an object pronoun. However, *who* is more common than *that* when defining people.

Explain also that commas are not put round the clauses, because they are *defining* relative clauses. It is only necessary to put a comma around a relative clause if it is a *non-defining* clause, e.g. *Mike, who is captain of the team, is unable to be here.* Non-defining relative clauses are not practised in this unit.

PRACTICE

Exercise 1

KEY
1 The man who lives next door lent me his hammer. *or* The man who lent me his hammer lives next door.
2 The girl who was standing behind me in the queue fainted. *or* The girl who fainted was standing behind me in the queue.
3 Have you met the family who have just moved in to the house next door?
4 A man whose company sells computers telephoned me this morning.
5 What was the name of the car which/that won the Car of the Year award?

Exercise 2

KEY
1 That's the man I was talking about last night.
2 Did you like the photo I took of you and your husband?
3 What did you do with the eggs I bought this morning?
4 The man you spoke to on the phone was my father.
5 The house they bought was very expensive.

Exercise 3

Divide the class into two groups. A person from Group 1 reads out one of the sentence openers and a person from Group 2 chooses the appropriate second half and converts it into a relative clause beginning with *where*. Work S–T first to give an example.

UNITS 29/30

KEY
1. That's the hotel where my sister spent her honeymoon.
2. Last night I went to a restaurant where you can eat as much as you like for ten pounds.
3. Over the road is the hairdresser's where I usually have my hair cut.
4. Why don't you go to the garage where I take my car to be serviced?
5. I went back to the part of the beach where I lost my watch but I couldn't find it.
6. That's the library where they usually have interesting art exhibitions.

Exercise 4

Ask students to look at the pictures and to pick out one or more identifying feature of each person. Practise phrases like: *the woman with the red hair/glasses*, *the woman in the red dress*, *the man in the hat*. Before starting the exercise, students should match each person in the picture with a suitable name and person, e.g. which of the women do they think looks as if she might have gone out with one of the waiters? Which of the men looks likely to have got badly sunburnt? etc.

Refer to the example and explain that it is not necessary to repeat *I told you about* each time, but it does give extra practice in this type of clause.

KEY
1. A: Who's the woman in the red dress?
   B: That's Ann. She's the one I told you about who overslept and missed the plane home.
2. A: Who's the woman with grey hair/with glasses?
   B: That's Sally. She's the one I told you about whose bed broke in the middle of the night.
3. A: Who's the man in the hat?
   B: That's Mark. He's the one I told you about who stayed in his hotel room most of the day.
4. A: Who's the woman with the headband?
   B: That's Lucy. She's the one I told you about who went out with one of the hotel waiters.
5. A: Who's the boy in/with the striped top?
   B: That's Robert. He's the one I told you about whose wallet was stolen on the beach.
6. A: Who's the woman with the red hair/glasses on her head/hooped earrings?
   B: That's Jan. She's the one I told you about whose hotel room caught fire.
7. A: Who's the man with the beard and glasses?
   B: That's Gordon. He's the one I told you about whose back got badly sunburnt.

WRITING

Ask questions about each of the subjects, e.g.

T: What was the last book you read?
S: The last book I read was a thriller called 'Eyewitness'.
T: What was it about?
S: It was about a woman who witnessed a murder while she was working late in her office.

EXTRA ACTIVITIES

1 Holiday photographs

Students bring interesting holiday photographs to describe for the class.

2 Biographies

Students find out biographical details of a famous person so that they can write a short biography, similar to the one about Billie Holiday in the linked Workbook exercise. They say who the person is, where he/she lived/lives and why he/she was/is famous and give brief details of the person's life. They should use relative clauses where suitable.

UNIT 30 READING
How to be an alien

PRESENTATION

Ask students if they know what *alien* means. Then ask them to look at the headings in the text and to say if they think the text is going to be serious or funny. Alternatively, start the lesson with the 'Talking point' and lead on to the text afterwards.

Cartoons

Discuss the cartoons and ask what aspect of the English character they are trying to portray. Explain that *Cruft's* is the name of the famous dog show held annually in Britain.

Introductory text and
COMPREHENSION 1–3

Read the introductory text aloud and check comprehension by asking Questions 1, 2, and 3. Ask if anyone has read the book in translation.

KEY
1. He came from Hungary.
2. *How to be an alien* was first published in 1946.
3. It is a funny/humorous book./It is a book about the English/about foreigners living in Britain.

 Text: How to be an alien and
COMPREHENSION 4

Play the tape of the main text, stopping after each section to check comprehension.

Many students will want to contribute their own opinions and experiences on each topic, so allow time for discussion after each section.

Play the whole tape again without stopping, while students follow the text. Encourage them to 'shadow' the voice on the tape by mumbling the words quietly to themselves.

KEY

The English language
It is difficult for foreigners to understand English as it is spoken in England. Possibly he means that it is spoken very fast and with many different accents, and that it is not like the English you hear from your teacher or on the radio.

The attitude to weather
The weather is not something you argue about or discuss seriously. The most common greeting is *Nice day, isn't it?*, even if the weather is awful. Maybe Mikes is also suggesting that as the weather is never very good in England, the English don't expect very much.

The habit of queuing
The English are very orderly.

Attitude to pets
They seem to prefer the company of their pets to fellow human beings.

Towns
It is impossible to find you way round English towns. They are not designed on a grid system (along straight lines) and streets are not just called streets but also lanes, avenues, etc. (c.f. Unit 13 Listening).

Ways of serving tea
The English spoil tea by adding milk, not lemon.

Tea drinking habits
The English like to drink tea at any time of the day or night.

VOCABULARY

Exercise 1
Those who finish the exercise quickly can try to think of more adjectives which are formed in the same way with *-less* and *-ful*.

KEY
1 homeless 2 heartless 3 careless 4 thoughtless
5 painless 6 shapeless 7 useless 8 jobless

the homeless the jobless

Exercise 2

KEY
careful painful useful thoughtful

Exercise 3
Ask students to look up any unknown words in a dictionary and to note where the stress falls.

KEY
Positive: true, funny, perceptive, affectionate, witty

Negative: stereotypical, cruel, silly, rude, superficial, xenophobic, old-fashioned

 LISTENING

Before you listen
To show that they have understood the dictionary definition, ask students to give an example of their own national stereotype. Ask if they can describe other stereotypes, e.g., the stereotype of a hen-pecked husband, the nagging wife, the sexy blonde secretary, the romantic hero.

Listen
Ask students how they see a typical Scotsman/Irishman/Englishman. Try to elicit the features which will be mentioned in the joke. Write on the board and explain: *Sahara Desert*, *precaution*, *bowler hat*, *car door*, *to wind down*, *offensive*, *over the top* (coll.).

KEY
National characteristics:
The Englishman: straight, formal, wearing a bowler hat at all times
the Scotsman: always drinking whisky
The Irishman: stupid
– It doesn't upset him in the slightest to hear jokes against the Irish.
– Racist and sexist jokes were thought to be more offensive.

TAPESCRIPT
Listen to some people discussing a joke based on national stereotypes of the Scots, the Irish and the English. Look at your Students' Book and follow the instructions.

MAN 1: (It's) quite good actually.
MAN 2: It's not bad.
MAN 1: Well, I've got one but you'll have to excuse my bad Irish accent. Er ... There's an Englishman, Irishman and a Scotsman and they're all going on this expedition to the Sahara Desert, right? Now ... Now ...
MAN 2: Mm.
MAN 1: ... there's a discussion before they leave the country, and during the discussion they discuss what precautions they're going to take for the sun and the heat and the weather, you know, er, and the Englishman's asked what precautions he's going to take and he says, erm: 'I'm going to take a bowler hat, to protect my head from the sun.'
MAN 2: Mmm.
MAN 1: And so the others say: 'Ah, right, yes.' Then the Scotsman's asked what he would take and he says: 'Ah, I'd take a bottle o' whisky.' Right?
MAN 2: Mmm.
MAN 1: And then the, er, Irishman was asked what

he would take and he says: 'Ah, I'd take a car door.' So the other two say: 'A car door?' …
MAN 2: Mm., uh huh.
MAN 1: … 'What's all that about?' And he says: 'Well, when it gets hot I can wind down the window.'
ALL: Mmm. Ah yes, yes … yes. Yes, mm.
MAN 3: Tell me, do you get upset about jokes in which Irishmen appear in a foolish light?
MAN 2: No, absolutely not. No, not at all.
WOMAN: Well, it's just the old story of the stereotyping, you know, like the mother-in-law jokes and all the rest. Everything is stereotyped so it just depends where you live.
MAN 1: Generalisation, isn't it?
WOMAN: I don't agree with people getting upset about it, though, because it happens, everybody's doing it. To start saying …
MAN 3: Sure, sure.
WOMAN: You know.
MAN 3: It can be offensive though, can't it?
MAN 2: Can be.
MAN 3: I mean, some of the things in the stories that are told about black people …
MAN 2: Yes …
MAN 3: … or Pakistanis can sometimes be really hurtful. Well, racist and, er, sexist jokes are particularly … offensive because it's such a big group you're …
MAN 2: Yes, national jokes in other words might be quite acceptable but racists jokes go over the top.

Ask the students if they have similar 'nationality' jokes directed against certain regions or nationalities in their own countries and what they think of them. Ask what sort of jokes make them laugh. If there is time, students can discuss types of humour and the sort of films, comedians and TV shows which amuse them.

TALKING POINT

Students work individually first, noting their opinions under the separate headings. After each opinion they should write *P* for positive or *N* for *negative*. Allow a time limit of three minutes. Students now form groups and compare their opinions according to the instructions in the Students' Book.

WRITING

Ask students to make a list of some popular stereotypes of their own nationality and to write about their reaction to them. They should try to write at least four separate paragraphs using the linking words suggested in the guide. If they like, they can write about a different nationality in each paragraph.

EXTRA ACTIVITIES

1 Is your pronunciation O.K.?

This short extract illustrates some of the difficulties of pronouncing English. It can be photocopied and distributed to the students. Write the following vowel sounds on the board and ask students to find different ways of spelling these sounds in the poem.

/iː/ /eɪ/ /ɪ/ /eə/ /ʌ/

Dearest creature in creation,
Studying English pronunciation,
I will teach you in my verse
Sounds like corpse, corps, horse and worse;
I will keep you, Suzy, busy.
Make your head with heat grow dizzy,
Tear in eye, your dress you'll tear;
So shall I. Oh, hear my prayer …
Finally: which rhymes with enough?
Though, through, plough, cough, dough or tough?
Hiccough has the sound of cup.
My advice is – give it up!

2 Joke corner

Each students must find a joke and tell it in English at the next lesson. It can be a joke translated from their own language if they like. Alternatively, they can bring to class a cartoon which they find funny and pin it up for display.

CHECK Units 21–30

(See notes for Check Units 1–10.)

KEY

Exercise 1

1 break/broke/broken
2 fall/fell/fallen
3 spend/spent/spent
4 steal/stole/stolen
5 bring/brought/brought
6 speak/spoke/spoken
7 spill/spilt/spilt
8 take/took/taken
9 drive/drove/driven
10 see/saw/seen
11 give/gave/given
12 write/wrote/written

Exercise 2

1 When did you buy/I bought
2 What have you done/I've just had
3 Have you ever been/I went
4 Have you seen/When did you have
5 I've already written
6 I've spilt

7 Have you seen/I saw
8 did you say/you spoke/I haven't spoken

Exercise 3

1 have you been cooking
2 She's already smoked
3 Have you seen
4 I've been crying/I've been peeling
6 have you put
6 I still haven't finished/I've been reading
7 I've been knocking
8 She's hurt

Exercise 4

1C 2G 3A 4D 5H 6E 7F 8B

Exercise 5

1 make 2 done 3 doing 4 make/do 5 made
6 make 7 make 8 do

Exercise 6

1 are grown 2 is exported 3 are being destroyed
4 was written 5 was assassinated
6 has not been corrected 7 I've been invited

Exercise 7

1 It's being cooked
2 it's made of
3 It's being repaired
4 Why are the children being sent
5 We're being met

Exercise 8

who which/that which/that who/which/that which/that

Exercise 9

1 dear 2 where 3 mean 4 ear 5 break

Exercise 10

1e 2i 3h 4g 5j 6l 7a 8k 9c 10b 11f 12d

Exercise 11

1b 2a 3b 4c

Exercise 12

2 5 4 6 1 3

USE YOUR ENGLISH
Units 21–30

Exercise 1

Before the students start the exercise, go through the list of time expressions and ask the students to call out if they are used with *for* or *since*. Work the first example T–S with one or two different students to show that several different answers are possible.

SUGGESTED ANSWERS

1 A: How long have you lived there?
  B: I've lived there since I was nineteen/1985/ since my eighteenth birthday.
2 A: How long have you had it?
  B: I've had it for three weeks/for a couple of months.
3 A: How long have you been driving/had your driver's licence?
  B: I've been driving/had it since last August/January of last year.
4 A: How long have you been learning/studying it/taking English lessons?
  B: I've been learning it/studying it/taking English lesson for quite a while/about eight years.

Exercise 2

Divide the class into As and Bs and direct the B students to the relevant page at the end of the book. Remind the students of a similar task in Exercise 1 of the previous Use your English (Units 11–20). Tell the students to read through the text as far as they can and to prepare their questions in advance.

KEY TO QUESTIONS
1 What was the man called?
2 Who did he plot to blow up?
3 What was the plot called?
4 When was it discovered?
5 When were Guy Fawkes and his friends executed?
6 What do people let off every 5th November?
7 What do they light?
8 What do they burn?
9 Where do some people have bonfire parties?
10 What is organised in most towns and villages?

Exercise 3

Ask students to keep to their A and B roles but ask all the A students and the B students to group together so that they can go through the pictures and work out how to say what is wrong, using the key word each time. When they are sure they know what to say, they can pair up as As and Bs and start the conversations.

KEY

1 A: Is there anything wrong with your trousers?
  B: Yes, I'm afraid the pocket is torn.
  A: Oh, I'm sorry. I'll change them for another pair.

2 A: Is there anything wrong with your jacket?
  B: Yes, I'm afraid there's a mark on it.
  A: Oh, I'm sorry. I'll change it for another one.

3   A: Is there anything wrong with your shoes?
    B: Yes, I'm afraid the heel is broken.
    A: Oh, I'm sorry. I'll change them for another pair.

4   B: Is there anything wrong with your salad?
    A: Yes, I'm afraid there's a caterpillar in it.
    B: Oh, I'm sorry. I'll remove the salad immediately.

5   B: Is there anything wrong with your soup?
    A: Yes, I'm afraid there's a fly in it.
    B: Oh, I'm sorry. I'll remove the soup immediately.

6   B: Is there anything wrong with your fish?
    A: Yes, I'm afraid it's not cooked.
    B: Oh, I'm sorry. I'll remove the fish immediately.

Exercise 4

KEY
d, k, b, g, a, e, i f, h, j, c

When they have finished the exercise, ask the students to compare the situation in Britain with that in their own country.

PROGRESS TEST Units 21–30

(See notes for Progress test Units 1–10.)

KEY

Exercise 1

1c 2a 3b 4a 5b 6c 7a 8c 9c 10c

Exercise 2

1 Have you found 2 for three years.
3 haven't written before 4 I'd better
5 this hamburger is overdone.
6 I would be grateful if 7 I made
8 who lives next door

Exercise 3

1 fired 2 temporary 3 valuable 4 shrunk 5 tear
6 broken down 7 favour 8 finally 9 cottage 10 tip
11 side by side 12 accompany 13 queue
14 careless 15 remarked

Exercise 4

1 who 2 good 3 in 4 shake 5 about 6 dealing
7 is 8 cause 9 thing 10 made 11 interviews
12 which

Eve

UNIT 31
Eve, a jewellery maker

Glossary
Refer to a map of Britain to show the county of Wiltshire, Bath and Avebury, and ask if any students have been to the antique market in Portobello Road in London.

> BACKGROUND NOTE
> *Avebury*: a village in Wiltshire which is surrounded by a stone circle called the 'Avebury Ring', one of Britain's most important prehistoric monuments.

Article about Eve
Students read the text silently first, looking at the questions in Exercise 1 as they do so.

Exercise 1

KEY
1 She first met Eve in a covered market in Bath.
2 She sells silver jewellery: necklaces, bracelets and earrings
3 She lives in Avebury, a village in Wiltshire.
4 She first visited Avebury as a student at art school. She had to some sketches of the prehistoric stones there.
5 She loves Avebury. It's peaceful and it's cheaper than living and working in London.
6 She takes commissions from people who want something special designed and made.
7 Because she enjoys being her own boss, she can choose the hours she works and she loves the creative part of her work.

Read the text again, working through it paragraph by paragraph. Ask for explanations, alternatives, paraphrases or translations of the following words, phrases and expressions: *a covered market, a stall, fingering the silver necklaces, on display, had her eye on the stall, I like the feel and look of it, go mad, an enormous rent, it would cut my profits considerable, to set up your own business, the antique side of the business, price tags, I do well enough, take commissions, lose my independence, being my own boss, make a fortune.*

Words to learn
Take care with the stress on the polysyllabic words: CONstantly, FASCinate, fiNANcial, unSCRUpulous, agGREssive and indePENdence. Students make sentences with these words.

Exercise 2

SUGGESTED RESPONSES
1 Because she thinks someone might steal her jewellery.
2 Because it is very hard work; there isn't any job security; you have to be strong-willed and disciplined about work; if your business fails, you can lose all your money.
3 Because the price can always be changed without the customer knowing.
4 Possible adjectives: *quite tough and business-like, honest, romantic, independent, creative, not very aggressive.*

Exercise 3
For Question 2, ask what sort of businesses people might like to go into.

Exercise 4 ABOUT BRITAIN
Refer to a map of Britain and point out the location of Bath. Ask students to read the short text about Bath and find at least two reasons why it is famous. Ask in what century the city first became famous. Explain that Georgian refers to an architectural period which was popular during the reigns of George I – IV (1714 – 1830). Ask if the students can name any spa towns in their country and whether they have ever swum in hot springs.

VOCABULARY

Exercise 1

KEY
1 talk informally = chat
  all the time = constantly
  drawings = sketches
  related to money = financial
  hard (of people) = tough
  dishonest = unscrupulous

Exercise 2

KEY
You wear:
1 earrings on/in your ears.
2 cuff-links on your shirt cuffs.
3 a necklace round your neck.
4 a brooch on the front of your sweater/dress/clothes.
5 a bracelet on your wrist.
6 a pendant round your neck.

UNIT 31

7 a ring on your finger.
8 a gold chain round your neck/waist/ankle.
9 a watch on your wrist.

Exercise 3
Provide the vocabulary needed for precious and semi-precious stones and metals: *gold, silver, platinum, bronze, copper, diamond, sapphire, emerald, ruby, jade, opal, amber, jet, amethyst, mother of pearl*

Exercises 4 and 5
Refer to the text and the sentence: *You have to be tough to set up in business.* Ask students how to pronounce *tough*. Then ask if they know any other words ending in *-ough* and how they are pronounced.

TAPESCRIPT
Listen to the pronunciation of the following words and check if you have put them in the correct sound groups.

though, bought, nought, rough, brought, cough, enough, fought, thought, although, ought, through

KEY
Group 1 /əʊ/ though ´although
Group 2 /ɔːt/ bought nought brought fought thought ought
Group 3 /ʌf/ rough enough
Group 4 /ɒf/ cough
Group 5 /uː/ through

Two other sound groups with this spelling not included here are:

Group 6 /aʊ/ plough bough drought
Group 7 /ʌ/ thorough borough

 LISTENING

Before you listen
Ask what the tools are normally used for and what they think Eve does with these tools in her work.

Listen
On the first listening, students note down the subjects Phil talks about, e.g. the sort of jewellery he makes and what materials he uses, etc.

After the second listening, when students have noted the questions, they can use them to reconstruct the interview. (Students may need to listen to the tape more than twice in order to complete the listening task in the Students' Book.)

TAPESCRIPT
Listen to Phil, a jewellery maker, talking about his job. Then listen again and each time you hear the bleep, note down the question which you think the interviewer asked.

Everything that could be classed as jewellery, from rings to pendants, earrings, cuff-links, brooches, neckpieces, anything really.
[bleep]

I only work in pure metals, that is silver, gold and platinum.
[bleep]

I've been doing this now for about fourteen years.
[bleep]

We used a whole range of tools. I have my files on one side and a, a set of pliers and pincers and tweezers on the other side, and they come in all different shapes and sizes as well.
[bleep]

Right, well, first of all, you have to select a piece of metal that is obviously big enough, and then you would cut out the design and then you would file it. If there's going to be anything that you would attach to it you would attach that by a soldering technique which is done with a gas torch.
[bleep]

Well, I sell to the whole range of public. I mean, I like to think that I make one-off individually designed pieces for the ordinary man in the street. I have made quite a lot of very exquisite pieces for celebrities – for very famous people.
[bleep]

I don't make a very good living. I don't think you'd ever get rich making, er, any hand-made objects but, erm, I get by.
[bleep]

KEY
What sort of jewellery/things do you make?
What materials/metals do you use?
How long have you been doing this?
What tools do you use?
What do you do when you make a piece of jewellery?/How exactly do you make a piece of jewellery?
Who do you make the jewellery for?/Who do you sell the jewellery to?/Who buys your jewellery?
Do you make a good living out of it?/Is it a good job?/Do you make a lot of money?

TALKING POINT

Exercise 1
With books closed, write students' suggestions on the board. With books open, students compare the list on the board with the one in their books and add any which they think are missing. They then rank-order the list.

Exercise 2
Explain that groups should try to agree on the top five most important things.

WRITING

Students choose a job and three reasons why they would like to do it. Ask one student to give you this information so that you can demonstrate how to link the ideas. Students write their sentences in class while you go round and check. Students with jobs can write about why they like or dislike them.

EXTRA ACTIVITIES

1 Who wrote it? (Follow-up to Writing)

Correct the students' paragraphs and select ten at random. Put each into a plain sealed envelope. When the class meets again, in turn, students choose an envelope and read the paragraph inside. The others students guess who wrote it.

2 Finish the sentences

Write the following sentences on the board and get the students to complete them.

1 When I go shopping for … I always go to … because …
2 The thing I really like about markets is …
3 My idea of a dream job is …
4 My perfect village is somewhere in … It is …
5 If I could live anywhere in the world I… because …

3 Portrait of a city

Students studying in Britain might like to make a field trip to Bath or another historic English city and do a project on it.

Workbook tapescript

Unit 31

Exercise 4

Look at your book, listen to the women talking and choose which jobs they do.

1
There are interesting parts of the job. I like organising everything and I think I'm quite an efficient person. You have to be really, if you want to be good at the job. And my boss tries to involve me in her work. She often discusses important decisions with me. But I must admit it can be boring at times. I have to do a lot of typing, which I don't really enjoy.

2
I love the job, but the hours are very antisocial and it's not very well paid. I enjoy looking after people, though it can be depressing when they're very ill. You have to have lots of energy in this job. It's hard just keeping up with the hospital routine.

3
Well, it's nice to be able to work at home and not have to go out to an office, but you do have to be very disciplined when there's no one telling you what to do. I enjoy being creative but there are some days when I just can't think of anything to write.

4
It's very hard work but I enjoy the challenge. I like to think that I am in a position to change things for the better in this world, but I do think a lot of very valuable time is wasted in Parliament. There are too many people who just like the sound of their own voices. I hope that my party will win the next election, and of course I would love to have post in the government. I'm quite ambitious – you have to be to get anywhere in this field.

UNIT 32 GRAMMAR
Second conditional *if* clauses

What's the difference in meaning?

In the first sentence it is quite possible the person will get a full-time job, whereas in the second sentence, it is unlikely.

Sentence 1 is a 'first conditional'. The main clause contains *will* + verb; the *if* clause contains the present simple tense.

Sentence 2 is a 'second conditional'. Here, the main clause contains *would* + verb; the *if* clause contains the past simple tense.

KEY
Second conditional sentences in the text about Eve:

I'd go mad if I have to live in London.
If I had a market stall in London, I'd have to pay an enormous rent.
If I were a man, I'd probably be more aggressive about selling.
My parents would prefer me to get a full-time job. (*If they had a choice in the matter* is understood.)
I'd lose my independence if I did that.

The sentences are a mixture of hypothetical or imaginary situations, and totally impossible situations.

FOCUS

Work through the Focus section, paying particular attention to the 'Points to note'.

PRACTICE

Exercise 1

Students discuss the first situation and report back their answers. Make sure that they are producing

UNIT 32

accurate sentences. If necessary, do choral practice of the verb phrases. Students now read the other three situations and choose one of them to think about and answer. When they have done this, ask them to stand up and walk round the class asking the other students which situation they have chosen and what they would do in it. They report back about the people they asked.

Exercise 2

Students first make a list of the questions they want to ask. Check these before students start pair work. Students who are asking the questions should note the information they get. Collect all the information and choose the two best suggestions for each situation.

SUGGESTED QUESTIONS
1 Where can I buy a good map of the town?
2 What do you think I should see?
3 How do you think I should get to … ? or What is the best way of getting to …?
4 What local food dishes do you think I should try?
5 Where is the best place to change money?

Exercise 3

As preparation, ask the students: *What are magazine questionnaires often about? Do they reveal anything useful about you? Do you take them seriously? Do you like doing them?*

Explain *assertive* (not afraid of saying what you want or think). When they have finished, students interpret each other's scores. Explain: *insist on*, *respect* (v) and (n), *pushy* and *submissive*.

ACT IT OUT

Students act out a confrontation in which one of the people is being assertive. Before they begin, revise complaints (Unit 23) and requests (Unit 13).

EXAMPLE CONVERSATIONS
1 The smoker and the non-smoker

A: Excuse me but this is a non-smoking area.
B: What do you mean? I can't see any notice.
A: It's there on the wall. That sign means No smoking. I'd be grateful if you could/would go outside and smoke.
B: I'll smoke where I want. This is a free country. Don't you tell me what to do.
A: In that case, I'll go and speak to the manager.

2 The two car drivers

A: Excuse me, but would you mind moving your car?
B: Why? What's the matter?
A: You're in my parking space. These are reserved for residents of this block of flats.
B: Oh, I'm sorry. I didn't realise it was private. I'll move it.

3 The manager of the shoe shop and the customer

A: Can I help you?
B: I bought these shoes from you last week. I only wore them once and the heels came off. Do you think you could change them for another pair, please?
A: I see. Have you got the receipt?
B: Yes, it's here.
A: Fine. I'll see if we've got another pair in stock.

4 The good friends

A: Oh, Sally. Have you got a moment to spare? I wanted to ask you something.
B: Yes, sure. What's up?
A: Well, I wondered if you could lend me some money.
B: Yes, sure. I'll just go and get my purse.
A: I'm afraid I need a bit more than that.
B: Oh, how much?
A: A hundred pounds.
B: A hundred!
A: Yes, it's the deposit on a car and I'm a hundred pounds short. I promise I'll pay it back.
B: Well … it's a lot of money …

TALKING POINT

As a warm-up, suggest some famous people from each of the progressional categories and ask what contribution these people make/have made to the world. To follow up the discussion, students can write a short essay: *The profession of my choice*.

LISTENING

Students should try and listen for gist. Do not pre-teach any vocabulary. Ask them later what clues the woman gave to indicate what she wanted to be.

KEY
Speaker 1: a composer; Speaker 2: a (creative) writer; Speaker 3: a doctor.

TAPESCRIPT
Listen to some people discussing a question about occupations. Note which occupations they choose and whether they give the same answers as you. The question which they're discussing is as follows:

'If you knew you could devote your life to any single occupation in music, writing, acting, business, politics, medicine, etc. and be among the best and most successful in the world at it, what would you choose and why?

S1: Well, what an intriguing question this is.
S2: Mmm.
S4: Do you, do you, um, actually compose, or, or, or is it to play a particular instrument?
S1: No, no. What I'd, what I'd like t… I do play, I play the piano, but I, what I would like to be I think , to answer this question, is, …erm, a, a, a composer …
S2: Mmm.

S1: ... I think, or perhaps, er, a player of a stringed, an expert player of a stringed instrument – the violin or cello.
S2: Mm mm.
S4: Mm mm.
S1: ... Er ... because I think, er, well, I know that music is, er, a language. Music is a, a, a wonderful way of communicating with everyone.
S4: Mm. What about you, Carol?
S2: Well, writing, er, you know, er, er, when I was at school I, I, guess like everyone, we all have to write school essays, and so on, but I wrote really very good ones.
S4: Mmm.
S2: Erm, but I think, because I was in the exam situation all the time, that it's kind of warped my, sort of, adult attitude to creative writing and it's something I've regretted and I'd really like to sort of sit down and do something re..., somehow recapture the talent that I had then.
S3: Er, have you, have you had any attempts to sit down and ...
S2: One or two, usually late at night, after, after too much wine, and then you look at it the next morning and you think 'Oh God, that was terrible'.
S3: Mm mm.
S4: Mm mm. There was something about you and medicine that I seem to remember.
S3: Oh well, it's just, er, I would, I would like to be a doctor and I, I would, I would like to be able to devote my life to making other people well. I mean, I can ..., it seems to me that there can be no greater satisfaction than, than, giving somebody back life, as it were, you know. Somebody who's, er, you can watch them through a process gradually getting better and I just feel there must be enormous satisfaction.
S2: Mmm satisfaction.

EXTRA ACTIVITIES

1 Who am I?

One player leaves the room while the rest of the group think of a famous person, living or dead, fact or fiction. The first player returns and asks other players questions using the second conditional, e.g. *If you were animal, what would you be?*

The answer must give a clue to the personality and identity of the mystery character. After a few questions, a personality pattern begins to emerge. The questions should concern things like choice of holiday, cars, shoes, clothes, music etc, e.g. *If you went on holiday, where would you go? If you wanted a new car, what make would you buy? If you were going out for the evening, what would you wear?* etc.

2 What would *you* do?

Students say what they would do if they knew or suspected their colleague or neighbour of:
– stealing stationery from the office.
– battering a wife.
– mistreating a child.
– being unfaithful to a partner.

Workbook tapescript

Unit 32

Speechwork: Pronunciation
Would and *will* contractions

Exercise 5

A
Listen to these sentences.
If she loses her job, she'll move out of London.
If she lost her job, she'd move out of London.

Now listen and repeat.
She'll [bleep]
She'll move out of London. [bleep]
She'd [bleep]
She'd move out of London. [bleep]

B
Now you say sentences with contractions.
Listen to the examples.

He will be here tomorrow.
He'll be here tomorrow.
They would help you.
They'd help you.

Now you do it.
He will be here tomorrow. [bleep]
He'll be here tomorrow.
They would help you. [bleep]
They'd help you.
I would like it [bleep]
I'd like it.
We will have to sell it. [bleep]
We'll have to sell it.
You would enjoy it. [bleep]
You'd enjoy it.
It will be a good day. [bleep]
It'll be a good day.

Exercise 6

Listen and write the correct word: *will* or *would*.

Example: I'd leave the job.

1 She'll understand.
2 It'd be awful.
3 We'd let you know.
4 Alison'll do it for you.
5 They'll like each other.

UNIT 33 COMMUNICATION
Polite requests for information

PRESENTATION

With books closed, pretend you are walking in the street and you want to find out the time. You go up to a stranger and say brusquely: *What's the time?*

Ask students what is wrong with the question. They will probably think that there is something grammatically wrong. Tell them that although it is grammatically correct, it sounds rude.

Ask them how to make it more polite so that you elicit: *Excuse me, can you tell me what the time is?* Or, give the first half and ask students to complete the question.

Write the question on the board so that you can point out the inversion of subject and verb.

Ask how to make a similar indirect question from *Is this seat free?* to draw out the use of *if* for Yes/No questions, i.e. *Can you tell me if this seat is free?* Write this question on the board underneath the other one.

Explain that it is very common to use indirect questions to make requests for information.

Ask the students if they know any other question openers such as: *Could you tell me …/Do you know …/Have you any idea …?*

Photograph
With books open, ask where Eve is and what she is doing.

 DIALOGUE

Ask the students to cover the dialogue and look at the questions while they listen.

KEY
1 She wants to speak to Dave Edgar.
2 He's still at work.
3 (b) The woman is his landlady.
4 She wants to know:
  – when he'll be back.
  – what his work number is.
  – if he received a parcel this morning.

Ask students to underline or tell you how Eve made these requests.

FOCUS
Students repeat the sentences, making sure the questions end in a rising intonation. Draw attention to the last 'Point to note' below the picture and give an example.

PRACTICE
When students give you the indirect question, insist that they say it politely as if they were asking the question to a stranger. They can select a fellow student to answer the question. They will have to use their imagination to supply a suitable answer.

KEY
1 Do you know how far it is to Bath?
2 Can you tell me if there's a hamburger restaurant around here?
3 Could you tell me where the nearest bank is?
4 Have you any idea what time the market closes?
5 Can you tell me where I can buy a phone card?
6 Could you tell me if there are any buses which go from here to the station?

ACT IT OUT
Remind students to make requests for information (not for things) and remind them of the last note in the Focus section.

EXAMPLE CONVERSATIONS
1 At a railway station

A: Excuse me, can you tell me what time the next train to Bath leaves?
B: Yes, it leaves at 10.15.
A: Which platform does it leave from?
B: It leaves from Platform 3.

2 In a post-office

A: Could you tell me how much it costs to send a postcard to Europe?
B: Yes, it costs 25p.
A: And do you know if I can make a telephone call abroad from here?
B: No, I'm afraid you can't. You'll have to use a public call box. There's one just down the road on the right.

3 At a sports stadium

A: Excuse me, can you tell me where the toilets are?
B: Yes, they're over there, next to the stairs.
A: And where can I buy a programme?
B: There are programme sellers at each entrance to the stadium.
A: Oh, O.K. Thanks.

 LISTENING

Before you listen

EXAMPLE QUESTIONS
Why do you want to sail the Atlantic alone?
How long is it going to take?
What food are you going to take?
Are you carrying a radio transmitter?
Who is sponsoring you and for how much?
When are you going to start?
Where are going to leave from? etc.

Listen

KEY

1 Could you tell us why you're doing this trip? (Indirect)
2 Can you tell us how you've been preparing for the trip? (Indirect)
3 How much have you received so far? (Direct)
4 Do you know how many times this has been done before? (Indirect)
5 Can you tell us when you're going to set off? (Indirect)
6 Have you any idea how long it's going to take you? (Indirect)
7 What does your family think of your trip? (Direct)

True or False?

Explain: *to challenge someone to do something*.

KEY

1 False 2 True 3 False 4 True 5 True 6 False

TAPESCRIPT

Listen to an interview with Adrian Taylor, who is planning to sail single-handed across the Atlantic. Look at your Students' Book and do the exercises.

INTERVIEWER: Thank you, Helen Allsop. Now let's talk to Adrian Taylor, who is planning to sail across the Atlantic single-handed. Adrian, welcome to our programme.
ADRIAN: Thank you.
INTERVIEWER: Adrian, could you tell us why you're doing this trip? After all, it is a bit extraordinary.
ADRIAN: Yes, it is. Er, I decided to do it because I felt I need a bit more challenge in my life – more adventure.
INTERVIEWER: Mm. Can you tell us how you've been preparing for the trip?
ADRIAN: I've been preparing the boat of course but I've also been training hard to get fit. And I've been writing letters to companies for sponsorship.
INTERVIEWER: How much have you received so far?
ADRIAN: About £800.
INTERVIEWER: Do you know how many times this sort of trip has been done before?
ADRIAN: Yes, quite a number of times. But not by me!
INTERVIEWER: Can you tell us when you're going to set off?
ADRIAN: Not exactly, no. It all depends on the weather. But it will be some time in the next month or so.
INTERVIEWER: Have you any idea how long it's going to take you?
ADRIAN: Well, I hope to do it in under two months but we'll see.
INTERVIEWER: And what does your family think of your trip?
ADRIAN: Oh, they're all delighted. The think it's terribly exciting.
INTERVIEWER: Well, Adrian, I don't think I'd like to be in your shoes – or rather in your boat ... But anyway I, and I'm sure all the listeners, wish you the very best of luck on your Transatlantic crossing.
ADRIAN: Thank you very much.

WRITING

Students use the statements in the True/False exercise and their list of interviewer's questions to help them to recall the interview. Encourage the use of the present perfect simple and continuous, and explain that they can include direct speech if they wish.

EXAMPLE ARTICLE
BON VOYAGE!
On Saturday 15th June, Adrian Taylor, aged twenty-two, is leaving Portsmouth in at attempt to sail singlehanded across the Atlantic. To prepare for the crossing, Adrian has been training hard to get fit. He has also been writing letters to companies and has so far managed to raise £800 in sponsorship. The start of the trip depends on the weather but Adrian says it will certainly be some time within the next month. 'I hope to do the trip in under a month,' says Adrian. Adrian's family are all delighted about his Transatlantic crossing. 'They think it's terribly exciting,' says Adrian, 'and so do I!'

ABOUT BRITAIN

Refer to the picture of Eve and ask if the students can see what she is holding in her hand. Point out the sign on the call box. Ask student to read the note on phonecards and to tell you how they work, using their own words as far as possible. Explain: *phone booth* (*call box*), *units*, *digital display*. Ask how this system compares with that in their own countries.

EXTRA ACTIVITIES

1 Whispered requests

Divide students into groups of about eight. Whisper a long indirect question to the first person in each group, e.g. *Excuse me, have you any idea where the nearest public toilets are?* and ask them to whisper it very quietly to the next person and so on until the whisper reaches the last person in the group. That person has to say aloud to the rest of the class what he/she heard.

2 Situation cards

Use some of the situation cards from Unit 13 Extra activity (e.g. Tourist information Office, Hotel Reception). In turn, students pick a card and make a request appropriate to the situation on the card, choosing someone in the class to respond, e.g. at the Tourist Information Office:

S1: Can you tell me where the Regent Hotel is, please?
S2: Certainly. It's in the High Street opposite the bank.

The student who responds is the next person to pick a card.

 Workbook tapescript

Unit 33

Speechwork: Stress and intonation
Requests for information

Exercise 2

Listen to these requests.
COULD you tell me what his WORK number is, PLEASE?
HAVE you any iDEa when he'll be BACK?
Do you KNOW if he received a PARcel this MORning?

Now listen and repeat.
what his WORK number is, please? [bleep]
COULD you tell me what his WORK number is, PLEASE? [bleep]
when he'll be BACK [bleep]
HAVE you any iDEa when he'll be BACK? [bleep]
received a PARcel this MORning? [bleep]
Do you KNOW if he received a PARcel this MORning? [bleep]

Exercise 3

Listen to the requests and write the one which sounds more polite: a or b.

Example:

a: Could you tell me where he is? [less polite]
b: Could you tell me where he is? [more polite]

1 a Do you know if she's gone out? [more polite]
1 b Do you know if she's gone out? [less polite]
2 a Have you any idea what time they left? [less polite]
2 b Have any any idea what time they left? [more polite]
3 a Do you know how long it takes? [less polite]
3 b Do you know how long it takes? [more polite]
4 a Could you tell me what her number is? [more polite]
4 b Could you tell me what her number is? [less polite]

UNIT 34 GRAMMAR
Have/get something done

PRESENTATION

With books closed, show magazine pictures of two well-known/glamorous Hollywood stars, one male and one female, and tell students you are going to talk about their appointments for today.

Write 'appointment diaries' on the board, e.g.

TIME	HE	SHE
10 a.m.	haircut and tint	pool cleaning
12 a.m.	photograph session	nail manicure
3 p.m.	foot massage	eyelash tinting
5 p.m.	palm reading	Cadillac service

As one of the stars, tell the class about your first appointment for the day: *This is going to be a busy day! At ten o'clock I'm going to have my hair cut and tinted.*

Now ask:

T: Is he going to cut his hair himself?
S: No. He's going to the hairdresser's.
T: That's right. He's going to have his hair cut at the hairdresser's. What else is he going to have done?
S: He's going to have his hair tinted.

Continue with the rest of the diary prompting with the time of day.

Refer to the diary entry: *Cadillac service* and discuss briefly what you can have done at a garage. Pre-teach *brakes* and *brake fluid*.

 DIALOGUE

With books open, ask students to look at the photograph and to tell you what the mechanic is doing. Tell them to cover the dialogue and look at the questions beneath the dialogue while you play the tape.

Listen and answer

KEY
1 Because the car needs some more brake fluid.
2 She's having the car serviced.
3 She'd like her tyres checked.

Read the dialogue again, highlighting the causative use of *have* and *get*. Ask further questions if you wish, e.g. *What's another word for adding more to something? When does the mechanic think the brake fluid should be topped up? Why?*

What's the difference in meaning?

In Sentence 1 you are servicing the car yourself, but in Sentence 2 someone else is servicing it for you, at your request.

UNIT 34

FOCUS

Explain that *have* and *get* are usually interchangeable. Explain that the use of *get* can be stronger than *have*, e.g. *I must get my car serviced soon.* Also explain that *get* can imply that some effort or difficulty is involved, e.g. *I finally managed to get my TV repaired yesterday.*, that *get* not *have* is used in orders, e.g. *Get your shoes cleaned!*, and that *get* is more informal than *have*.

PRACTICE

Exercise 1

Draw students' attention to the advertisement to the left of the article. Students take it in turns to say a sentence.

KEY
I'm going to have my/the tyres checked.
I'm going to have my/the oil checked.
I'm going to have my/the car waxed and polished.
I'm going to have my/the windscreen washed.
I'm going to have my/the battery checked.

KEY
I'd like my/the tyres checked, please.
I'd like my/the oil checked, please.
I'd like my/the car waxed and polished, please.
I'd like my/the windscreen washed, please.
I'd like my/the battery checked, please.

Show how to make this second part of the exercise into a conversation by responding with: *Yes, of course./Yes, certainly./Yes, sure.*

Exercise 2

Ask students to tell you what sort of work each of the tradespeople do. Point out that when the two verbs *get* and *have* are used causatively, they often occur with verbs like: *fix, mend, repair, service, clean, decorate, build, develop*.

The difference between the two lists of jobs is that the jobs in the left-hand column are assumed to occur fairly regularly, whereas the jobs in the right-hand column happen only occasionally. Hence the difference between *Do you …?* and *Would you …?*

Note the use of *own* in *do your own decorating*, etc. This means *do the decorating yourself*. (c.f. *We grow our own potatoes*, and *Peter cuts his own hair*.)

Encourage conversation around each item and, if possible, describe any 'Do-It-Yourself' disasters you, or anyone you know, have had. Ask: *Have you ever tried to do a job yourself and regretted it?*

 **LISTENING**

Before you listen

Use the questions to discuss the advantages and disadvantages of renting TVs. Discuss also good and bad picture reception and what causes TV pictures to go wrong.

KEY
Customer: Mrs Porter
Address: 5, Bedford Gardens
Complaint: Bad quality picture
Time of visit: Morning of Tuesday, October 20th

TAPESCRIPT
Listen to a woman who goes into a television rental shop with a complaint. Look at your Students' Book and follow the instructions.

WOMAN: Good morning. I was wondering if one of your engineers could come along and have a look at my television set.
MAN: It's one of ours, is it?
WOMAN: Yes, I rent it from you.
MAN: And what exactly is the problem?
WOMAN: It's the picture. The quality's awful. We can hardly watch it any more.
MAN: Mmm, perhaps you need to adjust the aerial.
WOMAN: I'm sure it's more serious than the aerial. I'd like the set checked out properly.
MAN: We're very busy at the moment but I'll send someone to go and look at it next week.
WOMAN: Next week! But I want it repaired now. Today.
MAN: I'm sorry, madam, but that's impossible. As I said, we're extremely busy and we try to deal with our calls in strict rotation. I can fit you in on … on Tuesday October 20th. All right?
WOMAN: Yes, I suppose so.
MAN: Now, can I have your name and address, please?
WOMAN: It's Mrs Porter. That's P.O.R.T.E.R. Porter. And my address is 5, Bedford Gardens.
MAN: 5, Bedford Gardens. Right, Mrs Porter. We'll have someone round on Tuesday the 20th in the morning at about eleven o'clock. Can you arrange for someone to be in?

READING

Before you read

> BACKGROUND NOTE
> *Time-Life*: An American publication company.
> *PR*: Public relations.

KEY TO EXPRESSIONS
put up with = tolerate, e.g. *I don't know how she puts up with her husband.*
out of order = not working, e.g. *I'm afraid the photocopier is out of order.*
vandalised = damaged so that it can't be used, e.g. *The sports centre lockers have all been vandalised.*

93

KEY TO COMPLAINTS
1 It takes a long time to get a telephone fixed/repaired in Britain.
2 Most of the public phones are vandalised.
3 It takes a long time to get a new telephoned installed.

TALKING POINT
Use the notes from the reading exercise to introduce the discussion questions.

WRITING
Read the example sentence and ask students to note how *whereas* is used. Give another example and write it on the board, e.g. *In our country children start school at the age of seven, whereas in Britain children start at the age of five.*

Students discuss one of the topics in each group, e.g. *education*, *entertainment*, *food* or *transport*, etc. Groups report back.

Collect ideas on the board under two headings: *Here* and *In the USA/Britain* (etc.) for students to copy for use in their writing.

EXTRA ACTIVITIES

1 Jumbled sentences
Write the following sentence in large writing on to a piece of stiff paper and cut it up into separate jumbled words:

Unless Jack turns up this evening to help me fix it, I'm going to get it done at the garage when I take it in to be serviced next week.

Students make a sentence out of the jumbled words.

2 Survey
Students conduct a survey among members of the class to find out how often people have things done, e.g. *How often do you have your hair cut?/teeth checked?/eyes tested?/ears tested?/blood pressure checked?*

After the survey, students can draw conclusions about people's priorities.

3 Car faults: discussion
Car enthusiasts may like to continue the discussion about cars with topics lie:
- things that can go wrong with cars
- 'horror' stories about bad service or repairs
- the relative merits of local garages
- the cheapest/best ways of getting things done
- the most reliable makes of car, etc.

First, build up vocabulary of parts of the car which can cause trouble and what can be done about them, e.g.

tyre	gets a puncture, goes flat	change
brakes	brake lining wears out	replace
brake fluid	leaks	top up
clutch	wears out	replace
gears	slip	replace gearbox
battery	goes flat	re-charge or replace
exhaust pipe	rusts	clean or replace

UNIT 35 READING
Friday Dressing

Before you read
Ask the students to look at the two photographs and the questions accompanying them. Ask them to describe the clothes the people are wearing in both the photos. Introduce the concept of 'body language' and ask the students what they understand by it and to give some examples of how it can convey meaning.

COMPREHENSION

Exercise 1
KEY
1 c)
2 Casual clothes my often reveal what the wearer is actually like and may show a character opposite to the one presented when wearing formal business clothes. Lack of taste in clothes could be thought to imply poor business judgement. For women, it is difficult to find a balance between the extremes of too much or too little make-up, too strong or too dull colours, etc. Wearing revealing clothes may lead others to form a mistaken opinion about a woman.

VOCABULARY
KEY
1 dress code 2 flourish 3 potentially
4 overestimated 5 daunting 6 fake
7 an exhibitionist 8 boring 9 sloppy
10 turn out to be

THINK ABOUT IT
Ask the first question to the class as a whole. Then divide the class into groups to work at the second question. Leave time for the groups to report back their lists of Do's and Don'ts.

 **LISTENING**

The passage falls into three natural parts. In the first part the speaker describes the image of a traditional businessman, in the second part he describes the image of a modern executive woman and in the third part he describes the difference between the traditional and the modern businessman.

Preparation

Before you play the tape, ask students to tell you what the stereotype of a English businessman is. Elicit: *briefcase, bowler hat, umbrella, pin-stripe suit*. Then play the first part of the tape and allow time to make notes. Repeat the same process for the executive woman and play the second part of the tape for comparison.

Revise the meaning of the word *yuppy* and play the last part of the tape. Ask if students agree with everything the speaker has said.

Discuss the question of clothes and what message they give to people. Ask: *If you work in business, is it important to look smart at all times? Can it be a disadvantage in some jobs to dress too formally?*

TAPESCRIPT

Listen to Andrew talking about business people and their image. Note how he describes the difference between the traditional and the modern image of a businessman.

ANDREW: I think there's … there's an image of a typical businessman and woman, erm, up to the middle of the nineteen eighties for example but, erm, in the last few years there's been emerging, erm, a secondary kind of … of new young business person, which is … generally seems to be called 'Yuppy'. The, the traditional image of the businessman is, er, three-piece striped, pin-stripe suit, black well-polished shoes, briefcase, umbrella, bowler hat. Er, very very smart appearance, always very punctual. Arrives at work at five to nine in the morning, leaves work at just after five and is very efficient and precise. But that's the stereotype, the image of the traditional businessman. I don't think there is an image of a traditional businesswoman, because, in the past, women didn't go into business. Erm, that's something that's changing rapidly nowadays.

INTERVIEWER: Well, what about the, the, the, the executive woman. Isn't there a look?

ANDREW: Yes, there is, there is, there is, erm, a look which is associated with the executive woman. I think, erm, the, the standard executive woman is very very well-dressed. She wears expensive designer clothes. She'll have a very smart modern hair-cut, probably quite short, er, very …

INTERVIEWER: Her hair?

ANDREW: … Her hair will be, yes, yes. Erm, she, she doesn't wear a lot of make-up in, at work. Er, not much jewellery that, the … whole image in one of, erm, smartness and efficiency, erm. Going on to what I was saying about the, the yuppy. The, erm, the yuppies seem to have been born and bred in, in the city, in London. And, er, they, they wear similar clothes to, to that of the traditional businessman but they're very dynamic, very high-powered. Erm, normally very intelligent and bright and they make an awful lot of money in a very short time.

KEY

Traditional image of a businessman: three-piece pin stripe suit, black well-polished shoes, briefcase, tie, umbrella, bowler hat. Smart appearance, punctual. Very efficient and precise.

Modern image of a businessman: the 'yuppy'; similar clothes to traditional businessman but very dynamic, high-powered, very intelligent; the sort of person that makes a lot of money in a very short time.

Modern image of a woman executive: very well-dressed, expensive designer clothes, modern short haircut, not a lot of make-up, not a lot of jewellery.

EXTRA ACTIVITIES

1 One minute speeches: Me and my clothes

Students have to prepare a 'One minute speech' on one the following clothes topics:
- My favourite outfit/clothes
- The clothes I like best on a girl/boy/man/woman (as appropriate)
- My worst (or most expensive) fashion mistake
- The awful secrets of my wardrobe
- How to dress well on a low budget
- School uniform

2 Game: Clothes surprise!

Write the following framework on the board:
1 At (name of place or event) last week …
2 (Name of a famous person) was wearing …
3 Describe the undergarments. (e.g. T-shirt, vest, shirt, etc.)
4 And … (describe the main items of clothing with accessories)
5 On top of this was … (describe an item of outdoor clothes)
6 And the whole outfit was finished off with … (describe the headgear)

This works like a game of consequences. Each student should write the first sentence at the top of a piece of paper, fold it over and pass it on to the

UNITS 35/36

student sitting next to him/her. This continues six times until the whole outfit is complete. The last person opens up the paper and reads out the description of the complete outfit for the person in question.

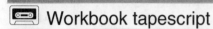 Workbook tapescript

Unit 35

Exercise 2

Look at your book and listen. Match the jobs with the people.

ALEX: Who did what in your house, Ellen? Were the jobs equally divided?
ELLEN: Oh no, by no means. My mother seemed to do most of the jobs. She did all the cooking and the cleaning and the washing up. And she did the shopping.
ALEX: Didn't your father do any of the housework then?
ELLEN: Not really. There were just a few jobs that he was responsible for. He always did the small repairs when things went wrong.
ALEX: Ah yes, so did my father. What about the gardening? Did you have a garden?
ELLEN: Yes, a small one, and it was my father who was responsible for it, but he really enjoyed doing that. Oh, and he looked after the car as well. He washed it at weekends, and he like fixing it when it broke down, which it seemed to do very often.
ALEX: And did your parents do the decorating themselves, or did they have it done professionally?
ELLEN: They did it themselves. And that was one of the few jobs that they did together. The only other job I can remember them doing together was packing when we went away for weekends or holidays.
ALEX: And who looked afer you when you were young?
ELLEN: My mother mostly. She gave up work, until we'd all gone to school.
ALEX: Are their roles still the same now that they've retired?
ELLEN: Oh yes. I think it's too late for them to change now.

UNIT 36 GRAMMAR
Past modal verbs: *should have*, and *ought to have*

Photograph and questions

KEY
1 They are (going to be) late.

2 Because he talked too long on the phone and so they left late.

Add to each answer respectively.
T: Yes, they should have left earlier.
That's right, he shouldn't have talked so long on the phone.

Write a table on the board for students to make sentences:

They	should ought to	have left earlier.
They	shouldn't oughtn't to ought not to	have left so late.

FOCUS

Ask students to read the Focus section and to tell you the difference between *ought to* and *should*.

To establish the continuous form, tell the story of a friend who cut her face badly in a road accident because she wasn't wearing a seatbelt. Write on the board a second table.

She	should ought to	have been wearing a seatbelt.
She	shouldn't oughtn't to ought not to	have been driving without a seatbelt.

Leave these two tables on the board throughout the lesson.

PRACTICE

Exercise 1

The sentence the students produce should be an extension of the sentence in the book, not a response to it.

KEY
1 You should have/ought to have phoned earlier.
2 You shouldn't have invited him.
3 You should have gone to bed a long time ago/hours ago/earlier.
4 He shouldn't have eaten it all/all the ice cream.
5 They shouldn't have got married (when they were) so young.
6 I should have worn something smarter/a dress/a suit.

Exercise 2

In this exercise, the new sentence reinterprets the original.

KEY
1 She shouldn't have been driving so fast.
2 He should have been wearing his helmet.

3 You should have been wearing your glasses.
4 You shouldn't have been walking on the grass!
5 He shouldn't have been cycling without lights.

TALKING POINT

Explain *test-drive* and *write off*. Students discuss and report back their criticisms.

SUGGESTED CRITICISMS
The car salesman:
– shouldn't have let the boys test-drive the car.
– should have asked their ages.
– should have asked to see their driving licences.
– should have gone with them in the car.
– shouldn't have allowed them to go on the motorway.
– shouldn't have believed them.
– should have been suspicious in the first place.
– shouldn't have been so eager to sell a car.

The boys:
– shouldn't have asked to test-drive the car. (It's very powerful and they probably didn't have the money to buy it.)
– shouldn't have driven so fast.

WRITING

Introduce the topic of football hooliganism. Discuss why it occurs, who the main offenders are and ways of preventing it. List ideas on the board to compare with those in the notes in the writing exercise. Explain *body search* and *weapons*. Students convert the notes into criticisms using *should/n't have*, before writing their letters.

EXTRA ACTIVITY

Who is to blame?

Copy the following situations and distribute them, one per student. Students find other students with the same situation and form groups to discuss their criticisms.

SITUATIONS
1 Playing with fire
A little girl was playing with a Christmas candle and burnt her hand badly. Her father immediately put some butter on the burn and then covered it with plaster.

2 Smoking in bed
A man who likes to smoke in bed woke one night to find his bedroom full of smoke. He immediately got out of bed and rushed to open the window to let the smoke out.

3 Hypothermia
During a very cold winter a man found his next door neighbour – an old age pensioner – suffering from hypothermia. He immediately poured a large glass of brandy, and gave it to her to drink.

Workbook tapescript

Unit 36

Speechwork: Pronunciation
Should have/ought to have

Exercise 4

Listen to these sentences.
We should have left earlier.
He ought to have phoned before.
You shouldn't have talked for so long.

Now listen and repeat.
should have [bleep]
We should have left earlier. [bleep]
ought to have [bleep]
He ought to have phoned before. [bleep]
shouldn't have [bleep]
You shouldn't have talked for so long. [bleep]

Exercise 5

Listen and tick the sentences which you hear.

Example: I shouldn't have eaten that meal.

1 I shouldn't have gone to the party.
2 You should have run faster.
3 You ought to have come earlier.
4 We should have told them our plans.
5 You shouldn't have hit that child.

UNIT 37 TOPIC
Ethics

PRESENTATION

With books closed, demonstrate the meaning of the words *ethics* and *ethical*. Say to the students: *Imagine you are a doctor treating a young patient who is dangerously ill. When the patient asks how ill he is, do you tell the truth? Is it always right to tell the truth?*

Before you read

With books closed, write the words on the board for students to discuss and predict what they think the text will be about.

Text: How far does friendship go?

Students read the text and see if their predictions were right. They then do Exercise 1.

Exercise 1

KEY
1 He wanted David to recommend him for a job in David's company.
2 He didn't think his friend would be able to handle the work.

3 He had to make a choice between refusing a request for help from a good friend and recommending someone for a job which he knew the person wasn't able to do.
4 He recommended his friend but only half-heartedly.
5 He should have (taken his friend out to dinner and) told him the truth.

Text: second reading

Go through the text in detail, paying attention to the 'Words to learn'. Gloss the expressions: *the lesser of two evils, not always clear cut, a half-hearted recommendation, it's pretty likely, get into a mess.*

Exercise 2

SUGGESTED ANSWERS

1 You need to be smart, tough, tactful, articulate, able to handle the press, able to think quickly.
2 You don't sound completely enthusiastic and you only talk about certain aspects of the person's ability, e. g. *I think he would be able to handle this part of the job quite well …* (*but not that part* is implied but not said).

Exercise 3

Discuss the first question with the whole class. The second and third can be discussed in pairs but prepare for the third question by explaining: *a (little) white lie* and building up on the board the following expressions: *to lie, to tell a lie, a liar.*

TALKING POINT

Either divide the situations among the pairs or groups, or ask students to discuss all of them. Each pair or group should have a secretary to report back. Develop any interesting point in discussion with the whole class.

VOCABULARY

Exercise 1

KEY

Noun	Verb
decision	decide
qualification	qualify
recommendation	recommend
reservation	reserve

Noun	Adjective
ability	able
capability	capable
possibility	possible
probability	probable

Exercise 2

KEY

deCISion	aBILity
qualifiCAtion	capaBILity
recommenDAtion	possiBILity
reserVAtion	probaBILity

TAPESCRIPT

Listen and repeat the words, to check if you have written the stress on the right syllable.

decision [bleep] qualification [bleep]
recommendation [bleep] reservation [bleep]
ability [bleep] capability [bleep]
possibility [bleep] probability [bleep]

LISTENING

Before you listen

KEY

1 A sum of money given by the government, or another institution, for example, to improve a building or to study at university.
2 An estimate is a statement of the probable cost of doing a job. It is submitted before the job is started.
  A bill shows the actual amount that must be paid.

Listen

After students have completed Questions 1 to 4, discuss Question 5 with the whole class. Introduce the words: *honest* and *dishonest.*

KEY

1 He agreed to take on the job of repairing (and decorating) the shop.
2 An improvement grant.
3 The newsagent asked Dennis to give him an estimate for £500 more than the newsagent had originally agreed to pay Dennis./The newsagent asked Dennis to give him a false estimate.
4 He refused to do it.

TAPESCRIPT

Listen to Dennis, a builder, talking about a recent dilemma, and answer the questions in your Students' Book.

I was in a bit of a dilemma some time ago. It was over money, of course. I'm a decorator. I do painting, repair jobs for people. Well a very good friend of mine bought a shop in the High Street … start up a newsagent's business. It was an old building … needed a lot of repair work doing on it. I agreed to take on the job and we agreed a price.

Anyway, you know you can get improvement grants from the local council – you know, they give you money to help you improve and repair your property if it's old. What you do is you send the council an estimate for the work to be done and if they approve it, they'll pay you the money. Well, the newsagent was trying to get one of these grants. So he asked me to give him an estimate that was £500 more than he had originally agreed to pay me. He wanted me to give him a false estimate on headed notepaper so he could send it to the council and get the money. I refused to do it ...

Never spoken to each other since then. It's sad really because our families were quite close. We used to go on holiday together.

WRITING

Discuss the sentences first, so that students get the idea of the different options available to them.

Exercise 1

EXAMPLE SENTENCES

1 On weekdays, I get up at seven o'clock. At the weekend, however, I sometimes stay in bed till midday.
2 Now and again we go out and have a meal in an expensive restaurant. However, most of the time we invite friends round to eat at home.
3 In the past, I used to go to the cinema once or twice a week. Recently, however, I've begun to be more interested in the theatre.
4 I used to think that living in the country must be very boring. However, nowadays I'm a completely changed person.
5 The Mediterranean was once clean and clear. Now, however, it's very polluted.
6 People think that the British are cold. However, when you get to know them they are friendly.
7 Nowadays in Russia people listen to pop music a lot. However, in the past it was banned.
8 In the USA there are some wonderful buildings. However, there are also some dreadful slums.

EXTRA ACTIVITIES

1 Scale of reaction

Students order the following ethical situations on a scale of reaction from 0 to 5.

0 = I don't react at all, 5 = I strongly disapprove.

Students form groups or pairs to discuss their reactions.

What is your reaction to the following?

In shops and restaurants:
- not telling a shop assistant he/she has undercharged you. ☐
- returning an item of clothing which you have worn once but you discover is not the right size. ☐
- trying on clothes, reading magazines, listening to records which you have no intention of buying. ☐
- booking a table at a restaurant and not turning up. ☐

At work:
- taking stationery for private use. ☐
- using the office phone to make private phone calls. ☐
- phoning work to way you are ill because you want to go on holiday a day earlier. ☐
- telling lies to save a friend's job. ☐

In your personal life:
- going out with a friend's boy/girl friend. ☐
- telling someone that their partner is being unfaithful to them. ☐
- cancelling a date or an engagement with a friend because something more exciting has turned up. ☐
- being unfaithful to your partner. ☐

2 Rank order

Write a list of personal qualities on the board. Students discuss the list and rank order the qualities from the most to the least important in their choice of friends.

PERSONAL QUALITIES

sense of humour	generosity
reliability	tact
honesty	intellectual ability
loyalty	assertiveness
adaptability	sincerity
sensitivity	ability to listen

UNIT 38 COMMUNICATION
Explanation and clarification

PRESENTATION

Ask students to suggest ways of asking for information in a language class, e.g. How to ask for:
- the meaning of a word or expression.
- advice on pronunciation or intonation.
- help with spelling.
- help with grammar or usage.

They may suggest the following direct questions.
What's the word for ... in English?
What does ... mean?
How do you pronounce/spell this word?
Why can't I say...?

Write these direct questions on the board. Now ask the students to rephrase each question beginning with *I don't know, I'm not sure* and *I don't understand*. Point out the change in the order of subject and verb in these indirect questions.

🔲 DIALOGUE

Find out if anyone has filled in a job application form recently. Introduce the idea of a curriculum

UNIT 38

vitae (CV) and the idea of a letter which supports an application. Ask why employers need this letter. Ask what the young man in the picture is asking his mother. Students look at the 'Listen and answer' questions and cover the dialogue while they listen. Play the dialogue.

Listen and answer

KEY
1 He's filling in an application form for a VSO job.
2 He doesn't know whether to type it or not.
3 Because you get a chance to say something more about yourself, and to say why you think you are suitable for the job.
4 Because he doesn't know what to say.

Go through the dialogue again, asking students to note all the requests for explanation, and all the indirect requests for help and clarification. Then ask them to give the direct form of the indirect questions.

– *Do/Should I type it or not?*
– *Why do they need more information about me?*
– *What shall I say?*
– *Do I want the job or not?*

Students read the dialogue in pairs.

FOCUS

Practise the example sentences chorally and point out how the intonation of the alternative indirect questions falls into two parts, with the second part starting on the word *or*. The intonation rises at the end of the first part, and falls at the end of the second part. This two-part intonation pattern is a feature of 'alternative' statements and questions with *or*.

PRACTICE

Exercise 1

Ask students where they would find the abbreviations. Students work S–T and then practise again in pairs when they are sure of the answers.

KEY
i.e. = *that is* or *that is to say* (from the Latin *id est*)
e.g. = *for example* (from the Latin *exempli gratia*)
etc. = *etcetera/and so on* (literally *and the rest* in Latin)
N.B. = *note* (from the Latin *nota bene* = *note well*)
P.S. = *post script* (something you add to the bottom of a letter, from the Latin: *post scriptum*)
R.S.V.P. = *Please reply.* (from the French: *Repondez s'il vous plait*)
EFL = *English as a foreign language*
UFO = *unidentified flying object*
EU = *European Union*
BBC = *British Broadcasting Corporation*
CIA = *Central Intelligence Agency*
AIDS = *acquired immune deficiency syndrome*

Exercise 2

This can be done as a game. In pairs, students think of three or four abbreviations. The class divides into two teams. Members from each team name an opposing player and ask her/him to give the full form of an abbreviation. There should be no consultation. Failure to give the full form means a point to the other team.

Exercise 3

Students may use dictionaries if they wish.

KEY
1e 2f 3g 4c 5b 6i 7h 8a 9d

Exercise 4

Practise the sentence openings before students ask for explanations across the class.

Exercise 5

Introduce the topic of special credit cards for shops and department stores and the sort of information which the shops require. Ask why this information is needed and if it is relevant or not. Ask students to study the information required on the form. Say: *I don't understand why they need this information. For example, ...* and give the example printed in the book. Mention again that subject and verb are not inverted in indirect questions.

Ask individual students to give you the questions. Encourage them to convert headings like *occupation/income* into verb phrases. (See the Key below.) Explain that *gross income* means your salary before tax is deducted. Although it is unlikely that people would object to giving their address and phone number, for practice students can start the exercise with the first section of the form.

KEY
I don't understand why they need to know:
– my address and phone number.
– if I'm married./single./widowed./divorced.
– if I've got any children./how old my children are.
– my occupation./what I do./what my job is.
– my gross income./monthly income./how much I earn a year./a month.
– if I own or rent my home.

After the exercise, encourage discussion as to why people object to revealing personal information.

Exercise 6

Explain that the advertisement asks for a formal letter of application. Ask the students how to write a formal letter. They may refer to the letter in Unit 23.

KEY
1 A: I don't know how to write the date in English.

B: You write it like this – 16th February.

2 A: I don't know whether to write my name at the top of the letter or not.
B: No, you don't need to. Only at the bottom of the letter when you sign it.

3 A: I don't know where to put the name and address of the person I'm writing to.
B: You put it at the top of the letter on the left-hand side.

4 A: I don't know how to start the letter.
B: You start it: 'Dear Sir/Madam, I would like to apply for the job of temporary Play Leader as advertised in …'

5 A: I don't know how to end the letter.
B: You end it: 'I look forward to hearing from you. Yours faithfully,' and sign your name.

6 A: I don't know whether to include a CV or not.
B: Yes, it's a good idea to include one.

WRITING

Discuss the sort of information that should be included and any useful expressions which students might need. Students exchange letters afterward and correct each other's work.

SUGGESTED LETTER

Dear Sir/Madam,

I would like to apply for the job of temporary Play Leader as advertised in 'The Guardian' of (Date).

I am twenty-one years old. I am (nationality) but I speak good English. I like children very much and think that this will be an ideal job for me. I come from a large family and so I am very used to young children. At the moment I am working as an au pair in England and I am looking after three boys aged thirteen, eleven and seven. The job finishes next month and so I am looking for another job from April until September.

If you want to interview me, I'll be available any afternoon after 3.30. I look forward to hearing form you.

Yours faithfully,

(Signature)

(Name)

 ## LISTENING

Exercise 1

KEY
What does CD stand for?
I'm afraid I don't know how to get to Room 6. Is it on this floor?
Could you explain what 'First Certificate class' means?

Exercise 2

Students need not reproduce the original exactly. The * in the following tapescript indicates where students speak.

TAPESCRIPT
Listen to a man enrolling on an English course. Note what he says when he asks for information or clarification.

MAN: I'd like to enrol on one of your English courses, please.
TEACHER: Well, you'd better see the CD.
MAN: *What does CD stand for?
TEACHER: Oh, sorry, it means the Course Director. She's in Room 6.
MAN: *I'm afraid I don't know how to get to Room 6. Is it on this floor?
TEACHER: Yes, it's at the end of the corridor on the left.
CD: Yes, can I help you?
MAN: Yes, I would like to enrol in an English class.
CD: Yes, have you been to any classes here before?
MAN: No, this is the first time.
CD: What about a First Certificate class?
MAN: *Could you explain what 'First Certificate class' means?
CD: It's a higher intermediate class leading to an exam. I think that would suit you very well.
MAN: All right. Could you enrol me in that class then, please?

Exercise 2
Listen again. When you hear a 'bleep', ask for the same information, using the language taken from this lesson.

MAN: I'd like to enrol on one of your English courses, please.
TEACHER: Well, you'd better see the CD.
MAN: [bleep]
TEACHER: Oh, sorry, it means the Course Director. She's in Room 6.
MAN: [bleep]
TEACHER: Yes, it's at the end of the corridor on the left.
CD: Yes, can I help you?
MAN: Yes, I would like to enrol in an English class.
CD: Yes, have you been to any classes here before?
MAN: No, this is the first time.
CD: What about a First Certificate class?
MAN: [bleep]
CD: It's a higher intermediate class leading to an exam. I think that would suit you very well.
MAN: All right. Could you enrol me in that class then, please?

UNITS 38/39

EXTRA ACTIVITIES

1 Job interview
Roleplay the interview for the job of Play Leader advertised in the unit. Select five students to apply for the job and a panel of six others to prepare appropriate questions to ask each applicant. Conduct the interview. The rest of the class act as 'observers' and make notes on the candidates' performances and say later if they agree with the decision of the interview panel.

As a follow up, ask if any 'candidates' were nervous in the interview and discuss what signs show when somebody is nervous. Discuss how one can prevent it.

2 I don't understand
Write on the board a selection of jobs and professions, e.g. *TV newsreader, airline pilot, croupier, nurse, vet, teacher.*

Students write a query for each job, e.g. *I don't understand how TV newsreaders never forget their words.*

3 Loan words and phrases
Students find out the meaning of five of the following expressions and say which languages they come from.

Latin: *ad nauseam, ad infinitum, incognito, modus operandi, post mortem, vice versa*

French: *avant garde, billet-doux, rendezvous, entre nous, double entendre, faux pas, fait accompli, pièce de résistance, tour de force, volte-face*

Students then write four English loan words or phrases which are used in their own language.

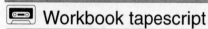 Workbook tapescript

Unit 38

Speechwork: Stress and intonation
Asking for advice and help

Exercise 3

Listen to this sentence.
I DON'T know whether to TYPE it or NOT.

Now listen and repeat.
TYPE it or NOT. [bleep]
I DON'T know whether to TYPE it or NOT. [bleep]

B
Now you make sentences. Listen to the example.

go
I don't know whether to go or not.

Now you do it.
go [bleep]
I don't know whether to go or not.
accept the job [bleep]
I don't know whether to accept the job or not.
invite them [bleep]
I don't know whether to invite them or not.
buy a new one [bleep]
I don't know whether to buy a new one or not.
apply [bleep]
I don't know whether to apply or not.

UNIT 39 GRAMMAR
Past modal verbs: *Could have/might have/must have and can't have*

Pictures
Explain or elicit the fact that the 'Odeon' is the name of a cinema. Students describe where the people are and the background to the dialogue.

Answer the questions

KEY
1 No, they don't.
2 He thinks she could have had a late meeting at the office.
3 She thinks Laura must have forgotten about their appointment/date/cinema visit.
4 Because he saw Laura write down the engagement/the date of the cinema visit in her diary.

FOCUS
Refer to the grammar table and practise a number of possible sentences chorally, making sure that *have* is always given a weak stress, e.g. /'maɪtəv/ /'kʊdəv/. Students read through the rest of the Focus section.

What's the difference in meaning?

KEY
1 *He might have left his glasses on the table.* = It is possible that he left them there.
2 *He must have left his glasses on the table.* = You have come to the conclusion that he definitely left them there.
3 *He can't have left his glasses on the table.* = You have come to the conclusion that he didn't leave them there.

PRACTICE

Exercise 1

KEY
1. She must have been asleep.
2. I can't have run out of petrol.
3. You must have wondered what had happened.
4. She must have won a lottery.
5. I can't have lost my glasses.
6. They must have cost you a fortune.
7. Alan can't have got lost.

Exercise 2

SUGGESTED ANSWER
He may/might/could have got caught in a traffic jam.
His watch may/might/could have stopped.
His car may/might/could have broken down.
He may/might/could have forgotten the day.
He may/might/could have overslept.
He may/might/could have had an accident.

ACT IT OUT

Go through each of the cues. Explain: *sick all night*. One or two pairs can perform their roleplays for the whole group.

SUGGESTED CONVERSATION
GERRY: Hello. 76884.
YOU: Gerry. It's me, John, here. Why aren't you here at the meeting?
GERRY: Well, I'm awfully sorry but I'm not feeling very well.
YOU: Is that all! We thought you might have had an accident or forgotten the day or something.
GERRY: No, I'm sorry. I was sick all night. I think it must have been the prawns I ate last night.
YOU: Well, I think you should at least have phoned Katie and told her you weren't coming to the meeting.
GERRY: Yes, I suppose I should have done. I'm sorry about that. Anyway, tell her I think I'll be able to get in to work tomorrow.
YOU: O.K. Well, take care and don't eat any more prawns!
GERRY: I won't! Bye.

WRITING

Refer to the business card at the top of the page. Explain the significance of AA (*Automobile Association*) and RAC (*Royal Automobile Club*). This hotel is recommended by these two motoring organisations and has been awarded three stars for its facilities by each of them. Students may like to comment on *Children and dogs welcome*. Go through the instructions to the writing task. Remind students of the layout of a formal letter (see Units 23 and 38). Alternatively, prepare the letter orally by asking students to provide sentences as instructed in the paragraph guide.

For variety, write a gapped 'cloze' version of the model letter below for the students to complete, or give it as a dictation.

EXAMPLE LETTER

(Your address)
(Today's date)

Mrs Sheila Nesbitt,
Assistant Manager,
The Salisbury Hotel,
Salisbury,
Wiltshire

Dear Mrs Nesbitt,

I was a guest at your hotel last Friday and Saturday night and I am writing to ask if my diary has been found.

It is a brown leather oblong diary with the initials (Your initials) in the corner. It has got my name, address and telephone number on the inside cover. I think I might have left it in my room (Room 402) or I could have left it on the reception desk when I was making a phone call on Saturday evening.

If you find it, or if someone hands it in, I would be very grateful if you could send it to me at the above address.

Yours sincerely,

(Your name)

 LISTENING

Before you listen

Refer to the dictionary entry and ask how mugging incidents are often carried out. Elicit words and phrases like: *snatch, grab, seize hold of, slash, thump, pick your pocket, throw to the ground*. Use the first two questions to focus the discussion. Students use dictionaries if necessary to find out the meaning of the words listed. Ask them which words can be used as both a noun and a verb, and what preposition follows the adjective *ashamed*.

Listen

> BACKGROUND NOTES
> ***Charing Cross Bridge*** is a railway bridge which crosses the Thames in central London. Pedestrians use the bridge to cross from Charing Cross Station on the north side of the river to the large cultural complex of the South Bank immediately opposite.

Write on the board and explain: *weak, spotted, prey, blow, turn up*.

Students make a chart (see the Key below) with the question words so that they can easily make notes.

UNIT 39

KEY

WHO?	Frances Thompson, a social worker.
WHEN?	Last November/just before her fortieth birthday/at about six in the evening/on her way to meet her husband at the National Theatre.
WHERE?	In London/on Charing Cross Bridge.
WHAT?	She was mugged and her bag was snatched.
HOW?	She was walking across Charing Cross Bridge. Someone – perhaps a girl in jeans, trainers and a leather jacket – hit her in the stomach and then snatched her shoulder bag.
WHAT EFFECT?	She is frightened of going out alone. She is ashamed of her fear.

TAPESCRIPT

Listen to Frances talking about a mugging incident on Charing Cross Bridge in London. Look at your Students' Book and do the exercise.

ANNOUNCER: We have called tonight's issue: 'When nasty things happen to nice people'. You will understand what we mean when you hear Frances Thompson, a social worker, recount an incident which happened to her last November in London.

FRANCES: Just before my fortieth birthday I was 'mugged'. I was attacked from behind and my handbag was snatched with all the things in it. Not valuable things, just the things which help me to arrange and order my life. I wasn't really hurt by the attack, but it has taught me just how weak and vulnerable we are.

I was on my own. It must have been about six o'clock in the evening. I was on my way to meet my husband at the National Theatre. I couldn't have been in a more public place – walking across Charing Cross Bridge. It was rush hour, too. There were hundreds of people around. My attackers must have planned their assault. They must have spotted my shoulder-bag and realised I'd be easy prey.

I felt a violent blow in my stomach. I cried 'Oh, sorry!', because I thought I must have bumped into someone. As I fell to the ground, I saw a slim person with blonde hair running away. It could have been a girl, I'm not really sure. But I do remember the smart-looking jeans and trainers and I can still smell the new leather jacket.

My cheque book turned up in Edinburgh in a TV shop, my credit cards in Amsterdam. The handbag was found – empty, of course – behind a toilet at Waterloo Station. But I lost more than material possessions. I lost my peace of mind. Now I take taxis from the station to my home. I jump whenever I hear a shout. I never go out at night on my own and never will again. I am deeply ashamed of my fear, but I can't stop myself feeling frightened.

EXTRA ACTIVITIES

1 Roleplays

1 Students roleplay the telephone conversation that they might have had with Mrs Nesbitt, the manager of the hotel, if they had not written the letter.
2 Students use their 'Listening' notes to roleplay the interview between Frances Thompson and the police inspector at Charing Cross police station after the mugging incident.

2 Deduction puzzles

Students discuss solutions to the following – or similar – deduction puzzles.

1 THE LIFT
Every day a man entered a lift of a ten-storey building. There were ten buttons. When he was alone in the lift, he always pressed the sixth button, left the lift and walked up the stairs of the remaining four floors. However, if there were other people in the lift he always got out at the tenth floor. Why did this happen?

(Solution: the man is very short and could only reach the 6th button.)

2 MURDER IN THE SAUNA
Two people with towels wrapped round their waists went into a sauna. One person was stabbed to death. By the body was a vacuum flask. The other person was arrested but was later released because no murder weapon was ever found. How was the murder committed?

(Solution: the murderer had a dagger of sharpened ice in the vacuum flask. After he stabbed his victim the ice melted and the water evaporated.)

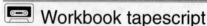

Workbook tapescript

Unit 39

Speechwork: Pronunciation
Could have/might have/must have/can't have

UNITS 39/40

Exercise 4

A

Listen to these sentences.
She could have had a late meeting.
She might have got the wrong day.
She must have forgotten.
She can't have got lost.

Now listen and repeat.
could have [bleep]
She could have had a late meeting. [bleep]
might have [bleep]
She might have got the wrong day. [bleep]
must have [bleep]
She must have forgotten. [bleep]
can't have [bleep]
She can't have got lost. [bleep]

B

Now you make sentences. Listen to the example.
You are talking about missing objects.

He might have dropped it.
left it on the bus
He might have left it on the bus.

Now you do it.
He might have dropped it.
left it on the bus [bleep]
He might have left it on the bus.
lost it [bleep]
He might have lost it.
can't [bleep]
He can't have lost it.
left it there [bleep]
He can't have left it there.
must [bleep]
He must have left it there.

UNIT 40 READING
Gather Together in My Name

PRESENTATION

Introduce the subject of black women writers. Ask is students have read any books by writers such as Maya Angelou and Alice Walker. Some students may have seen the film, *The Color Purple*, based on the book of the same name by Alice Walker. Explain that the text is an authentic extract from Maya Angelou's autobiographical novel: *Gather Together in My Name*.

Text: About the author

Write on the board the following question words.
1 *How old ...?*
2 *When and where ...?*
3 *Who ...?*
4 *How old ...?*
5 *Where ...?*
6 *What sort of jobs ... ?*

Students read the text and then ask and answer questions in pairs, using the question words as prompts.

KEY TO QUESTIONS ABOVE
1 How old was Maya Angelou when her first novel was published? She was forty-one.
2 When and where was she born? In 1928 in St. Louis, Missouri.
3 Who did Maya and her brother go to live with? Her grandmother.
4 Where did they move to later? To California.
5 How old was she when she gave birth to her son, Guy? She was sixteen.
6 What sort of jobs did Maya do after the birth of her son? She was a waitress, singer, actress, dancer and black activist as well as a mother.

Illustration

Ask students to describe the buildings and the café and to say what overall impression the picture gives. Ask them to try and describe what the restaurant might have been like inside and what sorts of dishes might have been served. Ask what the word 'Creole' means to the students (See 'Glossary') and if any have ever tasted Creole food.

 Text: Gather Together in My Name

Students first read the comprehension questions in Exercise 1 and then listen to the text while they follow it in their books.

COMPREHENSION

KEY
1 Creole food.
2 Seventy-five dollars.
3 Six days a week.
4 Yes.
5 Five o'clock.
6 It sounded like dark flashing eyes, hot peppers and Creole evenings, i.e. it sounded exciting and exotic. Her full name was Marguerite.
7 Reet.
8 She told three lies:
   Lie 1: She said she could cook Creole food.
   Lie 2: She said she like to go to church on Sundays.
   Lie 3: She said her name was Rita.

Text (Second reading)

Go through the text in detail with the whole class, pausing to let students discuss the choices in Exercise 2.

Exercise 2

KEY
1b 2c 3a 4c 5a 6c

UNIT 40/CHECK 31–40

THINK ABOUT IT

Remind students of the expression: *a little white lie* (Unit 37).

STYLE

Remind students of the explanation of similes in Unit 10 and ask if they can give any examples of similes and metaphors in their own language.

KEY

1 I gave her a lie as soft as melting butter.
2 Doubt hung on the edge of her questions.
3 Suspicion and doubt raced from her face.
4 My need for a job caught and held the denial.
5 Rita sounded like dark flashing eyes.

TALKING POINT

Ask students to try to project themselves into Maya's situation and help with ideas, e.g.

Maya's possible problems:
– prejudice against black people/women/ unmarried mothers
– finding somewhere to live
– living on her own
– difficulty in trying to get work
– no money
– possibly no social service support

WRITING

SUGGESTED BIOGRAPHY
Carson McCullers, American writer (1917–67)

Carson McCullers started writing quite early in life. She was twenty-three when her first book, 'The Heart is a Lonely Hunter', was published. She was born in 1917 in Columbus, Georgia. She originally wanted to be a musician. She married at the age of twenty. It was a difficult marriage which ended in her husband's suicide in 1953. She established her reputation as a writer with 'Reflections in a Golden Eye' (1941), and 'Member of the Wedding' (1946). She suffered from ill-health and alcoholism but wrote until her death in 1967.

EXTRA ACTIVITIES

1 Working at The Creole Café

In pairs or groups, ask students to plan a list of jobs for Maya to do at The Creole Café.

2 Biographies

Students carry out research and write a short biography of a writer of their choice.

3 Reading fluency

Play the tape of the text and ask students to 'shadow' the voice on the tape as they read the text. They should try and keep up with the voice even if it means leaving out a few words and phrases.

CHECK Units 31–40

(See notes for Check Units 1–10.)

KEY

Exercise 1

1e 2c 3f 4a 5b 6d

Exercise 2

1 didn't know
2 would you give
3 wouldn't wear
4 would get
5 had
6 Would you marry/wouldn't marry was /were
7 didn't want
8 wouldn't mind

Exercise 3

1 you're not 2 I had to 3 you'll be 4 she apologised 5 you cook 6 I phoned

Exercise 4

1 Have you any idea where John is?
2 Could you tell me how I get to/how to get to the station from here?
3 Can you tell me when the next programme starts?
4 Do you know if we've got any homework?
5 Have you any idea what time the last underground train leaves?
6 Do you know if Sam painted that picture?
7 Could you tell me why everyone is laughing?
8 Can you tell me where the nearest phone box is?

Exercise 5

1 I'd like my car serviced, please.
2 I'd like this watch repaired, please.
3 I'd like my hair cut, please.
4 I'd like these letters typed, please.
5 I'd like this leather jacket cleaned, please.
6 I'd like all that rubbish taken away, please.
7 I'd like my windscreen washed, please.
8 I'd like this computer system installed, please.
9 I'd like the door painted, please.
10 I'd like the tyres checked, please.

Exercise 6

1 a 2 c 3 c

Exercise 7

1 You should have seen
2 you ought to go
3 You shouldn't have taken
4 We should have thought
5 You ought to write

Exercise 8

1. You shouldn't have kept the change.
2. I shouldn't have got so angry.
3. They should have checked the time of the train.
4. I should have taken my swimming things.
5. He shouldn't have been drinking and driving.

Exercise 9

1. I can't find my keys anywhere. I think I must have lost them.
2. You shouldn't have driven when it was so foggy. You might have had an accident.
3. You never know. They might have taken the wrong bus.
4. She can't have telephone because I was in all day.
5. I'm glad you didn't come to see me yesterday. You might have caught my cold.
6. I can't have lost my passport. It was here on the table just a few minutes ago.

Exercise 10

1b 2c 3a

Exercise 11

1c 2e 3b 4a 5f 6d

Exercise 12

(Example responses)

1. Excuse me, could/can you tell me which platform the next train to Bath leaves from?
2. I'd like this (suede) jacket repaired, please.
3. Could/Can you tell/explain to me what Apex means, please?
4. Could you help me write a speech for my teacher's leaving party?/I don't know what to say in my speech. Could you help me?
5. I don't understand why you want to walk home alone.

USE YOUR ENGLISH
Units 31–40

Exercise 1

Ask the students to describe the picture and to say what the five characters are doing and where they are, if appropriate. Give an example of the first caption to show the different ways of completing it and to stress the need for subject-verb inversion in indirect questions.

KEY

1. Could you tell me what the exchange rate is for the dollar?
2. Can you tell me where the check-in desk is, please?/Can you tell me where I can find the check-in desk?
3. Do you know if there is a delay/why there is a delay/how long the delay is on the flight to Lagos?
4. Have you any idea where I can find the restroom?/where the restroom is?
5. Can you tell me where/if I can make a phone call, please?

When you have checked the accuracy of the students' questions, ask them to act out the questions and answers in pairs. The other half of the pair must think of a suitable answer each time.

Exercise 2

Divide the class into A and B roles and direct the B students to the relevant page at the back of the book. Let the students read the instructions through first, then check that they are sure how the exercise works. Work through a couple of examples so that the students are aware of the verb changes they must make, i.e. *would* in the main clause + past tense in the conditional clause.

KEY

1. If I got £100 for my birthday, I'd spend it on a pair of roller blades.
2. If I could go anywhere in the world, I'd go to Bali.
3. If I saw someone stealing in a shop, I'd tell the store manager.
4. If fire broke out in my house now, I'd save my photograph album.
5. If I suddenly lost my job, I wouldn't mind very much.
6. If I got tickets for the Cup Final, would you come with me?
7. I would be very surprised if I won a prize.
8. Would you marry me if I were rich and good-looking?
9. I would dive into ice cold water if you paid me £50.
10. My father would be very angry if he saw what had happened to his car.
11. Would you live abroad if you had the chance?
12. I would offer to help you if I knew something about computers.

Exercise 3

Remind the students of the meaning of the causative *have* using the example *service the car*. After the students have read their separate instructions, set them to work in pairs.

KEY
Ruth:
services the car herself
has her clothes altered
has her letters typed
has her hair cut
has the house decorated
cleans the house herself

Stuart:
has his car serviced
has his clothes altered
types his own letters
has his hair cut
decorates the house himself
has his house cleaned

Exercise 4

Ask the students to read the story through without paying any attention to the numbered gaps. Check the main events of the story and tell them that they must use their imagination to guess why certain things happened. Go through the first couple of examples with the whole class and ask them to complete the exercise in pairs.

SUGGESTED SENTENCES
1 You can't have got the correct timetable. *or* You must have got an out-of-date timetable.
2 They must have gone out.
3 There must have been some school children in the carriage previously. *or* There can't have been a wastepaper bin in the carriage.
4 They can't have got your message.
5 You must have left them at home.
6 You can't have screwed the top on properly.

PROGRESS TEST Units 31–40

(See notes for Progress test Units 1–10.)

KEY

Exercise 1

1c 2b 3a 4b 5a 6c 7b 8b 9c 10b

Exercise 2

1 shirt 2 harmless 3 petrol 4 wash 5 road 6 tailor
7 destroy 8 mugged

Exercise 3

independent, unforgettable, impersonal, unable, dishonest, unhappy, unscrupulous, impossible, unacceptable

Exercise 4

1 up 2 amount 3 example 4 but 5 hobby 6 might
7 eventually 8 agreement 9 for 10 down
11 broke 12 to 13 hated 14 promise 15 computer
16 worse

Errol

UNIT 41
Errol, a police officer

Before they read the text, discuss with the students what duties Errol's job involves. Ask students to think of other jobs which the police have to do and build up a list of these duties on the board. Introduce the phrase *be on the beat*. Ask which duties the students would find most interesting. In addition to discussing the printed questions, ask students if they know what equipment or weapons police carry in Britain. Discuss the words: *truncheon*, *handcuffs* and *radio*.

Photographs

Ask what image the photograph of Errol gives of the police. Then refer students to the photograph of the police car. Ask what the police are doing and what you can see and hear when police arrive at an emergency (*sirens* and *flashing lights*).

Text: So you want to join the police?

> BACKGROUND NOTE
> *Bristol*: A large city and port in the south west of England.

Students read the text silently, and answer the questions in Exercise 1.

Exercise 1

KEY
1 At the ice rink in the evening at eight o'clock.
2 They think the police spend most of their time chasing criminals in fast cars.
3 A truncheon, handcuffs and a radio.

Text: Second reading

Go through the text in detail, and check that students can use the 'Words to learn' in sentences of their own. Do not spend time on reported speech as this is presented in the next Grammar lesson.

Point out the use of the *-ing* form in the text. Ask students to note down how many times it is used and to say each time if it is the continuous form of the verb, a present participle, a gerund or just an adjective. Point out that one of the commonest uses of the *-ing* form is as a present participle after verbs, e.g.

> ... he spent a lot of his time playing ice hockey.
> ... we spend our time chasing criminals.
> You can be on the desk doing routine office work ...
> It really means ... walking round keeping your eyes open, ...

Exercise 2

KEY
1c 2a 3b 4a

Exercise 3

SUGGESTED ANSWERS
1 Because it is harder to sleep during the day because of noise and light/other people disturb you/the phone rings/you have to do your shopping/your 'body clock' is not adapted to it.
2 They form their opinions from TV, films and the news.
3 Because he likes meeting and talking to people/he likes fresh air/there is always something happening.
4 Because they need to be able to call for help quickly and send messages back to the police station.
5 If people are armed or behaving very violently or dangerously, e.g. in riots.

Exercise 4

Students may need to refer to the 'Vocabulary' section to answer Question 1, e.g. *I had to report a theft/burglary/robbery or I saw some burglars/thieves breaking into ...*

In Question 2, prompt with questions like: *How law-abiding are the police when they are off-duty? Are all police 'do-gooders'?*

VOCABULARY

Exercise 1

KEY
They are similar because they are all to do with stealing.

Burglary involves stealing from a house.
Shoplifting involves stealing from a shop.
Robbery is a general word involving stealing people's property.
Pickpocketing involves stealing money from people's pockets or bags, especially in crowds.
Mugging involves robbery, often with violence, in a public place.

Exercise 2

If there is time, extend the list to include the matching verbs, e.g. *to burgle/rob/rape/shoplift/ smuggle/murder/pick pockets/deal in drugs*. Make

UNIT 41

sure students are aware of how the words operate in a sentence, e.g. *to steal something (from somebody); to rob a place,* e.g. a bank.

KEY

Person	*Crime*
burglar	burglary
criminal	crime
thief	theft
robber	robbery
rapist	rape
shoplifter	shoplifting
smuggler	smuggling
murderer	murder
pickpocket	pickpocketing
drug dealer	drug dealing

 Exercise 3

KEY

poLICE OFFicer DRUG SMUggling
comMUNity poLIcing poLICE STAtion ARMED RObbery CRIminal investiGAtion

Ask students to use these words in full sentences, e.g. *The police officer left the police station to investigate a case of armed robbery/drug smuggling. The police officer said he preferred criminal investigation to community policing.*

TAPESCRIPT

Listen to the following nouns and copy them, writing the stressed syllables in capital letters.

police officer, drug smuggling, community policing, police station, armed robbery, criminal investigation

TALKING POINT

Question 1: Ask students to suggest parts of police work which might be unpleasant, e.g. attending a fatal accident, or dangerous, e.g. controlling riots/attempting to disarm terrorists.

Question 2: Ask if students think that police handle everyone in the same way, e.g. young people/children/women/'down-and-outs'/football fans, and whether students feel the police are prejudiced against any section of society.

Question 3: Raise the question of what sort of image TV series such as 'Hill Street Blues' and 'Miami Vice' give the police.

 LISTENING

Preparation

Refer to the opening paragraph about Errrol coming off night shift. Ask students if they know what shifts police work, i.e. the hours of the shifts. Remind students of the first question of 'Talking point'. Ask them if the police officer in the interview agrees with them about the most unpleasant part of the job. Write on the board and explain: *fatal accident, child abuse, beat a victim, snatch, abandon, stray* (of animals), *emaciated, limb, defenceless.*

KEY

The early shift = 6 a.m. – 2 p.m.
The late shift = 2 p.m. – 10 p.m.
The night shift = 10 p.m. – 6 a.m.

The worst part of her job is dealing with crimes concerning a) children, especially cases of child abuse; b) the elderly, when they are victims of robbery; and c) animals, when they are abandoned and starving (emaciated). She feels most sympathy for these three categories because the children haven't hurt anybody, the elderly are defenceless and the animals don't ask for harsh treatment.

TAPESCRIPT

Listen to a police officer talking about her work. Look at your Students' Book and follow the instructions.

INTERVIEWER: Now you spent, erm, quite some time, erm, as a beat officer or on the beat. Is that right?
OFFICER: That's right.
INTERVIEWER: When you were training?
OFFICER: Yes.
INTERVIEWER: How long was that for?
OFFICER: Approximately three and a half years before I specialised as such.
INTERVIEWER: And, and what would that involve?
OFFICER: It involved doing shift system which is early, lates, nights.
INTERVIEWER: Early, lates and nights. Can you explain what, what hours they are?
OFFICER: The early shift starts at six o'clock in the morning till two o'clock in the afternoon. Then you've got the late shift from two o'clock in the afternoon to ten o'clock at night. And then night duty from ten p.m. until six a.m., because obviously all stations have to be manned twenty-four hours a day.
INTERVIEWER: Is there any particular aspect of the work that you prefer?
OFFICER: Not really, erm. You do have your preferences. I mean, if it's pouring down with rain you prefer to be in a car than walking, but somebody has to do it.
INTERVIEWER: When you're out on the beat how often in fact, erm, do incidents occur that require your, erm, intervention?
OFFICER: You can't guarantee what's going to happen when you come on. You can come on duty thinking oh, you know: 'What a great day' and you end up with something terrible happening, erm. Every day's different.

INTERVIEWER: Have you ever had anything terrible or dangerous or unpleasant happening to you?
OFFICER: One or two things, yes. You obviously get involved with fatal accidents even just as a police officer, as a P.C.
INTERVIEWER: Would you say that was the worst part of the job, having to attend at fatal accidents?
OFFICER: For myself, no. They're not as bad as some things.
INTERVIEWER: But it's obviously, you say it's not what you consider the most unpleasant part. What is?
OFFICER: I think the worst things that you get involved with are the children, the elderly and the animals. You get cases of child abuse, children that have been beaten by parents, abandoned by parents. Again, you get the elderly people who are victims of robberies, snatches, where they've had their property literally wrenched from their hands or their necks. They're victims of burglaries. And then you get the other side of it where you get the dogs abandoned on the streets. You get the strays come in. They're emaciated some of them, erm. They've got broken limbs. And really those three categories … whereas obviously you get adult victims of crime that you can feel sympathy for … you tend to think: 'Well, the kids haven't hurt anybody, the elderly are, are defenceless and the dogs don't ask for the harsh treatment,' so I think your heart tends to go out to those groups, rather than the other side of society, although you are always sympathetic to the victims, but those are the three main things that, that get to you.

EXTRA ACTIVITIES

1 Crime and punishment

Duplicate the following list of beginnings of sentences or write them on the board. Divide the class into small groups. Set a time limit of five minutes for the groups to complete the sentences with an appropriate verb in the passive.

1 In Sweden children are not allowed to be …
2 Enemies of the French revolution were …
3 Until a few years ago, murderers in England were …
4 In the USA murderers are …
5 If you park your car in the wrong place it may be …
6 If you have a TV but not a licence in Britain, you may be …
7 In some schools in Britain boys are still …
8 If you are caught selling or using drugs at school, you will be …
9 Foreigners who commit crimes may be …

After the set time, give students a jumbled key to sort and match.

KEY
1 beaten/hit
2 executed/guillotined
3 hanged
4 electrocuted/gassed/shot
5 towed away/clamped
6 fined
7 caned
8 expelled
9 deported

2 Guess the activity

One student thinks of (or mimes) a particular duty of a police officer which the students have to guess in under twenty Yes/No questions.

3 So you want to join the police?

Students work in groups for two minutes to make a list of what they consider are the five most important qualities needed to be a police officer. After deciding on a final list with the other groups, students each make up a suitable advertisement to attract recruits into the police force.

UNIT 42 GRAMMAR
Reported speech (1)

PRESENTATION

With books closed ask a student:

T: Where do you live?
S: I live on North Street.
T: (to class). What did I ask him?
S: You asked him: 'Where do you live?'
T: Yes, I asked him where he lived. And what did he say?
S: (He said:) 'I live on North Street.'
T: That's right. He said he lived on North Street.

Write both the direct and the reported questions and statements on the board and label them.

Photograph

Ask students what Errol is going to do and ask a student to read the speech bubble aloud. Ask a different student: *What did he say?* and elicit: *He said (that) he spent most of his time playing ice hockey.*

UNIT 42

Look at the sentences

Draw attention to the change in pronoun and possessive adjective, and the optional *that*. Students then look back at the text in Unit 41 and find examples of reported speech. Let them call out the sentences while you write them in two columns on the board, one for reported statements, the other reported questions. Use these sentences to highlight the relevant points in the *Focus* section. Introduce the concept of tense changes by asking students to give you the direct speech in each case.

FOCUS

Many teachers feel that the need to learn verb tense changes and adverb changes in reported speech is overrated. This is because, in everyday speech, we often report speech very soon after it is spoken, and there is consequently no need for changes in tense or adverb, e.g. *John rang – he says he's coming tomorrow* or *John rang – he said he's coming tomorrow* or *John rang – he said he was coming tomorrow*. All these ways of reporting are possible.

However, when reporting speech some time after the words were spoken, e.g. when recounting an incident in the past, the verb tense and time adverb need to be changed, e.g. *... Then John rang and said he was coming the following day. Well, of course he didn't, so I ...* As students will often be required in examinations to 'report from a distance', the tables showing the necessary verb tense changes and other changes are included for reference. Do not expect the students to learn these changes by heart. The most important part for students to become familiar with is the change in word order in reported questions.

PRACTICE

Exercise 1

KEY
1 He told his mother (that) he was going to watch television.
2 She said (that) they had moved to Bristol three years ago/before/previously.
3 She told me (that) she would come at eight o'clock tomorrow/the next day/the following day.
4 She said (that) she had bought a new car.
5 The boy told his teacher (that) he couldn't think of anything to write.
6 They said (that) they were driving the car to France next summer/the following summer.
7 He said (that) he had to get some new glasses.
8 She said (that) she might sell her bicycle.

Exercise 2

Having to recall Errol's answers from memory will give the feeling of being more remote in time.

KEY
1 He said that it was hard to sleep during the day.
2 He said that it was one of the most interesting parts of his job.
3 He said that (normally) he carried a truncheon, handcuffs and a radio.

Exercise 3

 Dialogue

Explain: *initials*, *combination locks* and *computer discs*.

Exercise 4

The reporting of the conversation should be treated as an exercise and as a preparation for the writing exercise. In real life, the conversation would be summarised, and the verbs of speaking only used once or twice.

KEY
A: A man came in and said he had lost his briefcase. He asked if one had been handed in that morning.
B: Errol said that it hadn't. He asked the man where he had lost it.
A: He said he had lost it outside his house in Chester Street that morning. He said he had put it on the pavement, and then had driven off and forgotten about it.
A: Errol asked him if he could describe the briefcase/asked him to describe it.
B: The man said it was black leather with a combination lock and it had his initials D.B. on it.
A: Errol asked if there was anything valuable inside it.
B: He said there wasn't, except for a few papers and some computer discs.
A: Errol said that they would let the man know if they heard anything about the briefcase. He asked for the man's name and phone number.

Find out if any students have lost, or had stolen, anything valuable. Encourage the other students to ask them about the incidents.

WRITING

KEY
LOST PROPERTY REPORT

Time: 10 a.m. Date: Monday, 13th June ...

Item missing: one briefcase with personal contents

At approximately 10 a.m. this morning Mr D Barton reported the loss of his briefcase from outside his house in Chester Street. Mr Barton said he had put the briefcase on the pavement, and then had driven off and forgotten about it. The briefcase was black leather with a combination lock and the initials D.B. on it. It contained a few papers and some computer discs.

EXTRA ACTIVITIES

1 Witness in court

In pairs, one student is the witness and the other is the 'suspect'. Each witness first interviews the suspect to find out exactly how he or she spent the previous day. The witnesses must take notes and then assemble at the 'courtroom' to report their interviews with their suspects.

2 Fortune telling

Students work in pairs. One is the fortune teller and the other is the 'client'. The client must think of five questions to ask the fortune teller, who must answer the questions. After the interviews are completed, the pairs must report to the rest of the class the questions asked and the answers received.

UNIT 43 COMMUNICATION
Closing strategies

PRESENTATION

With books closed, ask students to tell you any leave-taking expressions they know and list them on the board. Then ask students for ways of signalling an end to a conversation before actually saying goodbye, e.g. *Goodness, look at the time!* List the expressions they suggest to the left of the leave-taking expressions on the board. Leave the expressions on the board.

The photographs

With books open, ask where the people are and what the relationship is between them. Ask students to roleplay what they think they are saying.

 DIALOGUES

Play the tape of the first dialogue and ask:

What does the boy want to find out? (If the girl is going to Steve's party tonight.)
What excuse does the girl give for leaving? (She says she's got an essay to write before tomorrow.)

Continue with the second dialogue. Ask:

What are the two girls talking about before they realise what time it is? (A problem one of the girls had with her boyfriend.)
What excuse does one of the girls give for leaving? (She says her parents want her home by six o'clock.)

Read and find out

Play the tape again, pausing for students to give you the information in the exercise. Add any new expressions to your list on the board.

Ask students to read the dialogues together in pairs.

FOCUS

Practise the 'signalling' expressions: *Look* and *Listen*, making sure that the students join them to the main sentence. Explain that too much of a pause makes the sentence sound like an order, e.g. *Listen! Look!* Even if the students find it hard to use these expressions naturally, they should be made aware of their function when used by native speakers.

PRACTICE

Exercise 1

Refer to the dialogue again and ask students to notice the responses to the leave-taking expressions. Ask students to look at the list of expressions on the board and to suggest ways of responding to these expressions.

KEY
1d 2c/g 3f 4a 5g/b 6e 7b

Exercise 2

Practise the example conversation. Then allow students time to prepare what they are going to say before starting their conversations.

 LISTENING

Play the tape and ask students to think first where the conversation is taking place and to select the relevant picture. Then play the tape again and ask what relation the speakers are to each other and what they think has been going on before the conversation. Play the extracts again and ask students to concentrate on the language used to end the conversations.

Conversation 1 = Picture b
Conversation 2 = Picture d
Conversation 3 = Picture a
Conversation 4 = Picture c

TAPESCRIPT
Listen to four conversations and match them to the correct pictures in your books.

Conversation 1

Airport announcement: American Airlines announce the departure of flight AA 128 to New York. Passengers please proceed to Gate 25.

BEN:	Listen, I've got to go. They're calling my flight.
DAD:	I want you to phone as soon as you arrive.
BEN:	I will. I promise.
MUM:	Now you take care. And give my love to Sal and Joe.
BEN:	OK. Bye!
MUM/DAD:	Bye! Safe journey!

Conversation 2

CAROL: Shall we watch a video?
TIM: No. We've got to be going.
SUE: Really? Must we?
TIM: Yes, the last bus goes in twenty minutes. Come on.
SUE: Oh, OK. Thanks for the meal.
JOHN: That's OK. Listen, Tim, I'll give you a ring about the Pink Floyd concert next week.
TIM: Fine. See you. Bye.
SUE: Yeah, bye!

Conversation 3

DAVE: Come on. Let's have a last dance.
EMMA: No, I'd better not. Look at the time.
DAVE: Have you really got to go?
EMMA: Yes, my mum will be waiting up for me.
DAVE: Shall I phone you tomorrow?
EMMA: Yes, please.
DAVE: All right, I'll phone you first thing in the morning.
EMMA: OK. Bye!
DAVE: Bye.

Conversation 4

MRS TAYLOR: Well, Kate, I think that's all I have to say. I'll be writing to you as soon as the exam results come out.
KATE: Yes, Mrs Taylor.
MRS TAYLOR: Well … good luck!
KATE: Thank you.
MRS TAYLOR: And have a good summer holiday.
KATE: Yes, I will.
MRS TAYLOR: Now, would you please send in the next person?
KATE: Yes, Mrs Taylor. Goodbye.
MRS TAYLOR: Goodbye, dear.

WRITING

Ask students if they can remember ways of ending letters from Unit 22. Go through the phrases and explain expressions like: *catch the post* and *look after yourself*.

Point out that *love from* is fairly neutral between friends, especially female friends, whereas *All my love* is much stronger, and is reserved for intimate friends or close family.

The letter can be written individually or as a 'chain-letter' in which each student writes a paragraph and passes the letter on to the next person. In the end, each finished letter will be a combination of four students' work. The letter should be corrected by the students who receives it last.

EXAMPLE LETTER

Dear (Terry),

Thank you very much for your letter, which came yesterday. I'm so sorry I haven't written earlier but I have been very busy with my English exams.

Fortunately, the exams are now over. I am enjoying my English classes very much, especially the lessons when we act situations. I think that's fun.

Did I tell you that I have joined a jazz dance class? I go every Monday and Wednesday evening. The teacher used to dance in 'Cats'. She's brilliant. I really enjoy those classes.

How are your parents and Mick? I hope his driving test was successful. How was your holiday in Portugal, by the way? I hear the weather wasn't very good in the Mediterranean this summer.

Well, I'd better stop. It's nearly five thirty and I must catch the post. Give my regards to anyone who knows me and please write back as soon as possible!

Love from

(Annika)

EXTRA ACTIVITIES

1 Farewell game

Divide the class into two teams. Make a list of farewell expressions equal to the number of students in each team. Call out one of the expressions, e.g. *Good luck on Monday!* and a person from either team has to answer appropriately, e.g. *Thanks*. The team member who gives the correct response first wins the point. If the response is wrong, the chance goes to the member of the other team. The winning team is the one whose members respond correctly the most times.

2 Good excuses!

Students work in groups to think of the most plausible excuse for:
- escaping from a conversation with a boring person at a party.
- not going out on a date when the person concerned has invited you three weeks in advance.
- ending a phone conversation with a very talkative aunt/uncle.

Workbook tapescript

Unit 43

Speechwork: Stress and intonation
Closing strategies

Exercise 3

A

Listen to this sentence.
Well, I suppOSE I ought to get ON.

Now listen and repeat.
WELL, I suppOSE I ought to get ON. [bleep]

B

Now you end conversations. Listen to the example.
go back to work
Well, I suppose I ought to go back to work.

Now you do it.
go back to work [bleep]
Well, I suppose I ought to go back to work.
get home [bleep]
Well I suppose I ought to get home.
start making the dinner [bleep]
Well, I suppose I ought to start making the dinner.

C

Listen to this suggestion.
LISten, WHY don't we meet for LUNCH?

Now listen and repeat.
meet for LUNCH? [bleep]
LISTEN, WHY don't we meet for LUNCH? [bleep]

D

Now you make suggestions. Listen to the example.
you come round tonight
Listen, why don't you come round tonight?

Now you do it.
you come round tonight [bleep]
Listen, why don't you come round tonight?
we go for a drink after work [bleep]
Listen, why don't we go for a drink after work?
we see each other on Saturday [bleep]
Listen, why don't we see each other on Saturday?

UNIT 44 GRAMMAR
Reported speech (2)

PRESENTATION

With books closed, ask a student:

T: Would you like some orange juice?
S1: Yes, please./No thank you.
T: What did I offer her?
S2: You offered her some orange juice.
T: Did she accept it or refuse it?
S2: She accepted/refused it.

Present the other verbs from the list in the Focus section in the same way, e.g. *advise*, *ask*, *persuade*, etc.

After the presentation, check that students have understood the meaning of the verbs and how to use them, by asking them at random to use them, e.g.

T: Hannah, remind Roberto to do his homework tonight.
H: Roberto, don't forget to do your homework tonight.
T: What did you do/say?
H: I reminded him to do his homework tonight.

Picture of Errol

With books open, ask students for alternative ways of offering a cup of coffee.

FOCUS

Students can now see how the verbs they have used in the Presentation are grouped together. Some students may be familiar with alternative structures with suggest, e.g. *He suggested that we met ...* or *He suggested that we should meet*. These are more commonly used when the subject of *suggest* is not included in the action suggested, e.g. *I suggested that they met outside the cinema*. Select verbs at random and ask students to make sentences with them. Point out that when a verb (e.g. *introduce*) is followed by two objects, the objects can be in either of the positions shown in the examples.

PRACTICE

Exercise 1

To make this into a game, divide all the sentences of reported speech and all the sentences of direct speech among the students. Call on someone with the letter a) to read out their sentence of direct speech. Then ask the student with the matching reported speech sentence to read that sentence aloud. Try to keep the pace going as as fast as possible.

KEY
1d 2f 3l 4g 5h 6i 7b 8j 9k 10c 11e 12a

Exercise 2

KEY
1 Mike: c   Jane: a
2 Ben: b   Sue: c
3 Mark: a   Mother: b

Exercise 3

KEY
1 Mike invited Jane to go with Greg and him to an open-air pop concert on Saturday.
   Jane accepted the invitation.
2 Ben asked Sue what he should do about his briefcase.
   Sue suggested going to the police station and reporting it. *or*
   Sue suggested that he went to the police station and reported it. *or*
   Sue suggested that he should go to the police station and report it.
3 Mark tried to persuade his mother to let him go to the carnival.
   His mother agreed but warned him not to take a lot of money in case there were pickpockets around.

UNIT 44

 **LISTENING**

Before you listen

Discuss whether babysitting is a peculiarly British or Northern European idea. If students are interested, discuss rates of pay, how to find babysitters, and what things can go wrong when you babysit.

Listen

1 Before they listen, students predict answers to the questions. Write on the board and explain: *turn up* (= to arrive). Play the tape for the first time.

KEY
1 Alan was going to babysit for Paul and his wife on Friday night.
2 Paul and his wife were going to a concert.
3 Alan didn't arrive until after nine.
4 Alan said he had been held up at work.
5 Paul felt really angry.

2 Play the tape again, pausing for students to note the verbs of reporting.

KEY
Verbs of reporting in the order of occurrence:

offered told asked warned (say) apologised said told

TAPESCRIPT
Listen to two people talking about a broken arrangement. Look at your Students' Book and follow the instructions.

MAN: I'm furious with Alan!
WOMAN: Why?
MAN: Well, you remember he offered to babysit for us on Friday night?
WOMAN: Yes?
MAN: Well, he didn't turn up!
WOMAN: What?
MAN: I told him that we were going to a concert and asked him particularly not to come late. I even phoned him the day before and warned him about the traffic on Friday night.
WOMAN: So what happened?
MAN: He didn't turn up till after nine.
WOMAN: What? So you didn't go to the concert?
MAN: No, it was far too late to go anywhere.
WOMAN: What did Alan say? He must have apologised.
MAN: Oh yes, he apologised. He said he had been held up at work.
WOMAN: That's typical of Alan.
MAN: Yes, I was really angry, I can tell you.

WRITING

Write on the board the verbs of reporting from the tape in the order in which they occurred, leaving plenty of space between each. Add a few more key words from the dialogue, e.g. *furious, concert, babysit, phone/day before, turn up, held up*. Ask students to reconstruct the incident orally, sentence by sentence, using the verbs and key words on the board.

SUGGESTED PARAGRAPH
I'm writing this in a very bad mood. You remember Alan? Well, he really let us down the other evening. We had tickets for a wonderful concert and Alan offered to babysit for us. I warned him about the traffic in the early evening and told him to be here in good time. Anyway, I put the children to bed and we were all dressed up and ready to go by seven o'clock. We waited and waited but Alan didn't turn up until 9.30! He apologised and said that he had been held up at work, but I think he just forgot. I was so angry I told him to go home and we haven't spoken to him since. That's the last time I'll ever ask him to babysit for us.

Anyway, how are things with you?

ACT IT OUT

Divide the class into As and Bs. Group the As and Bs together so they can prepare their roles and get help with words or expressions.

Explain that groups should not read the other role.

Pair As and Bs at random and ask students to try to do the roleplay without looking at the rolecards. Record one or two conversations for a later playback session.

SUGGESTED ROLEPLAY
A: Listen, have you heard about the new club called 'The Sound Store'?
B: Yes, I have. It's downstairs at the Electric Cinema, isn't it?
A: That's right. It sounds really good. Do you want to go and try it out this evening?
B: Well, no thanks. A friend of mine was mugged in that part of the city a few weeks ago. It's really dangerous. I don't want to go anywhere near there.
A: It's not dangerous there. You can get mugged anywhere. Anyway, we can get a taxi straight to the club.
B: I don't know.
A: Oh, come on. I really don't want to go alone. It'll be much more fun if we go together. Anyway, Mandi Knight and Summer Romance are playing. Please come.
B: But I've got to go to work early tomorrow and it goes on until 3 a.m.
A: We don't have to be late. We can go just for an hour or so.
B: Oh, O.K, I'll come. But let's not stay too late.
A: Oh thanks, I knew you'd say yes. What shall we wear?

UNITS 44/45

EXTRA ACTIVITIES

1 Noughts and crosses

Divide the class into Team A and Team B. Draw a noughts and crosses grid (3 x 3 squares) on the board and box it in. In each box write a verb of reporting, e.g.

remind	suggest	warn
introduce	ask	explain
apologise	advise	promise

Tell Team A to choose one of these squares and make a correct sentence using the word on that square. Team B must say if the sentence is correct or not. If Team A's sentence is correct, rub the word out and give them a cross in that square. If it is wrong, the word remains where it is and Team B have a chance to put it right. If Team B get it right, write an O in the square where the word was. The object of the game is the same as the original noughts and crosses game: to get three consecutive crosses or noughts either vertically, horizontally or diagonally.

2 Problem page letters

Collect some problem page letters and answers from a magazine. Divide the students into groups. Give one letter and its answer to each group, and ask them to summarise and report back the content of the original letter and its answer, using as many reporting verbs as possible.

UNIT 45 READING
The changing role of the police

PRESENTATION

With books closed, introduce the topic by referring to any recent incident in the news which has involved the police in a violent situation. Introduce or revise the words *demonstration* and *riot*. Copy the headlines from the Students' Book on to the board and discuss possible stories behind them. Explain: *march*, *gang* and *dawn raid*.

COMPREHENSION

> BACKGROUND NOTES
> **Home Counties**: The counties (Surrey, Buckinghamshire, Hertfordshire, etc.) surrounding London.
> **House of Commons**: The lower, but more powerful, of the two parts of the British Parliament. Its members are elected by citizens over eighteen years of age. Compare *House of Lords*.
> **Parliament Square**: The square in front of the British Houses of Parliament.

With books open, students skim read the three articles to find the key words in each which help to identify the headlines, i.e. A: *dawn raids* B: *nurses* C: *armed criminals*.

KEY
1B 2C 3A

Then ask students to read each article carefully and note any unfamiliar words. Ask which article was about:
- removing weapons. (A)
- police plans to protect themselves in the future. (C)
- police behaviour at a demonstration. (B)

VOCABULARY

Point out the use of the preposition *with* after the verb *deal* in Article C. Write the following verbs on the board and ask students to suggest how they are used in a sentence and which prepositions follow them: *prevent, arrest, accuse, sentence, warn, complain, face,* (*to be faced* …).

Encourage student to search the articles for examples of how some of these verbs are used, e.g. *deal with, sentenced to … for, faced with, complained of.*

KEY
1 The police often have to deal with dangerous criminals.
2 The protestors were prevented from entering Parliament Square.
3 The children were warned of/about the dangers of drugs.
4 The criminal was sentenced to five years in prison.
5 She was accused of armed robbery.
6 The nurses complained of/about unnecessary police violence.
7 The demonstrators were arrested outside the US embassy for disturbing the peace.
8 Even on the beat, a police officer might be faced with a dangerous situation.

 ### LISTENING

1 Play the tape as far as: *violence in general in London's underground system* for students to note the information. This may need to be played twice, especially the part which refers to: *robbing passengers at knifepoint.*

KEY
LRT are worried about violence on London's underground. Pop fans are causing the trouble. (They are robbing passengers at knifepoint.)

2 Before playing the rest of the tape, discuss with students how to make underground stations safer at night and list their ideas on the board. Include these words from the tape: *closed-circuit televisions, lookout boxes, alarm buttons.*

Discuss what these are and how they can improve safety. Play the second half of the tape once through without stopping, and a third time, pausing for students to make notes.

KEY

Measures being taken by LRT are:
1. installing better lighting.
2. repainting stations.
3. installing closed-circuit televisions.
4. building special lookout boxes/help points.
5. putting alarm buttons at many points along station platforms.
6. increasing the number of LRT police.

TAPESCRIPT

Listen to a radio news report, look at your Students' Book and follow the instructions.

ANNOUNCER: Today, London Regional Transport announced tough new plans to combat the violence of pop fans who are spreading fear throughout London's underground. Verity Harper reports.

VERITY: People are refusing to use public transport on Saturday nights, say LRT, because they are terrified of pop fans who go through the underground trains robbing passengers at knifepoint. I asked an LRT executive to explain their plans to deal with the problem of violence in general in London's underground system.

SPOKESPERSON: Firstly, we are installing better lighting and repainting the stations to create a friendlier environment. We are placing more closed-circuit televisions at key points along station platforms, particularly near escalators. Then there will be special lookout boxes or 'help points' where station staff will be able to see the maximum number of passengers. As well as these improvements, we are putting alarm buttons at many points along station platforms.
But in the end it comes down to staffing. So we're increasing the number of LRT police, especially on Saturday nights. We are trying to reassure the public that using the transport services isn't as dangerous as they think.

VERITY: This is Verity Harper at LRT's Central Office in London.

TALKING POINT

Ask students to discuss what usually happens at political demonstrations and at big football matches in their own country. How does this compare with Britain?

EXTRA ACTIVITIES

1 Headlines

In groups, students think of suitable headlines to 'shock the world' for front page newspaper articles about the following:
- a famous pop/film star or group.
- sport or the Olympic Games.
- politics or a famous politician.
- the British Royal family.
- the weather.
- fashion.
- any topic of their own choice.

2 The story behind the headlines

Divide the class into groups and give each the same headline, e.g. HEADMASTER IN EXAM SCANDAL or DOG IN CLIFF RESCUE DRAMA.
Each group composes a story to fit the headlines. Alternatively, use one or more of the headlines created in Extra activity 1.

3 A day in the life of ...

Students imagine they are either a nurse or a policeman at the nurses' march mentioned in Article B in the Students' Book. They use the article to write a diary account of the incident.

Workbook tapescript

Unit 45

Exercise 1

Listen to three people describing a demonstration. Look at your book and follow the instructions.

1
Well, it was a really successful day. Thousands of people turned out for it and there was a real feeling of being together and wanting the same thing. The atmosphere during the march was wonderful. We were chatting and singing and the mood was really peaceful. I didn't see any violence. We even exchanged a few jokes with the police. By the end of the day we all felt really positive. Let's hope we achieved something.

2
Well, I didn't know what was happening when I saw all these people marching past. A lot of them were carrying banners and shouting slogans but it took me a while to work out what they were demonstrating about. They looked all right, most of them, but some of them were a bit scruffy and dirty. There were police on either side of the road keeping an eye on everything, but I didn't see any trouble.

3
Well, there was just an enormous mob of people. Some of them were O.K., they were just marching, but some of them were shouting and screaming slogans at us and trying to get the rest of the protestors all worked up and angry. They looked really threatening and I thought they were going to start throwing things at us. I think a few were just hooligans who wanted an excuse to be aggressive. Anyway, I was certainly glad when it was all over.

UNIT 46 GRAMMAR
Past perfect simple

PRESENTATION

With books closed, make up an anecdote similar to the following:

I was very happy this morning. Last night I couldn't find my glasses anywhere. I searched and searched but I couldn't find them. Then this morning I was emptying the wastepaper basket and suddenly I found them. I had dropped them in the basket my mistake!

Ask: *What did I lose yesterday? Where did I find them? How did they get there?*

Draw a time line on the board and mark the events in the anecdote to illustrate the relationship between the past tense and the past perfect, e.g.

PAST	PAST		NOW
Monday 8 p.m. I dropped my glasses into the wastepaper basket by mistake.	Monday 10 p.m. I searched for the glasses.	Tuesday 8 a.m. I found the glasses in the wastepaper basket.	

Say and/or write: *The glasses were in the wastepaper basket because I had dropped them in it by mistake.*

BACKGROUND NOTES
Wembley Stadium: A large sports stadium and exhibition complex in Wembley, north-west London, which holds over 77,000 people. It is the main venue for important football matches, and is regularly used for pop concerts and similar events.
The Cup Final: This football match is always held at Wembley Stadium in May every year. It is the final match between the two teams which have won their way to the top of English football's principal knockout competition.

Refer to the Cup Final tickets and give the background to the Cup Final if the students are interested. Mention how difficult it is to get tickets for the Final and how lucky Errol and his girlfriend were to get them.

Put the events in order

KEY
Judy's father gave Errol and Judy two tickets for the Cup Final at Wembley.
They left the tickets at home.
They caught an early train to London.
They spent the morning shopping.
Errol and Judy arrived at Wembley Stadium.

What's the difference in meaning?

In Sentence 1, Errol was feeling pleased and then he bought the jacket. In Sentence 2, he was feeling pleased because he had bought himself a new jacket, i.e. he bought the jacket first.

FOCUS

Remind students of the use of the past perfect in reported speech.

PRACTICE

Exercise 1

Explain *cross* (adjective), *cut them off*, and *frontier*.

KEY
1 Judy and Errol were tired because they had spent the morning shopping.
2 He failed his exams because he hadn't worked hard enough during the year.
3 Mike was cross because he had left his wallet at home.
4 The telephone company cut them off because they hadn't paid their telephone bill.
5 They couldn't cross the frontier because they had left their passports at home.
6 She couldn't read the sign because she had lost her glasses.

Exercise 2

EXAMPLE SENTENCES
1 When I went to pay, I realised that I had left my purse/wallet/credit cards at home/I had lost my wallet, etc.
2 When he arrived at the station, he saw that the train had gone/that he had missed the train.
3 When they got home, they found that they had forgotten their door keys/the cat had escaped.
4 Soon after the wedding, she knew that she had made a terrible mistake/married the wrong man.
5 When I asked about the mess on the floor, she said that the children had been making cakes/painting/playing with their toys/they had had a party the night before.

UNIT 46

Draw the class together to compare sentences and choose the best ending for each sentence.

🔊 LISTENING

The notes in the 'Writing' exercise are based on the listening passage. To avoid students following these while they listen, it is suggested that the listening is conducted with books closed.

Ask if any students have ever crossed the English Channel by sea, and if they know the names of any British channel ports, e.g. *Dover, Folkestone, Portsmouth, Newhaven, Southampton*. Introduce the word *backpack*.

Write the questions from the Students' Book on the board. Explain that Errol's brother speaks with quite a broad West Country accent. Play the tape.

KEY
1 He was going to Austria to work in a hotel for the skiing season.
2 Michael missed the ferry because someone stole his passport and ticket from his backpack while he was drinking his tea.

TAPESCRIPT
Listen to Errol's young brother, Michael, talking to a friend about something which happened to him recently. Look at your Students' Book and answer the questions.

GIRL: Hi, Michael. It's a surprise to see you. I thought you were going off to Europe.
MICHAEL: I was. But things didn't work out.
GIRL: Really? What happened?
MICHAEL: Well, a hotel in Austria had offered me a job for the skiing season.
GIRL: Great!
MICHAEL: Right!
GIRL: Are you a good skier then?
MICHAEL: Yeah, not bad. I've been on lots of school ski trips. Anyway, I was all set to go and I took a train to Dover to catch the ferry to France.
GIRL: I know. You got on the wrong train!
MICHAEL: No, nothing as simple as that. I got to Dover quite early and went to have a cup of tea.
GIRL: And you fell asleep and missed the ferry!
MICHAEL: No! Worse than that. I put my backpack on the floor beside me while I was drinking my tea.
GIRL: And you forgot it!
MICHAEL: No! How could I forget my backpack! I finished my tea. I got up and went to the ferry. And when they asked me for my ticket and passport, I looked in the side pocket of my backpack and …
GIRL: I know! They weren't there!
MICHAEL: Right! Someone had taken them from my backpack while I was having tea.
GIRL: What on earth did you do?
MICHAEL: Well, I couldn't get on the ferry. I had to go back to London and go to the Passport Office about a new passport. I tell you, it was a real drag.
GIRL: But what about the job in Austria?
MICHAEL: You can imagine. They couldn't wait, so they took someone else. My lucky day, eh?

WRITING

SUGGESTED STORY
Michael was very excited because he had got a job for the skiing season in a resort in Austria. He was a good skier because he had skiied a lot at school. He went by train to Dover, and because he (had) arrived early, he went to a café to get something to drink. He put his backpack beside his chair while he was drinking his tea. When he went to catch the midnight ferry to France, he found to his horror that he had no ticket or passport. He realised that someone had stolen them.

EXTRA ACTIVITIES

1 Continue the story

Students give a sentence which must contain a verb in the past perfect tense to add to each of the following 'stories', e.g.
– *When I got to the party, there was nobody there.* (I had written the wrong day in my diary.)
– *When we finally got to the tiger cage, the door was wide open.* …
– *The child was sitting on the floor crying.* …
– *John was sweeping up some pieces of glass on the kitchen floor.*
– *I woke up screaming. But then I realised it was all right.* …

2 Write your own story

Write the following outline of a story on the board. Students work in groups to supply the missing information. They must use a past perfect tense when explaining or describing.

A WELCOME SURPRISE!
I woke up feeling depressed.
(Explain why.)
I looked out of the window at the pouring rain.
(Describe what the weather had been like recently.)
I went downstairs to the kitchen. It was in a terrible state.
(Explain why.)
I left for work and to my surprise when I got there, everyone was cheering and clapping.
(Explain why.)

3 Once upon a time …

Students work in groups and make notes about a well-known folk-tale, fairy story or legend, e.g. 'Cinderella', 'The Sleeping Beauty', 'The Little Mermaid', etc. They use the notes to tell the story, sentence by sentence, in a chain. Explain that the tense they will use most frequently will be the past simple but that they must try to find an occasion to use the past perfect at least once.

Workbook tapescript

Unit 46

Speechwork: Pronunciation
The past perfect

Exercise 4

A

Listen to this sentence.
They'd left the tickets at home.

Now listen and repeat.
they'd [bleep]
They'd left the tickets at home. [bleep]

B

Now you say sentences with contractions.
Listen to the example.
He had bought the tickets.
He'd bought the tickets.

Now you do it.
He had bought the tickets. [bleep]
He'd bought the tickets.
I had had a terrible day. [bleep]
I'd had a terrible day.
She had been at the airport for three hours. [bleep]
She'd been at the airport for three hours.
We had gone to bed late. [bleep]
We'd gone to bed late.

Exercise 5

Look at your book, listen and tick the sentence which you hear.

Example: They've lived here for three years.

1 Had you met her before?
2 We've had a lovely holiday.
3 She'd worked there for a long time.
4 They'd walked all the way.
5 They hurt themselves.

UNIT 47 TOPIC
Mysteries and thrillers

PRESENTATION

With books closed, ask students if they have read any of Agatha Christie's novels, or seen any films/TV series based on her books. Ask if they know the names of the detectives she created.

The background newspaper

With books open, ask students to scan the newspaper to say:
- when it was issued.
- what the sensational news story of the day was.
- who the story involved.
- who they think the person in the portrait is.

Text

Ask students to read the first paragraph only to find out:
- when Agatha Christie died.
- the names of two of her detectives.
- why she is popular.
- how much is known about her private life.

Students read the questions in Exercise 1 and tell you what they learn about Agatha Christie from the questions, and also what they don't know, e.g. they know that she disappeared, that she was distressed, that she had a companion called Carlo, etc. but they don't know why or how she disappeared, or where she went. Students read the rest of the text about Agatha Christie silently and answer the questions in Exercise 1.

Exercise 1

KEY
1 On Friday, 3rd December 1926.
2 Because she had found out that her husband was having an affair with another woman and wanted a divorce.
3 She told her companion that she wanted a day alone.
4 She found that the garage doors had been left open and that the maids were looking frightened.
5 Mrs Christie had come downstairs, had got into her car and had driven off quickly without saying anything to anybody.
6 The police found Agatha's car in a ditch with its lights on but there was no trace of Agatha.
7 The newspapers suggested that she had committed suicide, been kidnapped, run away with a lover, or even planned the whole thing as a publicity stunt.
8 Agatha reappeared in Harrogate in Yorkshire ten days later.
9 He said that she had lost her memory.

Exercise 3

If you prefer, write key words on the board instead.

Exercise 4

SUGGESTED ANSWERS
1 No, I don't. I think she planned it very carefully in order to make problems for her husband.
2 I think she met a friend secretly, and went in her car to a small village in Yorkshire where no one knew her.

3 Maybe it made her marriage worse. He was probably very angry with her and continued to see his lover.

VOCABULARY

After matching the books with their titles, ask students if they can name any real books in the same categories.

KEY

a detective story	Mystery at Highview House
a biography	The life of Jane Austen
an autobiography	Mainly Me, Myself and I
a thriller	Fear Strikes at Midnight
a travel book	In the steps of Marco Polo
a romantic novel	Long Lost Love
a collection of short stories	'Tramp' and other stories

TALKING POINT

Go through each point, elaborating where necessary. Point out that *ending* is used to describe the end of a story, film or play. Ask students to narrow down the list to the five most important features. Give some suitable sentence openers: *I think it's much more important to have a ... than a ..., I don't think it's necessary to have ..., I much prefer books which have ...*

WRITING

Linking devices

Provide a few more examples of your own, in contexts which are relevant to your students.

Exercise 1

Ask students first to note which of the sentences has two different subjects (number 4). Explain again that this is the only sentence in which *in spite of + -ing* cannot be used. Students can rephrase the other three sentences in two ways.

KEY

1 Although Carlos suspected that Agatha would not return, he waited up anxiously all night. In spite of suspecting that ..., Carlo waited up...
2 In spite of searching everywhere, they did not find Mrs Christie.
   Although they searched ..., they did not ...
3 Although Agatha Christie knew about her husband's affair with another woman, she still loved him.
   In spite of knowing about ..., Agatha Christie still ...
4 Although her husband said that she had lost her memory, nobody knows the truth.

Exercise 2

Students choose a book or film to write about. Before they write, ask them to say if there was anything they didn't like about the book/film. Show how a critical comment can be linked to, and contrasted with, a positive comment, e.g. *Although I thoroughly enjoyed the film, I thought the ending was rather weak.*

EXTRA ACTIVITIES

1 Detective game

Explain that to be a good detective you have to have an eye for detail. Find a wall chart/poster containing a lot of detail. Students look at this for thirty seconds. Remove the picture and ask detailed questions about it, e.g. *Where was the man with the moustache sitting? How many children were standing at the bus stop?* etc.

2 Unsolved mysteries

Students research information and write about one of the following unsolved mysteries: The Bermuda Triangle, The Loch Ness Monster, The Abominable Snowman, The Lost City of Atlantis, Shangri-la.

Workbook tapescript

Unit 47

Exercise 3

Look at your book and listen to the book reviews. Write which type of book the reviewers are talking about.

1
It was so exciting that I couldn't put it down until it was finished. There's a journey which is full of narrow escapes and terrible things, and when that's over, they reach the lost city where they find more danger still.

2
The writer obviously knows the prince and his family very well and provides us with all sorts of fascinating information about their day-to-day life. And he gives us a surprisingly honest description of the prince's ideas and beliefs and events in his life that formed these ideas.

3
Well, when they first meet, they know they want to be together forever, but it's not that easy. There are all sorts of obstacles in their way. Anyway, I won't tell you if their love wins through in the end. You can read it and find out.

4
This collection shows the writer at her best. The stories are very varied but they all share the poetic quality of her prose.

5
The plot is both exciting and surprising. Our hero doesn't find out who committed the murder until the last few pages. I bet when you read it, you'll be as surprised as I was. Anyway, I won't spoil it for you by giving you any ideas.

6
They make it sound like a wonderful country to visit. There are beautiful descriptions of the unspoilt countryside and of the warmth and hospitality of the people.

7
The stories she tells of her childhood are wonderful to read and I found they brought back all kinds of memories for me too. She's an unusual ability to remember the smallest details of her past.

UNIT 48 COMMUNICATION
Expressing regrets

PRESENTATION

With books closed, show a copy of a newspaper or the equivalent of the Radio/TV Times. Point to a film or programme and say: (*Name of programme*) *is on tonight but I'm going out. I'd like to watch it but I haven't got a video (recorder). I wish I had.*

Ask:
T: Have I got a video recorder?
S: No, you haven't.

Write on the board:

PRESENT
I wish I had a video recorder (but I haven't).

Now say: *I'm a bit upset today. Yesterday I bought a very expensive pair of shoes and after wearing them all day I realised they were too small. I wish I hadn't bought them now.*

Ask:
T: Did I buy some shoes yesterday?
S: Yes, you did.
T: What was wrong with them?
S: They were too small.
T: That's right. I wish I hadn't bought them.

Write on the board:

PAST
I wish I hadn't bought these shoes (but I did).

Photograph

With books open but with the dialogue covered, ask about the people. Ask:
– who and where they are.
– why the man looks tense and worried.
– what they are saying to each other.

DIALOGUE

Explain: *broke down*, *record*, *regret*. Students note sentences beginning with *I wish* and say which of these refers to the present time and which to the past.

Listen and answer the questions

KEY
1 Because the bus broke down.
2 No, he doesn't.
3 Because he hadn't got a car.
4 She feels tired because she went to bed very late last night.
5 Because she hasn't got a video recorder.

FOCUS

In order to sound plaintive, the students should use a fall-rise intonation, e.g.

I wish I lived nearer you.

What's the difference in meaning?

In Sentence 1, the speaker is complaining about a present habitual situation, where the boy doesn't write. In Sentence 2, the speaker is talking about a situation in the past where the boy never wrote any letters.

You may also like to introduce the structure: *I wish he/she/they/you wouldn't ...* when used to complain about annoying habits, e.g. *I wish you wouldn't smoke in your bedroom. I wish he wouldn't talk so much. I wish he'd phone when he's going to be late back.*

Ask students to supply a few more from their own experience of friends' and relatives' behaviour.

PRACTICE

Exercise 1

Explain that in reality it is unnecessary to add the *but ...* part of the sentence. Students do so here so that they understand when a wish refers to the present or to the past.

KEY
1 I wish I lived nearer town, but I don't.
2 I wish I was good at tennis, but I'm not.
3 I wish I'd bought some warmer clothes, but I didn't.
4 I wish I hadn't lent her my bike, but I did.
5 I wish I didn't live in the country, but I do.
6 I wish I could speak German, but I can't.

Exercise 2

Explain that students are now going to concentrate on wishes for the present. They make their complaints in note form first, choosing from the headings given, e.g.

JOB: don't earn enough money
STUDIES: too much homework

When students have finished, collect and write on the board all the complaints in note form under the separate headings. If students have already written full sentences instead of notes, omit the next exercise.

Exercise 3

Students convert the notes on the board into wishes, according to the example. Stress that the verb must be changed to the past tense.

EXAMPLE SENTENCES
JOB: I wish I earned more money.
FRIENDS AND SOCIAL LIFE: I wish I had a car. I wish my girlfriend didn't live so far away.
HOME LIFE: I wish I had my own room.
APPEARANCE: I wish I had thicker hair.
ABILITIES: I wish I could speak English better.
DAILY ROUTINE: I wish I didn't have to get up so early.

Exercise 4

Students now practise wishes about the past.

Give an example of something in your past life that you regret. Give the example using *I regret* ... first, and then convert it into a past wish, e.g. *I regret buying that expensive car. I wish I hadn't bought that expensive car.*

Write both sentences on the board.

After completing the exercise, ask students if there is anything they regret about their past lives, or if they identify with any of the regrets listed in the book.

KEY
1 I wish I'd worked harder at school.
2 I wish I hadn't given up piano lessons.
3 I wish I'd read more books.
4 I wish I'd taken up acting.
5 I wish I'd got to know my grandparents better before they died.
6 I wish I'd travelled when I had the opportunity.
7 I wish I hadn't gone straight into work from school.
8 I wish I hadn't spent all my money on records and clothes.

With a class of young students who might not identify with some of these regrets, make up a different list of regrets on the board, e.g.
– eating so much last night
– not getting tickets for the ... concert
– starting to smoke.

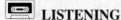 **LISTENING**

Refer to Unit 1 'Vocabulary' exercise to remind students of words to do with education, e.g. 'A' levels, *university*, *degree*, *pass*, *grades*. Write on the board and explain: *Modern Languages*, *easy option*, *revision*.

Read the rubric and ask what they think the young man regrets.

KEY
He chose to do Modern Languages at 'A' level.
He didn't do Science 'A' levels.
He studied Modern Languages at university.
He didn't change subjects at university.
His parents persuaded him to carry on.
He listened to his parents.

He expresses the regrets in the following ways:

I went to university to study the modern languages. Well that was a mistake.
I shouldn't have done the 'A' levels. I should have done Science.
I could have changed but my parents persuaded me to carry on ... and I listened to them, which I shouldn't have done.
The only option I've got in the future ... is to teach, which doesn't make me very happy.

The regrets could be expressed in this way:

He wishes he hadn't chosen to do Modern Languages at 'A' level.
He wishes he had done Science 'A' levels.
He wishes he hadn't studied Modern Languages at university.
He wishes he had changed subjects at university.
He wishes his parents hadn't persuaded him to carry on with Modern Languages.
He wishes he hadn't listened to his parents.
He wishes he hadn't started a teacher training course.

TAPESCRIPT
Listen to a young man talking about his university career. What does he regret about his education so far? Listen again, and note the different ways in which he expresses these regrets.

Er, when I was at school, erm, I was good at both Modern Languages and Science, er, so I had a bit of a problem to decide which one to do. Well, I chose to do Modern Languages because I was good at them and I figured that, erm, it would be the easy option really. I wouldn't have to do much revision, er. So I got my Modern Language 'A' levels. I got French, German and Spanish. And I went to university to study Modern Languages.

Well, that was a mistake. I shouldn't have done the 'A' levels in the first place. I should have ... I should've done Science, because I was about half-way through the first year at university doing Modern Languages when I got bored with it. I didn't like it. Erm, and, I also realised that a Science degree was going to be much more use to me in the future than a Modern Languages degree was.

Er, well I could've changed course at the end of the first year but my parents persuaded me to, er, carry on with Modern Languages. I don't know why, but they did, and I listened to them, which I shouldn't have done. So, I carried on doing Modern Languages and eventually, at the end of the course, I got a third class degree. It means I just ... only just passed.

Erm, and, right now I'm doing a teacher-training course and instead of the bright future in the sciences which I could've done, because I was good at it, er, all that really faces me – the only option I've really got in the future with this ... Modern Language degree – is to teach, which doesn't make me very happy.

WRITING

Students choose an opening line which interests them. Those who choose the same opening line discuss their ideas for the story in groups. Point out that the tenses which will be required most are the past simple, the past continuous and the past perfect. Explain that the story need not be more than 200 words long and that the last sentence must contain the climax.

TALKING POINT

Ask the questions to the class as a whole. Some of the differences which students may mention are: colour, size, privacy, simplicity of design, ease of cleaning, expense to install. Help students with any words or phrases they do not know. Ask them to compare telephone boxes in their own country with the modern one in the picture.

Encourage students to expand their *I wish* statements and to explain why they dislike the present situation. Introduce the word *nostalgic*, if appropriate.

EXTRA ACTIVITY

Funny captions

Collect, or ask students to collect, pictures from magazines, etc. of people in unusual situations, as strange as possible. Students write funny captions or thought bubbles for the pictures, using *I wish ...* The captions can be attached to the pictures.

 Workbook tapescript

Unit 48

Speechwork: Stress and intonation
Expressing regrets

Exercise 3

A
Listen to this sentence.
I WISH the office was NEARer the STAtion.

Now listen and repeat.
NEARer the STAtion. [bleep]
I WISH the office was NEARer the STAtion. [bleep]

B
Now you make sentences.
Listen to the example.

I don't live in a big city.
I wish I lived in a big city.

Now you do it.
I don't live in a big city. [bleep]
I wish I lived in a big city.
I can't drive. [bleep]
I wish I could drive.
I don't have a good job. [bleep]
I wish I had a good job.

C
Listen to this sentence.
I WISH I hadn't gone to BED so LATE.

Now listen and repeat.
gone to BED so LATE [bleep]
I WISH I hadn't gone to BED so LATE. [bleep]

D
Now you make sentences.
Listen to the example
I didn't go to the party.
I wish I'd gone to the party.

Now you do it.
I didn't go to the party. [bleep]
I wish I'd gone to the party.
I failed my exams. [bleep]
I wish I hadn't failed my exams.
You saw that letter. [bleep]
I wish you hadn't seen that letter.

UNIT 49 GRAMMAR
Third conditional *if* clauses

Notes on the structure

The concept of the third conditional is relatively easy to understand, but it is often one of the most difficult ones for students to produce fluently. There are so many grammatical elements, all of which are important, that students are forced to concentrate on the production of sentences syllable-by-syllable. For this reason, the structure needs continually reviewing.

Students should be familiar with the pattern: *might/could/must have* + past participle, so the introduction of the third conditional *would have* is a logical next step. However, some students tend to forget the *'d* (= *had*) in the *if* clause and others will use *would have* in both clauses. Although this is sometimes spoken by native speakers, it is only done so in contracted form, e.g. *If I'd've known, I'd have told you.* Therefore, it is safer to tell students that it is ungrammatical to use *would have* in the *if* clause.

Photograph

Ask students to describe what is happening. Elicit or explain the words: *traffic warden, (parking) ticket, fine* and *double yellow line.* Students read the speech bubbles and answer the questions. Explain the meaning of *caught* in the driver's 'thought bubble'.

What's the difference in meaning?

In Sentence 1, the speaker is giving advice about a general hypothetical situation, whereas in Sentence 2, the speaker is talking about a specific situation that has already happened in the past, i.e. in Sentence 1, the person may not have parked anywhere yet, but in Sentence 2 the person did park, but on a meter.

FOCUS

Check the concept of the structure by asking questions about each sentence, e.g. *Did you park on a meter?/Did you get a ticket?* Rephrase the facts and lead in to the conditional, e.g. *You didn't park on a meter so you got a fine, but if you had parked ... you wouldn't have got ...*

PRACTICE

Exercise 1

Allow students time to think about these sentences before writing. Point out that the verb changes when the sentence is changed into a conditional sentence. Negative verbs become positive. Positive verbs become negative.

If students find this exercise difficult, supply the first half of the sentence (the *if* clause) yourself, and ask them to supply the main clause. Then go through the exercise again. Start with the main clause and ask students to supply the *if* clause. In this way, students will become familiar with the idea that conditional sentences can be reversed.

KEY
1 If I hadn't borrowed the money, I wouldn't have been able to buy the bike
2 If I'd/I had caught the bus, I wouldn't have been late for work.
3 If I hadn't watched the late-night film on television, I wouldn't have overslept.
4 If I'd/I had worked hard at school, I would have got to university.
5 If we'd/we had been able to find a babysitter, we'd/we would have gone to the party.
6 If she hadn't gone out with wet hair, she wouldn't have caught a cold.

Exercise 2

Note that in Sentences 2 and 3, students do not need to change the tenses in the *if* clause, and that in Sentence 5, they will need to use the continuous form of the verb. In Sentence 4, students need to assume that the day is nearly over, i.e. conceptually in the past, otherwise a mixed conditional is necessary, e.g. *If I hadn't eaten so much last night, I wouldn't feel so awful today.* Practise one or two sentences of this type before students start the exercise.

KEY
1 If you hadn't reminded me about Jack's birthday, I'd have forgotten about it.
2 If I'd left earlier, I wouldn't have missed the train.
3 If I'd taken more money with me, I would have/could have bought that jacket.
4 If I hadn't eaten so much last night, I wouldn't have felt so awful today.
5 If you hadn't been wearing seatbelts, you might have got hurt.
6 If the car hadn't broken down, I would have/could have gone to the party.

 LISTENING

Explain: *dropped off, trace* and *vanish into thin air.* Remind the students that the last expression was in the Agatha Christie text in Unit 47.

KEY
1 He was carrying a briefcase full of money/bank notes.
2 He'd been to the bank.
3 He got out at the London Hilton Hotel.
4 He discovered he had left the briefcase with all the money it in on the back seat of the taxi. He called the police.
5 He drove off with all the money and vanished into thin air.

TAPESCRIPT
Listen to two people talking about an incident which happened recently in London, involving a businessman and a taxi driver. Look at your Students' Book and answer the questions.

JOHN: Did you read the story about that businessman who left his briefcase in the back of the taxi with thousands of pounds in it?
WENDY: No.
JOHN: It was in the papers last week. Apparently, the businessman had picked up £300,000 in notes from a bank and had hailed a taxi ...
WENDY: So he had the bank notes in his briefcase?
JOHN: Yes. He was dropped off at the London Hilton Hotel and then he remembered the briefcase. He'd left it on the back seat of the taxi. He called the police but they

couldn't trace the taxi or the driver.
WENDY: Had the taxi driver gone off with the money?
JOHN: Yes, he'd taken the lot and vanished into thin air.

TALKING POINT

1 Treat the first question in a light-hearted way: the object is not to test who is honest or dishonest, but to stimulate discussion.
2 Encourage use of: *might have/could have/must have* in the discussion.
3 Try to elicit: *I would have wanted to know/I would have asked the man why he had so much money on him and what he wanted it for.*

READING

Ask if students have ever been on an aeroplane when the flight has been extremely bumpy and if they were frightened. Then ask what the physical effects of fear are.

Exercise 1

Students look at the questions while reading the article. Explain: *collapse, strap themselves in, turbulent, asthma* and *panic*.

KEY
1 Sixty-five-year-old Ivan Kowalski.
2 He collapsed from lack of oxygen on a flight to Warsaw. The plane had flown into a storm and he had panicked. This had brought on a bad attack of asthma.
3 A doctor on board helped him by giving him oxygen.

Exercise 2

Students discuss possible endings to the conditional sentences, based on the article.

SUGGESTED ANSWERS
1 The flight wouldn't have been so bumpy if the plane hadn't flown into a storm.
2 If Mr Kowalksi hadn't panicked, he wouldn't have had an asthma attack and collapsed.
3 Mr Kowalski might have died if there hadn't been a doctor on board the plane.
4 The doctor wouldn't have been able to help him if there hadn't been oxygen on board.

Ask if students have ever been on board a ship or plane in an emergency when a doctor has been needed.

WRITING

Groups work on the details behind the story. Prompt ideas by asking:

Where was the boy rescued from?
How had he got there?
Why was he there?
How long did he have to wait before help came?
what did he say when the helicopter came?

Each member of the group should take notes in preparation for the writing. When the group is satisfied with the outline of the story, one person gives an oral summary. Students then write their story for homework. Arrange for members of the same group to exchange their stories for comment before handing them in.

EXTRA ACTIVITIES

1 The dinner party

Write a list of famous, topical names on the board, e.g.

Julia Roberts	*Tom Cruise*
Agatha Christie	*Princess Diana*
Nelson Mandela	*Prince*
André Agassi	*Whitney Houston*

Ask the students: *If you had been invited to the dinner party, which two people would you have chosen to sit next to and what would you have talked about?*

2 What would you have done?

Photocopy the situations below. Distribute these among the students. They should choose one to comment on specifically. Students walk around talking to other students about the situations. They should say which one they have chosen and discuss what they would have done in the same situation.

What would you have done?

1 A mother discovered that her son/daughter had been taking hard drugs like heroin and cocaine. She called the police to arrest him/her.
2 A forty-five-year-old man decided he wanted a change in life. He said he had always wanted to write a best-selling novel so he gave up a steady job and bought himself a word-processor.
3 A woman/man discovered that their marriage partner was having an affair with someone else. She/He took an overdose of sleeping tablets but was discovered before the tablets had time to take effect.
4 A person who was on a strict diet to lose weight was invited out to dinner. When the food was served, it was very rich and fattening, but the person ate it, and even asked for more, so as not to appear to be rude.

Workbook tapescript

Unit 49

Speechwork: Pronunciation
The third conditional

UNIT 49/50

Exercise 5

A

Listen to this sentence.
If you'd worked harder, you'd have passed your exams.

Now listen and repeat.
you'd have [bleep]
you'd have passed your exams [bleep]
If you'd worked harder, you'd have passed your exams. [bleep]

Listen to this sentence.
If you'd stayed at home, you wouldn't have been ill.

Now listen and repeat.
wouldn't have [bleep]
you wouldn't have been ill [bleep]
If you'd stayed at home, you wouldn't have been ill. [bleep]

B

Now you make sentences. Listen to the example.

I spent all my money. I didn't go on holiday.
If I hadn't spent all my money, ...
If I hadn't spent all my money, I'd have gone on holiday.

Now you do it.
I spent all my money. I didn't go on holiday.
If I hadn't spent all my money,...
If I hadn't spent all my money, I'd have gone on holiday.
We took a taxi. We weren't late.
If we hadn't taken a taxi, ... [bleep]
If we hadn't taken a taxi, we'd have been late.
She bought a newspaper. She missed the train.
If she hadn't bought a newspaper, ... [bleep]
If she hadn't bought a newspaper, she wouldn't have missed the train.
You didn't ask her. She didn't help you.
If you'd asked her, ... [bleep]
If you'd asked her, she'd have helped you.

UNIT 50 READING
A Judgement in Stone

Introduction

Explain to the students that they are going to read a short extract from a novel by Ruth Rendell, (pronounced RenDELL), a highly-respected British crime novelist. Ask them not to worry about the title of the book until after they have read the extract.

Students read the introduction to the book. Ask:
Why did the Coverdales employ Eunice?
What job did she have?
Did Eunice like the Coverdales? Why not?
What did she do to them? Why?
What do you think her secret could have been?

Encourage students to speculate over the last question.

LISTENING

Play the tape for students to take notes.

KEY

1 Eunice was unable to read or write.
2 Because you know what is going to happen right from the beginning.

Play the tape again and ask what sort of thriller the book could be called and why. Ask if students can remember the word that was used to mean *not able to read or write* (*illiterate*). Ask if they know another word which is similar to this, which is used in a medical context and means that people have difficulty in reading (*dyslexic*).

TAPESCRIPT

Listen to an extract from a radio programme about the latest crime books. The panel are discussing 'A Judgement in Stone' by Ruth Rendell.

TONY: And now 'A Judgement in Stone' by Ruth Rendell. Hilary, perhaps you'd like to introduce the book?
HILARY: Yes, the plot is quite simple. It's about a woman called Eunice Parchman who gets a job as a housekeeper with the Coverdales, a kind and loving middle-class family. But because they discover that she can't read and write, she murders all four of them, quite brutally, I might say.
TONY: And the plot centres around the fact that Eunice Parchman is illiterate and that she'll do anything to stop her secret from being revealed?
HILARY: Yes, and, and what's unusual about his book is that the reader knows what is going to happen right from the beginning. Ruth Rendell takes you inside the mind of her central character so that the interest is not so much in what is going to happen next, but in why Eunice did the terrible things she did.
TONY: So you'd class the book as a sort of psychological thriller?
HILARY: Yes. Yes, I think I would.

Main text: A Judgement in Stone

Play the tape of the text while students follow it in their books.

COMPREHENSION

Some of the answers will need discussion, e.g. Questions 2 and 5. Ask students to explain the significance of the 'plain glass' in the glasses.

KEY
1 A questionnaire to test if you are really in love.
2 Because she didn't want to do the questionnaire and show Melinda that she couldn't read.
3 She wanted Eunice to read out the questions to her and score.
4 She said she hadn't got her glasses.
5 No. They were in her pocket.
6 Taking the glasses out of Eunice's pocket, she looked through them and saw that they were of plain glass.
7 She had noticed that Eunice never read books, looked at newspapers, left notes or got letters.

THINK ABOUT IT

KEY
1 Because she wanted everyone to think that she could read.
2 Because she was embarrassed and terrified. She realised that Melinda was about to discover her secret.

At this point, refer to the title of the book. Ask students what they think is characteristic about things written in stone. Then ask or explain what the words *judge* and *judgement* mean. Ask if they can make a connection between the title and what they have read, i.e. that Eunice Parchman felt that the world would forever judge her as a worthless and wicked person if they knew that she was illiterate, and they they would never forgive or forget this 'sin'.

TALKING POINT

SUGGESTED ANSWERS
1 I would have left the room pretending I wasn't feeling well or I had something important to do.
2 I wouldn't be able to fill in any forms, write a cheque, do homework, help my children to do homework, read a map, road signs or recipes. I couldn't read or answer any letters, etc. My choice of job would be very limited.
3 The first step is for the dyslexic person to admit to the disability, and stop feeling guilty about it. They can then go to special clinics/doctors/counsellors.

Some students may be dyslexic themselves, of may know of people who are, or have been dyslexic, and will be able to offer advice here. You may like to discuss degrees of dyslexia and how widespread this handicap is among children.

STYLE

Explain that it is quite common in speech to omit verbs and articles, but that it is less common in writing. Students should be wary of attempting the same stylistic device in their own writing. Students can study the text in pairs to spot the verbless sentences or you can play the tape again pausing at the relevant places.

KEY
(There was) A firm shake of the head from Eunice.
The tortoise-shell ones (were in her pocket).
(These were) The pair the Coverdales knew as her reading glasses.
(She was) Too busy for what?
(She didn't know) What to do, how to get out of it?

VOCABULARY

Exercise 1

Check the spelling of the last three adverbs and give more practice in spelling changes of this type, e.g.

heavy – heavily, pretty – prettily,
fantastic – fantastically,
romantic – romantically,
joyful – joyfully, wonderful – wonderfully

KEY
nervously, suspiciously, rudely, angrily, enthusiastically, hopefully

Exercise 2

An adverb is often used after the verb *said* to describe the way something is spoken.

Read the sentences with the appropriate intonation. Expect more than one adverb in some cases for each utterance.

KEY
1 'I don't care who you are,' she said rudely/angrily.
2 'Perhaps she'll be on the next train,' she said hopefully/nervously.
3 'Get out of here,' he said angrily/rudely.
4 'Is it my turn now?' he asked nervously/hopefully.
5 'We've got a terrific timetable this term,' said the girl enthusiastically.
6 'What have you put in here?' she asked suspiciously/rudely.

 ### Exercise 3

KEY
NERVously susPICiously RUDEly ANGrily enthusiASTically HOPEfully

TAPESCRIPT
Listen and repeat the adverbs. Notice where the main stress falls and write it in capital letters.

nervously, suspiciously, rudely, angrily, enthusiastically, hopefully

WRITING

Exercise 1

Revise the main rules of punctuation before the students start the exercise, e.g.:

Use capital letters when starting a new sentence,

for names of people and places, titles, days of the week, months and religious holidays.

When punctuating direct speech, use inverted commas, commas, etc.

Use apostrophes for contractions.

Put commas on either side of phrases in parenthesis, or between the subordinate and the main clause.

KEY

The silence endured for a full minute. Melinda, too, had blushed. 'Why didn't you tell us?' she said as Eunice got up. 'We'd have understood. Lots of people are dyslexic. I did a study of it in my last year at school. Miss Parchman, shall I teach you to read? I'm sure it could be fun. I could begin in the Easter holidays.'

Eunice took the two mugs and set them on the draining board. She stood still with her back to Melinda. Then she turned round slowly and fixed Melinda with a stare. 'If you tell anyone I'm what you said, I'll tell your dad you've been going with that boy and you're going to have a baby.'

Exercise 2

Students discuss how they think the story might continue. To prompt ideas, ask:

Did Melissa get angry or embarrassed?
Did she plead with Eunice not to say anything?
Did she promise not to say anything about Eunice's dyslexia?
What was going through their minds?

The writing should preferably be done in class, and different versions read out or exchanged, or pinned up on a board for everyone to read.

EXTRA ACTIVITIES

1 Top of the list

Ask students to look back at the following six reading texts: *Cider with Rosie*, *Blackberries*, *Fever Pitch*, *How to be an alien*, *Gather Together in My Name*, and *A Judgement in Stone*. Ask them to discuss in groups which of these:
- was the most difficult.
- was the easiest.
- was the funniest.
- sounded the most effective when read aloud on tape.
- contained the most useful words.
- was the most interesting, i.e. gave them most to talk about.
- they would have liked to have read more of.

After the discussion, students can vote for the best extract.

2 In the manner of the word (Guess the adverb)

One student chooses an adverb. Others guess which it is by asking the student to perform different actions in the manner of the word, e.g. *Eat an apple in the manner of the word. Walk across the room in the manner of the word.*

To help with the choice of adverbs, write a selection on the board.

CHECK Units 41–50

(See notes for Check Units 1–10.)

KEY

1 He told me that one of my relatives was ill in hospital.
2 He told me that I had been worrying a lot lately.
3 He told me that a friend of mine had just had a baby.
4 He told me that I had received an important letter the week before.
5 He told me that I was going to travel abroad the following summer.
6 He told me that I would meet and fall in love with a stranger.
7 He told me that he could see a wedding in my life.
8 He told me that I was improving at English.

Exercise 2

1 I asked him what he could see in my palm.
2 I asked him what my career chances were.
3 I asked him how long I was going to live.
4 I asked him if I had (got) any hidden health problem.
5 I asked him where I would be the following year/the year after.
6 I asked him when I was going to get married.
7 I asked him if I had passed my exam the previous day/the day before.
8 I asked him if my parents were going to move house.

Exercise 3

1 The teacher told us that the following day's/the next day's class was cancelled.
2 She invited me to go/come to the café with them.
3 The man refused to let them into the match without a ticket.
4 She promised to phone that evening.
5 The caretaker reminded them to double-lock the front door.
6 He suggested buying her/that we should buy her a bunch of white roses.
7 She warned him not to cycle on the main road.

Exercise 4

1. I wish I had a different job.
2. I wish I didn't have to get up so early.
3. I wish I earned more money.
4. I wish I was interested in a career.
5. I wish I had somewhere to live.
6. I wish I knew what I wanted to do with my life.

Exercise 5

1. I wish I'd gone to Scotland.
2. I wish I'd known about the Edinburgh festival.
3. I wish I'd had time to see a typical English village.
4. I wish I hadn't stayed with our group all the time.
5. I wish I'd taken my camera.
6. I wish I'd managed to get a ticket to see 'Phantom of the Opera'.

Exercise 6

1g 2f 3h 4a 5b 6c 7d 8e

Exercise 7

(Example responses)
1. If I'd known you needed the eggs for the cake, I wouldn't have used them all.
2. If she hadn't gone to Mexico, she wouldn't have met her future husband.
3. If you'd taken my advice, you wouldn't have lost your wallet.
4. If he'd sent off the form in time, he would have got a prize.
5. If she hadn't hurt her ankle, she would have won the match.
6. If it hadn't been foggy I wouldn't have arrived late.
7. If you hadn't told me the ending, I would have enjoyed the film.
8. If I'd known the time of your train, I could have met you at the station.
9. The fire would have spread if there had been a lot of/more wind.
10. If I hadn't cleared out my handbag, I wouldn't have lost your telephone number.

Exercise 8

1c 2b 3a 4b

Exercise 9

(Example responses)
1. Look, I'm afraid I really must be going. I've got to get back to work/Someone has just arrived to see me.
2. There's someone at the door. I'm afraid I must go/I'll give you a ring later.
3. Listen, why don't we meet for lunch some time?
4. Have a lovely holiday/time. (Take care!)

USE YOUR ENGLISH
Units 41–50

Exercise 1

Ask the students to use dictionaries to guess the meaning of any new words. Explain that there is more than one possible version. Get students to agree on which sounds the most convincing order.

SUGGESTED ORDER
1c 2f 3b 4e 5a 6d

Exercise 2

Divide the class into A and B roles and direct the B students to the relevant page at the back of the book. Let the students read the instructions though first, then check that they are sure how the exercise works. Work through a couple of examples so that the students are aware that they must insert a subject for the main clause and that there will be some verb changes, i.e. *would have* in the main clause + past perfect tense in the conditional clause. Go round and listen as the students perform and note any errors to take up with the whole class later.

KEY
1. If the weather had been better, we would have gone on a picnic.
2. If you'd looked both ways before crossing the road, you would have seen the lorry.
3. If your birthday had fallen on a Saturday, I would have taken you out dancing.
4. If I hadn't spent all my money, I would have taken you out for the evening.
5. If I hadn't eaten so much last night, I would have slept better.
6. If the film had been worth seeing, I would have bought a couple of tickets.
7. I would have been on time if I hadn't lost my keys as I was leaving.
8. I wouldn't have got so worried if you'd phoned me earlier.
9. I wouldn't have spent so long on the phone if I'd known you wanted to make a call.
10. I would have been sick if I'd eaten any more.

Exercise 3

Explain that there are several possible ways of completing the poem but that each line should make grammatical sense.

Ask a few students to read out their finished versions to the rest of the class.

SUGGESTED POEM
If she had kissed me
I would have cried
If she had smiled at me

I would have written a poem for her
If she had asked me to
I would have carried her bag
If she had wanted
I would have kissed her hand
but if she had laughed at me
I would have died.

PROGRESS TEST
Units 41–50

(See notes for Progress test Units 1–10.)

KEY

Exercise 1

1 had 2 her name was 3 had already left
4 I'll give 5 to me 6 not to touch 7 me
8 her to stay 9 sitting 10 had lost 11 hadn't gone
12 had stood

Exercise 2

1 got nervous 2 must go 3 in 4 the same
5 for being late 6 reminded me 7 from going
8 accused of

Exercise 3

1b 2c 3a 4c 5b 6a 7b 8c 9b 10c

Exercise 4

1 has 2 on 3 employ 4 summer 5 bring 6 series
7 students 8 carry 9 advised 10 recent 11 station
12 now

Grammar index

	Example sentence	Unit
A		
after	After graduating I went to Madrid.	7
allowed to	We're not allowed to go in.	4
already (with present perfect)	I've already done it.	22
as ... as	... as separate as the notes of a piano ...	10
as soon as	I'll phone you as soon as I get home.	16
as well as	She likes watching football as well as playing it.	5
B		
be able to	Although the sea was rough, they were able to swim to the shore.	14
besides	Besides, I enjoy travelling.	31
be used to	I'm used to eating salads.	9
both ... and	She likes both watching football and playing it.	5
C		
can (ability)	She can sing well.	14
can (+ verbs: *remember, understand, smell, hear, feel, taste, see*)	I can smell something burning.	14
can't have	She can't have forgotten.	39
causative *have*	I'm having my car serviced on Friday.	34
conditionals	(See first, second and third conditionals.)	
contact clauses	That's the man I was talking about.	29
could (ability)	When I was young, I could dance quite well.	14
(request)	Could you take this to the Computer Centre, please?	13
	Do you think you could hurry?	13
could have	She could have had a late meeting.	39
D		
defining relative pronouns	(See *who, which, that, whose, where*.)	
do (contrasted with *make*)	He did his homework	24
during	During the eighties we worked together closely.	7
E		
expected to	Am I expected to wear an evening dress?	28
F		
first conditional	If it starts to rain, we'll play inside.	16
for (with present perfect)	She's lived here for three years.	22
future tenses	(See *will* and *going to*.)	22
G		
gerund (after time adverb)	After graduating ...	7
(+ main verb)	He suggested meeting at the rink.	44
(after preposition)	He apologised for being rude.	44
get (+ adjective)	I'm getting tired.	21
(+ past participle)	I got fired.	21
going to future		
(plan/intention)	I'm going to ask for a rise.	12
(prediction)	It's going to rain.	12

GRAMMAR INDEX

	Example sentence	Unit
H		
have to	Do I have to wear a black tie?	28
have something done	(See causative *have*.)	
however	We usually stay at home in the summer. However, this year we are …	37
I		
I'd like (+ noun phrase + past participle)	I'd like my tyres checked, please.	34
in case	I'll take some coins in case I need to phone.	19
indirect questions	Could you tell me what time the next train leaves, please?	33
	I don't know whether to type it.	38
	I don't understand why they need more information.	38
infinitive (after question words)	I don't know what to say.	38
(in indirect commands)	He warned me not to stay.	44
(+ object + infinitive)	He advised me to leave.	44
-ing form	(See gerund.)	
inversion	So/Nor do I.	1
L		
like (= similar to)	… like birds in a nest …	10
M		
make (contrasted with *do*)	He made a delicious cake.	24
might have	She might have got the wrong day.	39
modal verbs	(See *can, could, will, should, must, can't have, could have, might have, must have, ought to have, should have*.)	28
must	You mustn't have bare arms.	28
must have	He must have left his glasses on the table.	39
N		
negative questions	Isn't there a pool in Lansbury Park?	18
neither … nor	Football is neither fun to play nor very exciting to watch.	5
not only … but also	We will not only have to build a new (motorway) but also (improve the parking facilities.)	17
O		
ought to have	We ought to have left earlier.	36
P		
passive tenses	Wine is produced in France.	26
	It was directed by Trevor Nunn.	26
	The house is being demolished.	26
	Taxes will be reduced.	26
	Have you ever been stopped by the police?	26
past continuous	While she was paying, a boy stole her wallet.	6
past perfect	They realised they had left the tickets at home.	46
past simple	She arrived and had breakfast.	6
present continuous	Nick is playing the guitar.	2
present simple	Nick plays the guitar.	2
present perfect continuous	He's been working in Stratford.	22
present perfect simple	He's worked in Stratford.	22

	Example sentence	Unit
R		
relative pronouns	(See *who*, *which*, *that*, *whose*, *where*.)	
reported questions	I asked him when we could meet.	42
	She asked if he was ever frightened.	42
reported statements	He said/told me (that) he lived in Bristol.	42
reporting verbs	(See verbs of reporting.)	
S		
second conditional	What would you do if you won £100?	32
should	I think we should take a present with us.	28
should have	You should have been wearing a seatbelt.	36
since (with present perfect)	I've worked here since 1987.	22
supposed to	You're not supposed to block the street.	4
	I'm supposed to be revising.	4
T		
tag questions	The 49 bus goes there, doesn't it?	18
that (relative pronoun)	This is the dog that followed me all over the Lake District.	29
third conditional	If you'd parked on a meter, you wouldn't have got a ticket.	49
time clauses	(See *when* and *as soon as*.)	9
U		
unless	Unless you go now, you'll miss the train.	16
used to (+ infinitive)	I used to eat a lot of red meat.	9
(+ gerund)	I'm used to eating salads.	9
V		
verbs of reporting (+ infinitive)	They agreed to come.	44
(+ *ing* form)	He suggested meeting at the rink.	44
(+ object + infinitive)	He advised me to leave.	44
(+ two objects)	She introduced me to her husband.	44
W		
when	I'll phone you when I get home.	16
where (defining relative pronoun)	This is the village where I stayed.	29
whereas	In New York you can … whereas in Britain …	34
which (defining relative pronoun)	This is the dog which followed me all over the Lake District.	29
while	(See past continuous.)	
who (defining relative pronoun)	This is the baker who gave me some fresh bread.	29
whose (defining relative pronoun)	That's the man whose cauliflowers won first prize.	29
will future (decision)	I'll tell him tonight.	22
(future fact)	Steve will be thirty next birthday.	12
(prediction)	It'll be like Manhattan.	12
wish	I wish I hadn't gone to bed so late.	48
would you mind (request)	Would you mind asking them to call me?	13
Y		
yet (with present perfect)	I haven't done it yet.	22
	Have you done it yet?	22

Vocabulary and expressions

This list contains all the words in the *Guess the meaning*, *Words to learn* and *Vocabulary* sections of the Students' Book. Pronunciation is shown in the system used in the *Longman Dictionary of Contemporary English*. The number following each word indicates the unit in which it first appears. The symbol /ʳ/ at the end of a word means that /r/ is pronounced in British English when the next word begins with a vowel sound.

A

ability /əˈbɪlɪti/ **37**
able (v) /ˈeɪbəl/ **37**
act (of a play) (n) /ækt/ **25**
actor /ˈæktəʳ/ **25**
adore /əˈdɔːr/ **30**
affectionate /əˈfekʃənɪt/ **30**
aggressive /əˈgresɪv/ **31**
alien /ˈeɪliən/ **30**
although /ɔːlˈðəʊ/ **31**
amazing /əˈmeɪzɪŋ/ **20**
angry /ˈæŋgri/ **50**
appalled /əˈpɔːld/ **15**
applaud (v) /əˈplɔːd/ **20**
appreciative /əˈpriːʃətɪv/ **20**
armchair /ˈɑːmtʃeəʳ/ **10**
aromatic /ˌærəˈmætɪk/ **30**
at all costs /ət ɔːl kɒsts/ **17**
athletics /æθˈletɪks/ **17**
attic /ˈætɪk/ **7**
audience /ˈɔːdiəns/ **25**
autobiography /ˌɔːtəbaɪˈɒgrəfi/ **47**
awful /ˈɔːfəl/ **7**

B

beat (v) /biːt/ **20**
beautiful /ˈbjuːtɪfəl/ **7**
biography /baɪˈɒgrəfi/ **47**
blank /blæŋk/ **50**
block (v) /blɒk/ **27**
block of flats /blɒk əv ˈflæts/ **27**
boarding school /ˈbɔːdɪŋ ˌskuːl/ **1**
bookcase /ˈbʊk-keɪs/ **10**
borough /ˈbʌrə/ **31**
bothered (to be) /ˈbɒðəʳd (tə bi)/ **1**
bow (v) /baʊ/ **25**
box (in a theatre) /bɒks/ **25**
boxing /ˈbɒksɪŋ/ **17**
box-office /bɒks ˈɒfɪs/ **25**
bracelet /ˈbreɪslɪt/ **31**
brave /breɪv/ **5**
brilliant /ˈbrɪljənt/ **37**
bring up /brɪŋ ˈʌp/ **11**
brooch /brəʊtʃ/ **31**
bully /ˈbʊli/ **5**
bungalow /ˈbʌŋgələʊ/ **27**
burglar /ˈbɜːgləʳ/ **41**
burglary /ˈbɜːgləri/ **41**
bursting out /ˌbɜːstɪŋ aʊt/ **10**

C

candle /ˈkændl/ **10**
candlestick /ˈkændl ˌstɪk/ **10**
cap (n) /kæp/ **15**
capability /ˌkeɪpəˈbɪlɪti/ **37**
care /keəʳ/ **30**
careless /ˈkeələs/ **30**
chapter /ˈtʃæptəʳ/ **25**
chase (v) /tʃeɪs/ **14**
cheat (v) /tʃiːt/ **17**
chest of drawers /tʃest əv drɔːz/ **20**
circle (of a theatre) /ˈsɜːkəl/ **25**
claim /kleɪm/ **1**
cluster (n) /ˈklʌstəʳ/ **15**
comedy /ˈkɒmɪdi/ **25**
commentary /ˈkɒməntəri/ **25**
competitive /kəmˈpetɪtɪv/ **17**
complicated /ˈkɒmplɪkeɪtɪd/ **30**
confess /kənˈfes/ **17**
conformist /kənˈfɔːmɪst/ **5**
conspirator /kənˈspɪrətəʳ/ **25**
conspire /kənˈspaɪəʳ/ **17**
constantly /ˈkɒnstəntli/ **31**
contradict /ˌkɒntrəˈdɪkt/ **30**
costume /ˈkɒstjʊm/ **7**
cottage /ˈkɒtɪdʒ/ **27**
cough /kɒf/ **31**
courier /ˈkʊriəʳ/ **11**
course (golf) /kɔːs/ **17**
court (tennis) (n) /kɔːt/ **17**
crack (v) /kræk/ **15**
crackle /ˈkrækəl/ **10**
crawling /ˈkrɔːlɪŋ/ **21**
crime /kraɪm/ **41**
criminal (n) /ˈkrɪmɪnəl/ **41**
cruel /ˈkruːəl/ **30**
cry (v) /kraɪ/ **20**
cuff-links /ˈkʌf ˌlɪŋks/ **31**
curtain (in a theatre) /ˈkɜːtn/ **25**
curtain call /ˈkɜːtn kɔːl/ **25**

D

dagger /ˈdægəʳ/ **25**
daunting /ˈdɔːntɪŋ/ **35**
day school /ˈdeɪ ˌskuːl/ **1**
decide /dɪˈsaɪd/ **37**
decision /dɪˈsɪʒən/ **37**
degree /dɪˈgriː/ **1**
deliver /dɪˈlɪvəʳ/ **11**
demonstration /ˌdemənˈstreɪʃən/ **41**
detached house /dɪˈtætʃt ˈhaʊs/ **27**
detective story /dɪˈtektɪv ˌstɔːri/ **47**
develop /dɪˈveləp/ **11**
dilemma /dɪˈlemə/ **37**
director (of a play) /dɪˈrektəʳ/ **7**
discouraging /dɪsˈkʌrɪdʒɪŋ/ **35**
disease /dɪˈziːz/ **50**
distraction /dɪˈstrækʃən/ **25**
district /ˈdɪstrɪkt/ **27**
do someone a favour /duː ˌsʌmwʌn ə ˈfeɪvəʳ/ **21**
dreadful /ˈdredfəl/ **7**
dress code /dres kəʊd/ **35**
dressing room /ˈdresɪŋ ruːm/ **7**

E

ear (a good ...) /ɪəʳ/ **7**
earrings /ˈɪəˌrɪŋz/ **31**
emergency /ɪˈmɜːdʒənsi/ **41**
eminent /ˈemɪnənt/ **30**
energy /ˈenədʒi/ **23**
enough /ɪˈnʌf/ **31**
enthusiastic /ɪnˌθjuːziˈæstɪk/ **50**
entire /ɪnˈtaɪəʳ/ **20**

136

VOCABULARY AND EXPRESSIONS

essential /ɪ'senʃəl/ 37
ethical /'eθɪkəl/ 37
evening class /'iːvnɪŋ ˌklɑːs/ 1
exaggerated /ɪɡ'zædʒəreɪtɪd/ 35
exclusive /ɪk'skluːsɪv/ 17
exhausted /ɪɡ'zɔːstɪd/ 41
exhibitionist /ˌeksɪ'bɪʃənɪst/ 35
experiment /ɪk'sperɪmənt/ 30
extrovert /'ekstrəvɜːt/ 5

F

fail (an exam) /feɪl/ 1
fake (adj) /feɪk/ 35
fan (football) /fæn/ 20
fanatic /fə'nætɪc/ 11
fascinate /'fæsɪneɪt/ 31
finally /'faɪnəli/ 21
financial /fɪ'nænʃəl/ 31
fine (v) /faɪn/ 17
fireguard /'faɪəɡɑːd/ 10
fireplace /'faɪəpleɪs/ 10
fixation /fɪk'seɪʃən/ 20
floodlit /'flʌdlɪt/ 27
flourish (v) /'flʌrɪʃ/ 35
flushed /flʌʃt/ 50
football /'fʊtbɔːl/ 17
footlights /'fʊtlaɪts/ 25
foyer /'fɔɪeɪ/ 25
free kick /friː kɪk/ 20
funny /'fʌni/ 30

G

get (a pass/good grade/degree) /ɡet/ 1
get into college /ˌɡet ɪntə 'kɒlɪdʒ/ 1
glamorous /'ɡlæmərəs/ 7
golf /ɡɒlf/ 17
gold chain /ɡəʊld 'tʃeɪn/ 31
go to college /ˌɡəʊ tə 'kɒlɪdʒ/ 1
go up /ˌɡəʊ 'ʌp/ 11
grade /ɡreɪd/ 1
graduate (v) /'ɡrædʒueɪt/ 7
grandly /ɡrændli/ 25
grin (n) /ɡrɪn/ 41
ground (football) /ɡraʊnd/ 20

guilty /'ɡɪlti/ 20
gymnastics /dʒɪm'næstɪks/ 17

H

half-hearted /ˌhɑːf 'hɑːtɪd/ 37
handle /'hændl/ 37
hard /hɑːd/ 5
hardworking /ˌhɑːd'wɜːkɪŋ/ 5
head (v) (a ball) /hed/ 20
heart /hɑːt/ 30
heartless /'hɑːtləs/ 30
helpful /'helpfəl/ 7
home /həʊm/ 30
homeless /'həʊmləs/ 30
hopeful /'həʊpfəl/ 7
house /haʊs/ 27
hurricane /'hʌrɪkən/ 30
hut /hʌt/ 27

I

ice rink /'aɪs rɪŋk/ 17
ice skating /'aɪs ˌskeɪtɪŋ/ 17
immensely /ɪ'mensli/ 7
important /ɪm'pɔːtənt/ 37
impress /'ɪmpres/ 1
independence /ˌɪndə'pendəns/ 31
instantly /'ɪnstəntli/ 27
iron bar /'aɪən 'bɑːʳ/ 17

J

job /dʒɒb/ 30
jobless /'dʒɒbləs/ 30

K

kick (v) /kɪk/ 20

L

leap (v) /liːp/ 7

M

mark (v) /mɑːk/ 1
mantlepiece /'mæntlpiːs/ 10
matting /'mætɪŋ/ 10
medal /'medl/ 17
motor racing /'məʊtə ˌreɪsɪŋ/ 17

mugging /'mʌɡɪŋ/ 41
murder (v) /'mɜːdəʳ/ 41
musical (n) /'mjuːzɪkəl/ 25
mutter /'mʌtəʳ/ 15
mysterious /mɪ'stɪəriəs/ 20

N

necklace /'neklɪs/ 31
nervous /'nɜːvəs/ 50
noisy /'nɔɪzi/ 5
nought /nɔːt/ 31

O

obsession /əb'seʃən/ 20
obviously /'ɒbvɪəsli/ 20
offstage /ɒf steɪdʒ/ 25
off duty /ɒf 'djuːti/ 41
office block /'ɒfɪs ˌblɒk/ 27
old-fashioned /əʊld 'fæʃənd/ 30
one-bedroom flat /'wʌn bedrʊm 'flæt/ 27
orchestra /'ɔːkɪstrə/ 25
outstanding /aʊt'stændɪŋ/ 37
overestimate /ˌəʊvər'estɪmeɪt/ 35

P

package /'pækɪdʒ/ 11
pain /peɪn/ 30
painless /'peɪnləs/ 30
palace /'pælɪs/ 27
pass (an exam) /pɑːs/ 1
pass (n) /pɑːs/ 1
parlour /'pɑːləʳ/ 20
path /pɑːθ/ 15
patrol (n) /pə'trəʊl/ 41
peak /piːk/ 15
penalty /'penlti/ 20
pendant /'pendənt/ 31
perceptive /pə'septɪv/ 30
perfectly /pə'fɪktli/ 20
persecute /'pɜːsɪkjuːt/ 21
pickpocketing /'pɪkˌpɒkɪtɪŋ/ 41
piles /paɪlz/ 10
pitch (football) (n) /pɪtʃ/ 17/20
play (n) /pleɪ/ 7

player /'pleɪəʳ/ 20
plump /plʌmp/ 15
pool /puːl/ 17
portrait /'pɔːtrət/ 25
possibility /ˌpɒsɪ'bɪlɪti/ 37
potentially /pə'tenʃəli/ 35
pour /pɔːʳ/ 20
power /'paʊəʳ/ 27
praise (v) /preɪz/ 20
prevent /prɪ'vent/ 27
primary school /'praɪməri ˌskuːl/ 1
prison sentence /'prɪzən 'sentəns/ 17
private school /'praɪvɪt ˌskuːl/ 1
privilege /'prɪvɪlɪdʒ/ 25
probability /ˌprɒbə'bɪlɪti/ 37
producer (of a play) /prə'djuːsəʳ/ 25
protect /prə'tekt/ 37
puzzled /'pʌzəld/ 50

Q

qualification /ˌkwɒlɪfɪkeɪʃən/ 37
quarrel (n) /'kwɒrəl/ 15

R

raise /reɪz/ 7
rape /reɪp/ 41
rebel (n) /'rebəl/ 5
receive /rɪ'siːv/ 25
recommend /ˌrekə'mend/ 37
recommendation /ˌrekəmen'deɪʃən/ 37
reduce /rɪ'djuːs/ 5
refreshing /rɪ'freʃɪŋ/ 30
reservation /ˌrezə'veɪʃən/ 37
resign from /rɪ'zaɪn frəm/ 17
revise /rɪ'vaɪz/ 1
rink /rɪŋk/ 17
ring /rɪŋ/ 17/31
riot /raɪət/ 41
rise (n) /raɪz/ 11
rival (n) /raɪvəl/ 17
robbery /'rɒbəri/ 41
romantic novel /rəʊ'mæntɪk 'nɒvəl/ 47
root /ruːt/ 7

137

VOCABULARY AND EXPRESSIONS

rough /rʌf/ 31
rude /ruːd/ 30
ruin (v) /'ruːɪn/ 15

S

scandal /'skændl/ 17
scene /siːn/ 25
scenery /'siːnəri/ 7
score (v) /skɔːʳ/ 20
scrambling /'skræmblɪŋ/ 17
scrape /skreɪp/ 27
scratch (v) /skrætʃ/ 15
secondary school /'sekəndri ˌskuːl/ 1
semi-detached house /ˌsemɪdɪ'tætʃt 'haʊs/ 27
sensible /'sensɪbəl/ 7
shame (n) /ʃeɪm/ 17
shape /ʃeɪp/ 30
shapeless /'ʃeɪpləs/ 10/30
shoot (at a goal) /ʃuːt/ 20
shoplifting /'ʃɒpˌlɪftɪŋ/ 41
short stories /ˌʃɔːt 'stɔːriz/ 47
shout (v) /ʃaʊt/ 20
show off /ʃəʊ ɒf/ 35
shrill /ʃrɪl/ 15
silly /'sɪli/ 30
skating /'skeɪtɪŋ/ 17
skiing /'skiːɪŋ/ 17
skyscraper /'skaɪˌskreɪpəʳ/ 27
slope /sləʊp/ 17
sloppy /'slɒpi/ 35
soak /səʊk/ 15
sober /'səʊbəʳ/ 35
smuggling /'smʌglɪŋ/ 41
spectacular /spek'tækʊələʳ/ 20
spirit /'spɪrɪt/ 17
spoil /spɔɪl/ 15/30
spotlights /'spɒt laɪts/ 25
stadium /'steɪdiəm/ 20
stage (of a theatre) /steɪdʒ/ 25
stain (v) /steɪn/ 15
stalls /stɔːlz/ 25
stand (n) /stænd/ 20
stand up for himself /stænd 'ʌp fə hɪm'self/ 5
star (v) /stɑːʳ/ 7

stare (at) /steəʳ/ 20
startle /'stɑːtl/ 20
state school /'steɪt skuːl/ 1
steadily /'stedɪli/ 20
stereotypical /ˌsteriəʊ'tɪpɪkəl/ 30
storm (n) /stɔːm/ 21
strong /strɒŋ/ 5/37
succession (in quick) /sək'seʃən/ 7
suffer /'sʌfəʳ/ 5
suitable /'suːtəbəl/ 11
superb /suː'pɜːb/ 20
superficial /ˌsuːpə'fɪʃəl/ 30
suspicious /sə'spɪʃəs/ 50
swimming /'swɪmɪŋ/ 17
symbol /'sɪmbəl/ 27

T

tablecloth /'teɪbəlˌklɒθ/ 10
table tennis /'teɪbəl ˌtenɪs/ 17
take (an exam) /teɪk/ 1
take to extremes /teɪk tə ɪk'striːmz/ 17
talented /'tæləntɪd/ 1
tall /tɔːl/ 5
tangle (n) /'tæŋgəl/ 15
team /tiːm/ 20
tear (v) /teəʳ/ 15
tease /tiːz/ 5
tennis /'tenɪs/ 17
terraced house /ˌterɪst 'haʊs/ 27
terrific /tə'rɪfɪk/ 37
theft /θeft/ 41
though /ðəʊ/ 31
thought /θɔːt/ 30
thoughtless /'θɔːtləs/ 30
thriller /'θrɪləʳ/ 47
through /θruː/ 31
tired /'taɪəd/ 37
tough /tʌf/ 7/31
track /træk/ 17
track (running) (n) /træk/ 17
traffic jam /'træfɪk ˌdʒæm/ 11
tragedy /'trædʒɪdi/ 25
transform /træns'fɔːm/ 30

travel book /'trævəl bʊk/ 47
trip (v) /trɪp/ 17
trod (tread) /trɒd/ 10
truck /trʌk/ 20
true /truː/ 30
truly /'truːli/ 20
tunnel (n) /'tʌnl/ 20
turn out to be /tɜːn aʊt tə bi/ 35

U

undermine /ˌʌndə'maɪn/ 25
under pressure /ˌʌndəʳ 'preʃəʳ/ 5
uneven /ʌn'iːvən/ 20
unscrupulous /ʌn'skruːpjʊləs/ 31
use /juːz/ 30
useless /'juːsləs/ 30

V

vaguely /'veɪgli/ 50
vampire /'væmpaɪəʳ/ 7
victim /'vɪktɪm/ 7
volleyball /'vɒlibɔːl/ 17

W

walk-on /wɔːk ɒn/ 25
warehouse /'weəˌhaʊs/ 27
washbasin /'wɒʃˌbeɪsən/ 10
windowsill /'wɪndəʊˌsɪl/ 10
witty /'wɪti/ 30
wonderful /'wʌndəfəl/ 7
wrestling /'resəlɪŋ/ 17

X

xenophobic /ˌzenə'fəʊbɪk/ 30

Workbook key

Unit 1
1 1 got 2 has been working/has worked 3 like 4 'll/will probably go 5 went 6 didn't like 7 was 8 left 9 won't send 10 'll/will send 11 didn't get 12 don't need 13 's/is studying 14 comes 15 want

2 1 D 2 C 3 E 4 G 5 F 6 A

3 1 a 2 b 3 a 4 b 5 b 6 b 7 a 8 b 9 b 10 a

4 1 approve 2 agree 3 educate 4 think 5 live

5 1 uniVERsity 2 acaDEMic 3 OPPosite 4 aNNOY 5 muSIcian 6 magaZINE 7 COMpany 8 comPUter 9 riDIculous 10 eduCAtion

Unit 2
1 1 're/are studying 2 plays 3 visit 4 don't understand 5 Are you going out 6 's/is staying

2 1 love 2 like 3 enjoy 4 's/is 5 Do you write 6 don't know 7 's/is looking for 8 Do you play 9 'm/am learning 10 needs 11 're/are making 12 Are you rehearsing 13 're/are working 14 're/are giving 15 have to 16 Do you get on well 17 don't argue

3 1 Helen 2 Peter 3 Alice 4 Sarah

4 1 Helen is holding a ball. She lives in Brighton.
2 Peter is running out of the water. He plays football for his local team.
3 Alice is making a funny face. She works in Sarah's office.
4 Sarah is reading. She has her own business.

6 1 a 2 b 3 b 4 a 5 a

Unit 3
1 1 compact DISC 2 ALbum 3 SINgle 4 PAPerback 5 MARker pen 6 HARDback 7 reCEIPT 8 magaZINE 9 caSSETTE 10 WRIting paper

2 1 £9.99 2 £110 3 £2 4 50p 5 £43,000

Unit 4
1 2 You're not allowed to drink alcohol.
3 You're not allowed to smoke.
4 You're not allowed to put posters on your bedroom walls.
5 You're not allowed to have lights on after 9.30 p.m.

2 7 You're not supposed to play music in the study rooms, but everyone does.
8 You're not supposed to eat in the study rooms, but everyone does.
9 You're not supposed to talk in the library, but everyone does.
10 You're not supposed to take trips into town without permission, but everyone does.

3 1 A 2 F 3 B 4 D 5 C

Unit 5
1 1 conformist 2 extrovert 3 tease 4 talent 5 shy

2 because and both because as well as and

Unit 6
1 1 came in was leaving called out started
2 saw Were they playing weren't were running Did you say shouted didn't answer didn't see

2 1 were watching 2 rang 3 went 4 opened 5 was

2 1 was sleeping 2 was 3 woke up 4 were arguing/shouting/having an argument/having a row 5 threw 6 screamed 7 was/went

3 ACROSS: 1 passport 5 take 6 lock 8 or 10 have 12 leave 14 it 15 musician 16 interview
DOWN: 2 see 3 oil 4 ticket 7 she 9 return 11 visa 13 voice

5 1 Do 2 Were 3 Is 4 Do 5 Was 6 Did 7 Are

Unit 7
1 1 houseproud 2 homesick 3 house-warming 4 home-made

2 1 when 2 at the age of 3 at first 4 for a time 5 after 6 in 7 at 8 during 9 eventually 10 now

Unit 8
1 1 b 2 b 3 b 4 b 5 b 6 a 7 a

2 **Example dialogue:**
ALAN: Oh no! I'm terribly sorry, Bob!
BOB: That's all right, Alan.
ALAN: Is the jacket washable?
BOB: Well no, I'm afraid it isn't.
ALAN: Oh dear! Look, I'll pay the dry cleaning bill.
BOB: No, it's O.K. Really.
ALAN: Well, I really am sorry.
BOB: Never mind. It's nothing to worry about.

4 1 a 2 b 3 b 4 a

Unit 9
1 1 aren't used to 2 used to 3 Didn't she use to 4 am not used to 5 is used to 6 used to

2 1 used to 2 'm/am used to 3 used to 4 'm/am not used to 5 used to 6 're/are used to

3 1 F 2 T 3 T 4 F 5a F 5b T 5c T 5d T 5e F 5f T

Unit 10
1 1 in 2 on ... in 3 in 4 on 5 on 6 in

2 1 a procession of half-seen figures 2 showing the marks of our boots 3 collection of fine old china 4 But most of the time 5 potatoes of unusual shape 6 coal and sticks of beech wood 7 six tables of different sizes

3 ACROSS: 2 coal 5 piano 7 as 9 candle 10 else 14 modern 15 awake 16 pot
DOWN: 1 crackle 2 cottage 3 attic 4 sofa 5 plant 8 silent 11 low 12 to 13 nest 14 me

Unit 11
1 1 cost of living 2 afford 3 rich 4 money 5 cost 6 pay 7 rise

2 photography acting journalism hairdressing science engineering physics

Unit 12
1 1 's/is going to 2 will 3 'll/will 4 'll/will 5 'll/will 6 will

2 **going to:** 2 We're going to spend the whole summer by the sea.
will: 4 I'll send her a card this afternoon.
5 I'll phone every day.

WORKBOOK KEY

6 I'll carry one for you.
7 I'll get a place at university.
8 Millions of people will die of hunger again next year.
3 1 F 2 F 3 T 4 F 5 F 6 F 7 T 8 T
5 1 b 2 a 3 a 4 b 5 a

Unit 13
1 1 turn it down, (please)? 2 borrow yours, (please)? 3 could use yours, (please)? 4 could post it for me, (please)? 5 typing it again, (please)? 6 moving it (please)?
2 receptionist 4E receipt 2D urgent 5B deliver 1A sign 3C

Unit 14
1 1 will be able to/can ... can't 2 couldn't/wasn't able to 3 was able to 4 be able to 5 couldn't/wasn't able to 6 have been able to
2 1 could/was able to 2 could/was able to 3 was able to 4 couldn't 5 will be able to

Unit 15
1 1 wonderful 2 delicious 3 spectacular 4 magnificent 5 fantastic
2 1 terrible 2 dreadful 3 awful
3 unhappy incorrect impolite irresponsible
   unable inexpensive imperfect unclear
   informal impatient unforgettable improbable
4 1 among 2 on 3 along 4 through 5 on 6 across 7 to 8 From 9 along 10 past

Unit 16
1 1 catch 2 'll/will take 3 catch 4 'll/will arrive 5 miss ...'ll/will 6 catch 7 'll/will catch
2 1 What'll you do if you can't find anywhere to stay?
   2 What'll you do if you lose/spend all your money?
   3 What'll you do if you're ill?
   4 What'll you do if you get lost?
3 1 E 2 B 3 A 4 C 5 D
4 1 If you go by bike, you'll have to be careful.
   2 If you go by underground, you'll get to your destination quickly./you won't see much of the city.
   3 If you go by taxi, you'll have a very comfortable journey.
   4 If you walk, you'll be able to stop and look at anything that interests you./it'll give you a sense of the 'atmosphere' of London.
   5 If you go by bus, you'll get a good view of the city.

Unit 17
1 **Sports:** running, skiing, cycling, windsurfing, swimming, golf, skating, tennis
   Places: pool, slope, ring, court, arena, pitch
2 **Example sentences:**
   She plays football on Sundays.
   She goes running on Mondays.
   She goes cycling on Wednesdays.
   She goes swimming on Thursdays.
   She plays golf on Fridays.
3 Agadir 5 windsurfing, sailing, waterskiing, tennis, horseriding
   Gran Canaria 6 tennis, golf, swimming, windsurfing, horseriding, camel-riding

Unit 18
1 1 doesn't she? 2 haven't I? 3 didn't you? 4 aren't they? 5 won't you? 6 didn't you? 7 isn't he?
2 1 Doesn't she come from Italy?
   2 Haven't I met you before?
   3 Didn't you leave school last year?
   4 Aren't they going to get married soon?
   5 Won't you be twenty next birthday?
   6 Didn't you use to have a car like that?
   7 Isn't he supposed to be at work?
3 **Possible questions:**
   1 You're a journalist, aren't you?
   2 You were born in Manchester, weren't you?
   3 You were born in 1960, weren't you?
   4 You live in England, don't you?
   5 You're 1.82 metres tall, aren't you?
   6 You've got a scar on your left arm, haven't you?
   7 You've got a son, haven't you?
   8 His name's Colin, isn't it?
   9 He was born in 1985, wasn't he?
   10 You're a political correspondent, aren't you?
   11 You work for The Daily News, don't you?
   12 You live in Camden Town, don't you?
   13 Your address is 210, Lyme St, Camden Town, isn't it?
   14 Your work address is 410, Cannon St, London EC4, isn't it?
4 shallow/deep put on/take off
   offer/refuse lengthy/short
   sunny/cloudy simple/complicated
5 1 didn't speak was putting rang
   2 Are you going to come are staying I'll try
   3 were able to
   4 came used to is used to
   5 come 'll have
   6 heard jumped ran

Unit 19
1 1 Why don't you take some sandwiches in case there isn't a buffet car on the train?
   2 Take this map in case you get lost.
   3 I'll take my sunglasses in case it's sunny.
   4 You should always phone before you come round in case I'm not in.
   5 I always use my alarm clock in case I don't wake up.
   6 I'll stay at home in case Pat calls.
   7 We'll have to take out insurance in case we have an accident.
2 1C Phone me when/as soon as you arrive.
   2E We'd better be quiet in case we wake the baby.
   3F I'll phone you as soon as/when I get my results.
   4A She should pass the exam if she works hard.
   5B I'll leave this job unless they give me a rise.

Unit 20
1 Clare Andrews, Cambridge, Hostel for the Homeless, 3rd
   Tim Hunter, Brighton, Old People's Home, 4th
   Alec Jones, London, Children's Hospital, 1st
   John Stevens, Bristol, Animal Rescue Society, 2nd
2 **Adverbs:** badly, perfectly, noisily, lovingly, unhappily, slowly, beautifully, excitedly
   Adjectives: likely, hilly, lovely, lively, jolly, friendly, lonely

Unit 21

1 *Table 5*
1 tomato juice
1 cereal – cornflakes
1 mushrooms on toast
1 scrambled egg on toast
Toast
2 teas

2 1 getting dark. 2 getting excited. 3 getting worried. 4 getting old. 5 got accepted. 6 getting better. 7 got fired (last week). 8 get lost.

Unit 22

1 1a ✘ b ✔ 2a ✔ b ✘ 3a ✘ b ✔ 4a ✔ b ✘
5a ✔ b ✘ 6a ✘ b ✘ 7a ✘ b ✔ 8a ✔ b ✘
9a ✘ b ✔ 10a ✔ b ✘

2 1 What have you been doing in the last few months?
2 What other countries have you visited?
3 Have you (ever) been a waiter before?
4 What other jobs have you had?
5 Why do you want to work as a waiter?
6 How long have you been looking for a job?
7 When are you going to leave Stratford?

3 1 She hasn't written to me yet.
2 They have already done all the washing-up.
3 Have you seen that film yet?
4 Sarah has just told me the good news.
5 Haven't we already this programme?

4 **for:** three months, a week, ten years, a term, a few minutes, an hour and a half
since: I finished school, 1984, 3rd August, the beginning of the year, 9 o'clock, I was a child

Unit 23

1 1 is 2 is 3 has 4 has 5 has 6 has 7 is 8 has

2 1 This soup is salty. 2 This meat is underdone. 3 This zip has broken. 4 The coffee machine doesn't work. 5 This shirt has shrunk.

3 Example complaints and requests:
1 I'm afraid this soup is salty. Would you mind taking it back to the kitchen?
2 I'm sorry but this meat is underdone. Would you mind grilling it for a bit longer?
3 I'm afraid this zip has broken. Could you put in a new one, please?
4 I'm afraid the coffee machine doesn't work. Could you give me my money back, please?
5 I'm afraid this shirt has shrunk. Would you mind changing it for a different one?

4 1 happy 2 naughty 3 pretty 4 silly 5 ugly

5 Example dialogue:
ASSISTANT: Can I help you?
ANN: Yes, I bought some trousers here last week and when I washed them, they shrank and the button came off.
ASSISTANT: Oh, I'm sorry about that.
ANN: Well, could you give me a refund, please?
ASSISTANT: I'm afraid the shop doesn't give refunds.
ANN: Well, I think you should give refunds.
ASSISTANT: Look, I'm sorry about the trousers. Shall I change them for you?
ANN: No, thank you. I'd like to see the manager, please.

Unit 24

1 Make: a cake, friends, a noise, a meal, a mistake, the bed, an arrangement

Do: the washing-up, my homework, my hair, some repairs the shopping, a course, the cleaning

2 1 I've got to do the shopping.
2 I've got to make the beds.
3 I've got to do the washing-up.
4 I've got to do the cleaning.
5 I've got to make the dinner.

3 hope big   work
    hole bag   word/fork
    hold bar   wood/ford
    told car   food

Unit 25

1 1 f 2 c 3 g 4 i 5 e 6 d 7 h 8 b

Unit 26

1 A news story is selected by the director and producer. Then a reporter and a camera crew are sent to the story location. The news script is written by the director and the story is told by the reporter. The film is sent to the studio by motorbike and the length of the story is agreed by the director and producer. After that, the film is cut by the director. It is then introduced by a newsreader.

2 1 A lot of T.V.s are being stolen at the moment.
2 I was never given homework when I was your age.
3 This school is going to be closed soon.
4 Do you think it will be knocked down?
5 Tea has to be made with boiling water.
6 Our rooms were being prepared when we arrived.

3 Example article:
At Broad Street Junior School yesterday, a dangerous snake was found in Class 6's room. It was discovered by six-year-old Renny Astley when she put her feet under her desk. After the discovery, the class were sent home for the day, the classroom was locked and the police were called. An animal rescue team was then sent from the local zoo and the snake was caught and taken to Chester Zoo. No-one knows how the snake got there. The police are now investigating. The snake was a boa constrictor and was two metres long.

Unit 27

1 St Thomas's Hospital 7, County Hall 5, Cleopatra's Needle 2, Houses of Parliament 6, National Theatre 1, Hispaniola 3

2 1 (Texas is situated in the south-west of the USA) above Mexico and the Gulf of Mexico.
2 (It became part of the United States) in 1845.
3 (The official language is) English.
4 Spanish (is also widely spoken).
5 (A lot of) oil (is produced there).
6 (The oil is exported to) other American states.
7 (The state (is headed by a governor but) is governed by) the President of the USA and the Congress.

3 Six: is situated, is (also widely) spoken, is produced, (is) exported, is headed, is governed

5

Suzi	Hal	Mo	
Kay			Mel
			Ali
	Jo		Brad

1 Two 2 Hal 3 Ali

6 1 rectangle 2 square 3 cube 4 diamond 5 circle 6 triangle 7 oval

Unit 28

2 Example sentences:
You're not supposed to take off your coat or sit down without being asked.
You're not supposed to ask for a drink.
You're supposed to wait until everyone is served before you start to eat./You're not supposed to start first.
You shouldn't ask for more.
You're not supposed to pour yourself a drink.
You're expected to ask if you can smoke.
You're not supposed to get up during the meal.
You're expected to stay until the end of the meal.

Unit 29

1 1 – 2 where 3 whose 4 which 5 – (who) 6 which 7 – (which)

2 1 S 2 O 3 O 4 S 5 O 6 S

3 This is the shop I described to you.
This is the friend I knew as a child.
This is the house we're going to buy.

Unit 30

1 ACROSS: 1 published 7 too 8 refreshing 10 who 11 reporter 13 pie 14 ever 15 industries 17 ours 19 ear 20 violin 22 as 23 ice 24 on 26 low 29 eighteen 30 fear
DOWN: 2 before 3 inexpensive 4 dance 5 at 6 colourless 9 horror movie 12 reason 16 during 18 ran 21 ill 24 owe 25 me 27 of 28 or

Unit 31

1 1 ambitious ambition 2 flexible flexibility 3 creative creativity 4 energetic energy 5 patient patience 6 tactful tact (tactfulness) 7 disciplined discipline 8 outgoing 9 hard-working

2 Example adjectives:
1 flexible 2 efficient 3 energetic 4 creative 5 hard-working 6 outgoing 7 tactful 8 ambitious

3 Example sentences:
1 A police officer has to be flexible, and energy is also important.
2 A secretary has to be efficient, and tact it also important.
3 A rock musician has to be energetic, and creativity is also important.
4 A writer has to be creative, and discipline is also important.
5 A nurse has to be hard-working, and patience is also important.

4 2 nurse 3 writer 4 politician

Unit 32

1 1 had … would apply 2 would you do … saw 3 would help … had 4 were … would change 5 had … would you live 6 would go … was/were 7 would be … had 8 would go out … weren't/wasn't 9 would do … worked 10 wouldn't marry … didn't love

2 Example sentences:
1 If I were the Prime Minister, I'd build more houses.
2 If I pass my exams, I'll have a party.
3 If I have time this weekend, I'll write some letters.
4 If I owned a yacht, I'd sail round the world.
5 If I spoke English fluently, I'd get a job as an interpreter.
6 If it rains next Saturday, I'll go to the cinema.

3 1 443 kg 2 63 kg 3 Three years 4 Thirty-two sausages, half a kilo of bacon, twelve eggs, a loaf of bread and a pot of jam 5 Fruit and nuts 6 Lying in bed

4 Example sentences:
If I were you, I'd take more exercise.
If I were you, I'd find some new interests.
If I were you, I'd give myself a target each week.
If I were you, I wouldn't eat any more chips.

6 1 will 2 would 3 would 4 will 5 will

Unit 33

1 1 Could you tell me/Do you know is it's possible to take the Cambridge First Certificate exam, (please)?
2 Could you tell me/Do you know how many classes there are altogether, (please)?
3 Could you tell me/Do you know how many students there are in each class, (please)?
4 Could you tell me/Do you know if it is possible to study in the afternoons, (please)?
5 Could you tell me/Do you know what time the morning classes start, (please)?

3 1 a 2 b 3 b 4 a

Unit 34

1 check – tyres
install – telephone
cut – hair
repair – television, telephone, car
service – car
decorate – flat
alter – dress, jacket

2 Example sentences:
1 I'm going to have my tyres checked.
2 I'm going to get a telephone installed.
3 I'm going to have my hair cut.
4 I'm going to get the television repaired.
5 I'm going to have my car serviced.
6 I'm going to have the flat decorated.
7 I'm going to get this dress altered.

3 1 garden 2 plain 3 clouds 4 apple 5 eggs

Unit 35

1 disgusting, brilliant, fantastic impossible, awful, terrific, essential, terrible

2 Ellen's mother: cleaning, washing-up, shopping, decorating, packing, looking after children
Ellen's father: gardening, car washing, car maintenance, decorating, packing

3 Example questions:
1 Who would you live with if your parents got divorced?
2 What would your parents say/do if you got home at three o'clock in the morning?
3 What would you do if some people tried to rob you?
4 What would you do if there was a fire in your house?

Unit 36

1 1 They shouldn't have/oughtn't to have drunk all the milk.
2 She should have/ought to have worked harder.
3 We shouldn't have/oughtn't to have spent all the money yesterday.
4 They shouldn't have been/oughtn't to have been smoking in the classroom.
5 He shouldn't have been/oughtn't to have been lying

WORKBOOK KEY

in bed at 11.00.
6 I should have been/ought to have been working (when the boss came into the office).

2 1 glass 2 attendant 3 immediately 4 stereo 5 foolish 6 plaster

3 Example sentences:
She should have worn a skirt and blouse./She shouldn't have worn jeans.
She shouldn't have tried to cycle to the interview. She should have taken a bus.
She shouldn't have been eating crisps when the manager came in.
She should have thought about what to say before the interview.
She should have listened more carefully to the manager's questions.
She shouldn't have asked only about the pay and the holidays.

5 1 b 2 a 3 b 4 b 5 a

Unit 37

1 1 don't live 2 got 3 are you doing 4 'm/am visiting 5 'm/am going (to go) 6 's/is 7 Have you ever been 8 haven't 9 've/have often heard 10 lived 11 was 12 are you going to stay/staying 13 don't know 14 think 15 'll/will be 16 'll/will come

2 1 D 2 E 3 A 4 C

3 1 E 2 F 3 A 4 B 5 G 6 C

4 1 I'm feeling really tired today so I must go to bed early tonight.
2 They've got very little money. However, they seem very happy.
3 I didn't like Sue when I first met her. However, I really like her now.
4 I can't do any shopping today because I've spent all my money.
5 Jerry's failed his exams so he'll have to take them again.

Unit 38

1 1 At the London Club, Xenon. 2 She's a bouncer. 3 She asks people to keep calm. 4 No, only very occasionally. 5 (She uses) Wing Chun.

2 1 I don't know whether to look aggressive or not.
2 I don't know what to say to anyone who's arguing.
3 I don't know whether to talk to people or not.
4 I don't know what to do if there's a fight.
5 I don't know whether to use force or not.

Unit 39

1 1 She can't have seen you.
2 She might/could have left it at home.
3 You must have met Helen before.
4 They must have been watching us.
5 They might/could have been sitting in the garden.
6 She can't have been working all night.

2 Example sentences:
He must have had some bad news.
He might have failed his exams.
The letter might be from his girlfriend.
His girlfriend might have decided to leave him.

4 1 F 2 T 3 T 4 F 5 F 6 T 7 T 8 F

5 1 must have 2 must have … can't have 3 can't have 4 could/might have 5 could/might have

Unit 40

1 ripe, sour, sweet juicy *orange*
mild, ripe, hard, salty, strong *cheese*
tender, fatty, lean, tough *meat*
oily, salty *fish*
mild, spicy, strong, hot *curry*

2 At: bedtime, 9 o'clock, the beginning of the lesson
In: August, 1988, the morning, the 1930s, the twentieth century
On: Friday, my first day at school, New Year's Day, your birthday

3 1 to 2 ago 3 to 4 for 5 When 6 ever 7 so 8 in 9 to 10 to 11 until 12 of 13 by 14 takes 15 of 16 but 17 used 18 getting 19 makes 20 of

Unit 41

1 1 A 2 G 3 F 4 C 5 D 6 E

Unit 42

1 1 She told me (that) they had spent a week there.
2 She told me (that) they were going to the same place next year.
3 She asked me if I/we had ever thought of going there.
4 I told her (that) I/we could join them the following year.

2 1 They asked me why I was so late.
2 They asked me how I had got home.
3 They asked me what I had been doing.
4 They asked me if I had been out with you again.
5 They asked me when I was going to do my homework.
6 They asked me if I was staying in tonight.

3 1 It's for a summer camp. 2 You have English lessons. 3 You can swim at the beach, 100 metres away. 4 It's ten minutes' walk.

4 Example sentences:
The brochure said that the beach was only 100 metres away but it was at least a kilometre away.
The brochure said that the beach was sandy but it was stony.
The brochure said that the teachers were all native speakers of English but my teacher was Italian.
The brochure said that a wide range of activities was arranged but there was nothing arranged.
The brochure said that the town was full of things to do but there was nothing to do.
The brochure said that the town was ten minutes' walk from the camp but it was half an hour away.

Unit 43

1 2 B 3 D 4 H 5 A 6 E 7 C 8 F

2 1 Good luck on Monday. 2 Have a good weekend. 3 See you tomorrow. 4 Speak to you soon.

Unit 44

1 1 c 2 c 3 b 4 a 5 b 6 b

2 1 I suggested going out for a meal.
2 She offered me a piece of cake.
3 I promised to be there by nine o'clock.
4 He apologised for being late.
5 She advised me to look for a new job.
6 I agreed to talk to her.

3 1 If I were you, I'd see a doctor.
2 I'm sorry I have to leave early.
3 Don't forget to buy the tickets.
4 Why don't we got for a swim?

WORKBOOK KEY

5 Don't go there.
6 Would you like to come round and see the new baby?
7 I promise I'll post it for you./Don't worry, I'll post it for you, I promise.

4 1 1 He phoned to invite her and Ann round for dinner.
2 Next Friday./The following Friday.

5 John phoned earlier. He invited us to dinner on Saturday but I explained that our grandparents were coming to stay, so he suggested going next Friday and I accepted. He offered to come and pick us up but I reminded him that you had bought a car. Oh, he warned us not to use the A6 because of some roadworks. Anyway, I thanked him for inviting us and he apologised for not inviting/not having invited us before.

Unit 45

1 demonstrator 1 bystander 3 police officer

2 **Police officer:** aggressive, mob, screaming, hooligans, angry
Demonstrator: wonderful, peaceful, singing, successful, jokes

3 **Example sentences:**
1 A sixty-five-year-old woman attacked two robbers when they entered her home late on Saturday night.
2 The teachers have ended their strike after one month and are returning to work on Monday.
3 A comprehensive school in West London burnt down in a huge fire early yesterday morning.
4 The Queen left London this morning for a two-week tour of Australia.

Unit 46

1 1 was 2 had already been 3 knew 4 had never been 5 went 6 had 7 had studied 8 had 9 rained 10 were 11 had packed 12 was 13 came 14 felt 15 had had

2 Two years ago, on 1st June, it was Mrs Ambler's one hundredth birthday. She was still living at 17 Laburnum Gardens, in the house where she had lived all her life. She said she had never wanted to live anywhere else. All her memories from childhood to old age were there in that house. She had been a child there and then had had her own three children there. All of them had left many years before and her daughters were now grandmothers. Mrs Ambler's husband had died ten years before, so she had lived alone since then, She never felt lonely, however, because she had many friends and relations who came to visit her.

3 1 She is a policewoman, head of the Paris Arts Theft Squad.
2 a) Because four stolen Corot paintings had been returned to France.
b) The people who had bought the paintings in Japan.
c) Three armed criminals had hidden themselves there.
3 Five: paintings had been returned.
successes had been
the people who had bought
she had finished
criminals had hidden

5 1 b 2 a 3 b 4 b 5 a

Unit 47

1 1 Although he had a heart attack last year, he seems to be quite healthy. In spite of having/having had a heart attack last year, he seems to be quite healthy.
2 Although she's very old now, she can still look after herself. In spite of being very old now, she can still look after herself.
3 Although he's very intelligent, he's very boring to talk to. In spite of being very intelligent, he's very boring to talk to.
4 Although she works very hard, she doesn't earn much money. In spite of working very hard, she doesn't earn much money.

2 1 playwright 2 poet 3 author 4 journalist

3 2 biography 3 romantic novel 4 short stories 5 detective story 6 travel book 7 autobiography

Unit 48

1 1 I wish we hadn't had an argument.
2 I wish I could speak English very well.
3 I wish I'd/had helped them.
4 I wish I didn't have to go to school.
5 I wish I lived near a swimming pool.

2 **Example sentences:**
I wish I had worked harder.
I wish I hadn't spent the evenings playing pinball.
I wish I had got up early in the mornings.
I wish I had gone to all the lectures.
I wish I had written an essay every week.
I wish I had revised harder for my exams.

Unit 49

1 1 hadn't rained … would have gone
2 would have called round … had known
3 would have got … had applied
4 would have done … had known
5 hadn't seen … wouldn't have bought
6 would have been killed … hadn't been
7 wouldn't have left … hadn't been

2 1 if you had the money?
2 I'd/would have seen them.
3 if I'd wanted it.
4 I'll tell her the news.
5 if she knew about this letter.
6 if we don't hurry.
7 if you'd/had asked her.

3 1 It's amusing.
2 Shakespeare would have written better if he'd had a Berol.

4 1 Albert Einstein would have found the answers more quickly with a Techno Computer.
2 Florence Nightingale would have saved more lives with Allcure medicine.
3 Queen Victoria would have looked more beautiful in Goldmark designer clothes.
4 Sherlock Holmes would have been able to see better with 'Clearview' glasses.

Unit 50

1 1 didn't you? 2 aren't you? 3 have you? 4 won't you? 5 should I? 6 had he? 7 mustn't we? 8 doesn't she? 9 were you? 10 is he?

2 **Example question:**
1 Would you rather be with him than with anyone else?

3 1 Eton 2 A musician 3 Motorcycle courier 4 The Docklands 5 Stratford-upon-Avon 6 Shakespeare 7 Jewellery maker 8 Stones 9 Ice hockey 10 They left the tickets at home.